KNOWLEDGE AND THE KNOWN

SYNTHESE HISTORICAL LIBRARY

TEXTS AND STUDIES IN THE HISTORY OF
LOGIC AND PHILOSOPHY

VOLUME 11

JAAKKO HINTIKKA

KNOWLEDGE AND THE KNOWN

Historical Perspectives in Epistemology

D. REIDEL PUBLISHING COMPANY

DORDRECHT-HOLLAND/BOSTON-U.S.A.

Library of Congress Catalog Card Number 74–76473

ISBN 90 277 0455 4

Published by D. Reidel Publishing Company,
P.O. Box 17, Dordrecht, Holland

Sold and distributed in the U.S.A., Canada, and Mexico
by D. Reidel Publishing Company, Inc.
306 Dartmouth Street, Boston,
Mass. 02116, U.S.A.

c c

Printed in The Netherlands by D. Reidel, Dordrecht

TABLE OF CONTENTS

Introduction   VII

On the Origin of the Essays   XI

CHAPTER 1 / Knowledge and Its Objects in Plato   1
CHAPTER 2 / Plato on Knowing How, Knowing That, and
             Knowing What   31
CHAPTER 3 / Time, Truth, and Knowledge in Aristotle and
             Other Greek Philosophers   50
CHAPTER 4 / Practical vs. Theoretical Reason – An Ambiguous
             Legacy   80
CHAPTER 5 / 'Cogito, Ergo Sum': Inference or Performance?   98
CHAPTER 6 / Kant's 'New Method of Thought' and His Theory
             of Mathematics   126
CHAPTER 7 / Are Logical Truths Analytic?   135
CHAPTER 8 / Kant on the Mathematical Method   160
CHAPTER 9 / A Priori Truths and Things-In-Themselves   184
CHAPTER 10 / 'Dinge an sich' Revisited   197
CHAPTER 11 / Knowledge by Acquaintance – Individuation by
             Acquaintance   212

Index of Names   235

Index of Subjects   238

INTRODUCTION

A word of warning concerning the aims of this volume is in order. Otherwise some readers might be unpleasantly surprised by the fact that two of the chapters of an ostensibly historical book are largely topical rather than historical. They are Chapters 7 and 9, respectively entitled 'Are Logical Truths Analytic?' and 'A Priori Truths and Things-In-Themselves'. Moreover, the history dealt with in Chapter 11 is so recent as to have more critical than antiquarian interest. This mixture of materials may seem all the more surprising as I shall myself criticize (in Chapter 1) too facile assimilations of earlier thinkers' concepts and problems to later ones.

There is no inconsistency here, it seems to me. The aims of the present volume are historical, and for that very purpose, for the purpose of understanding and evaluating earlier thinkers it is vital to know the conceptual landscape in which they were moving. A crude analogy may be helpful here. No military historian can afford to neglect the topography of the battles he is studying. If he does not know in some detail what kind of pass Thermopylae is or on what sort of ridge the battle of Bussaco was fought, he has no business of discussing these battles, even if this topographical information alone does not yet amount to historical knowledge. Likewise, a historian of ideas is in the most favourable instance seriously handicapped if he does not master the topical aspects of the problems with which earlier philosophers were grappling, and at worst he is incapable of doing justice to his predecessors. To be more specific, a discussion of Kant's claim that most mathematical truths are synthetic cannot be successful, it seems to me, if it is not based on knowledge of the sense or senses in which deductive truths can in fact be informative ('synthetic'). Nor can an analysis of a philosopher's attitude to the distinction between knowledge of facts (knowing that) and knowledge of objects (knowing + direct object) be definitive unless its author understands what the logic of this distinction really is. For such reasons, historical inquiries often vitally need the backing of analytical and

critical studies even when they have a purely historical aim. I believe that
the interrelations of the several essays collected in this volume illustrate
this need. For the same reason I have called my essays historical perspectives in epistemology rather than studies in the history of epistemology.

My emphasis on our knowledge of conceptual topography is compatible with the belief that earlier philosophers' maps of this intellectual
landscape were frequently drawn in accordance with principles entirely
unlike ours. If anything, I have been impressed by certain large-scale
differences between the epistemological and conceptual assumptions of
the old Greeks and ourselves. (Since these presuppositions often remained
tacit, they should perhaps be called ways of thinking rather than assumptions.) According to my lights, the most interesting features of
Plato's or Aristotle's epistemology are not anticipations of Frege or
Wittgenstein, but hints of underlying differences between their conceptual
system and ours. The first three chapters of this book are accordingly
attempts to delineate some of these peculiarities of the ancient Greeks as
they appear in the epistemological thought of the Socratic school. It is
clear that the limits of applicability of whatever results are obtained in
these chapters need further investigation. It already seems clear to me,
however, that we cannot begin to appreciate the epistemology of Plato
and of Aristotle if we are not aware of the peculiarities noted here.

Chapter 4 is an all too brief sketch of an important epistemological
idea whose perennial significance is underestimated in our days, an idea
which connects knowledge with power à la Bacon but unlike him tends
to think of the latter as a precondition of the former, and not vice versa.
One of the most important adherents of this tradition was Kant, to whom
most of Chapters 6–10 are devoted. It is there argued, or at least suggested,
that important new avenues into his thought are opened by such recent
studies in epistemological and logical analysis as concern deductive
information and perceptual cross-identification (cross-identification by
acquaintance). The ubiquity of the latter subject is illustrated in Chapter
11 where the same problem is argued to form the gist of Russell's concern
with 'knowledge by acquaintance'. An unexpected connection with the
Greek predilection of viewing knowledge as some sort of direct acquaintance is also reached there.

It is hopeless to try to anticipate all criticisms of essays which are
intended to be just that – essays in the old sense of experiments. How-

ever, I have encountered one particular type of misunderstanding too
often to let it pass. I propose to dub it the fallacy of monolithic concepts.
It amounts to the assumption that an interpretation or a rational reconstruction of an earlier thinker's concept (distinction, argument,
assumption, or whatnot) is ipso facto mistaken if it does not cover
everything he said of it. This assumption is fallacious because a philosopher's concepts and arguments are rarely monolithic in the last analysis.
On the contrary, one of the most frequent discoveries a serious student
is likely to make on a closer scrutiny of a historical figure's conceptual
map is that several different features are run together in it. A major
argument or distinction we find in conceptual history is often a conglom-
erate of several superimposed arguments or distinctions. In such cases, it
simply cannot be given a uniform interpretation. Yet the contrary is
being assumed when (to take an actual rather than a synthetic example)
my partial reconstruction of Kant's famous definition of analytic and
synthetic truths is criticized by reference to simple truths of the kind
W. V. Quine would call analytical but not logical. (For a case in point,
see the review of my book *Logic, Language-Games, and Information* in
the *TLS*, 20 July, 1973.) I had explained Kant's distinction as applied
within the class of logical and mathematical truths in terms of a need of
importing new individuals into the argument for these truths. (Cf.
Chapter 8 below.) Of course this does not imply that Kant drew the
distinction according to the same principles when it came to judgments
of an entirely different sort, for instance the step from 'all bodies are
extended' to 'all bodies are heavy'. Or, rather, the imputation of such an
implication depends on the fallacious premise that Kant drew his
distinction in accordance with the same principles always and everywhere. This premise is implausible a priori and is easily disproved by a
closer examination of the evidence. Likewise, I seem to detect the same
fallacy of monolithic concepts in more than one earlier criticism of my
interpretations of such ideas as Descartes' *cogito*-argument (cf. Chapter 5
below), W. D. Ross' distinction between prima facie obligations and
absolute obligations (presented in the last chapter of my *Models for
Modalities*, D. Reidel, Dordrecht, 1969), and Kant's notion of *Ding an
sich* (cf. Chapter 9 below), to mention only a few. In all these cases, it
seems to me, the original argument, distinction, or concept is too many-
splendoured a thing to admit of a unique interpretation. A partial

interpretation therefore ought not to be criticized only because it catches only one facet of the original. Further examples of the same sort are easily found. I am more upset by this kind of criticism than I perhaps ought to be because it seems to me to involve a form of ahistoricity which is particularly pernicious because it tries to hide under the guise of historical accuracy. I cannot help feeling that a failure to recognize the ambiguities of the history of philosophical ideas is an especially dangerous form of anachronism. I hope that I shall in future encounter it less often.

The earlier history of the different chapters of this book is indicated in a separate note below. Some of the intellectual debts incurred in working on them are indicated in them or are apparent from them. Others must unfortunately be left unacknowledged. In editing these essays for republication – and in some cases in writing them in the first place – I have enjoyed the help of Mr. Juha Manninen and Mr. Unto Remes. This help, like virtually all my recent research opportunities, has been made possible by the support of the Academy of Finland.

Finally, I hope that Marjorie Grene will forgive me for stealing the best part of the marvellous title of her epistemological book, *The Knower and the Known*. The temptation was simply overwhelming.

Helsinki, November 1973

ON THE ORIGIN OF THE ESSAYS

Chapter 1 first appeared in *Ajatus* **33** (1971) 168–200, and was subsequently reprinted, with small corrections, in *Patterns in Plato's Thought*, edited by Julius M. E. Moravcsik (Synthese Historical Library, D. Reidel Publishing Company, Dordrecht and Boston, 1973), pp. 1–30. It is reproduced here with the permission of the Philosophical Society of Finland.

Chapter 2 is a greatly expanded version of my contribution to *Modality, Morality, and Other Problems of Sense and Nonsense: Essays Dedicated to Sören Halldén*, edited by Bengt Hansson (CWK Gleerup Bokförlag, Lund, 1973), pp. 1–12, with the title 'Knowing How, Knowing That, and Knowing What: Observations on Their Relation in Plato and Other Greek Philosophers'. The earlier material is reprinted here with the permission of the Editorial Committee for the *Festschrift* to Sören Halldén.

I have covered some of the same ground in a still earlier paper, 'Tieto, taito ja päämäärä' ('Knowledge, Skill, and Purpose', in Finnish), *Ajatus* **27** (1965) 49–67. Although the present paper is a new start, a few of its sentences are translated from that earlier Finnish version.

Chapter 3 first appeared in the *American Philosophical Quarterly* **4** (1967) 1–14, under the title 'Time, Truth, and Knowledge in Ancient Greek Philosophy'. It is reprinted here with the permission of the Editor of the *American Philosophical Quarterly*. The present version incorporates the additional material which first saw the light of day when this paper reappeared (under its present title) as Chapter 4 of my book, *Time and Necessity: Studies in Aristotle's Theory of Modality* (Clarendon Press, Oxford, 1973), pp. 62–92. The Clarendon Press has authorized the republication of this material.

Chapter 4 is an expanded version of my contribution to the 1972 Bristol Colloquium on Practical Reason. It is due to appear in the Proceedings of that meeting, edited by Stephan Körner (Basil Blackwell, Oxford, 1974), pp. 83–102. It is reprinted here with the permission of Professor Körner and of Basil Blackwell, Publisher.

Chapter 5 first appeared in the *Philosophical Review* **71** (1962) 3–32, and has been reprinted repeatedly. The present version incorporates a couple of small changes made in one of these reprintings. Like Chapter 7, it appears here with the permission of the Managing Editor of the *Philosophical Review*.

Chapter 6 is reprinted from *Ajatus* **27** (1965) 37–47 with the permission of the Philosophical Society of Finland. It was originally presented as a talk in the BBC Third Programme Series on Kant in 1964.

Chapter 7 is reprinted, with the appropriate permission, from the *Philosophical Review* **74** (1965) 178–203.

Chapter 8 is reprinted from *The Monist* **51**, Number 3 (July, 1967), La Salle, Illinois, pp. 352–375, with the permission of the publisher.

Chapter 9 first appeared in the *Journal of Philosophy* **65** (1968) 640–651, under the title 'Are Mathematical Truths Synthetic A Priori?'. This title was occasioned by my paper's being a contribution to an APA Symposium on Mathematical Truth, 29 December, 1968. Its appearance here has been authorized by the Managing Editor of the *Journal of Philosophy*.

Chapter 10 is scheduled to be my invited contribution to the Fourth International Kant Congress (Mainz, April 1974) and to appear as a part of the preprinted Proceedings of the Congress in a *Beiheft* of *Kant-Studien*, edited by Gerhard Funke (de Gruyter Verlag). It appears here with the kind permission of Professor Funke. A few passages have been added to the Congress paper.

Chapter 11 was my invited contribution to *Bertrand Russell: A Collection of Critical Essays*, edited by David Pears (Anchor Books, Doubleday and Company, Inc., Garden City, New York, 1972) pp. 52–79. I used it also as my contribution to the 1970 Meinong Colloquium in Graz, which explains its appearance in *Jenseits von Sein und Nichtsein: Beiträge zur Meinong-Forschung*, edited by Rudolf Haller (Akademische Druck- und Verlagsanstalt, Graz, 1972), pp. 205–221. The essay appears here with the permission of Mr. Pears and of Doubleday and Company, Inc.

All the different reprint permissions are gratefully acknowledged.

CHAPTER 1

KNOWLEDGE AND ITS OBJECTS IN PLATO

1. WHAT HISTORY OF PHILOSOPHY IS AND WHAT IT OUGHT TO BE

What we find in texts and treatises of the history of philosophy is by and large information as to what theses or opinions different philosophers put forward at different times. All too seldom do we find any interesting clues as to *why* they adopted these views and *why* it was important for them to propound them as a part of their explicit teaching. However, if history of philosophy is to be something more than the graveyard of more or less forgotten doctrines, it ought to offer us some insights into the reasons why different problems were problematic for different thinkers, why the way in which they used to attack them differed from one philosopher to another, and why the standards of successful solutions to problems have varied. Often, though not always, answers to these questions depend on the conceptual assumptions which the thinkers in question more or less tacitly adopted. Often, these conceptual assumptions and conceptual preferences were common to all or most thinkers of the same period or even of the same culture. However, attempts to study such hidden conceptual assumptions and the characteristic modes of argumentation to which they give rise are few and far between, and successful attempts seem to me still rarer. One does find, it is true, some interesting and illuminating observations concerning, for instance, Aristotle's typical modes of philosophical discussion. At the same time, there are respectable scholars who seriously compare Aristotle's notion of analogy with Wittgenstein's concept of family resemblance, or Aristotle's concept of *aporia* with the Kantian idea of antinomy, oblivious to the fact that in both cases the concepts assimilated to each other not only exhibit dissimilarities in addition to similarities but in reality also belong to different and almost diametrically opposite conceptual contexts.

2. Two Problems in Plato's Epistemology: Plato's Interest in Them is Not Primarily Polemical

In this essay I shall venture a few suggestions concerning certain tacit presuppositions that lurk in the background of Plato's theory of knowledge. These presuppositions can be seen from Plato's discussion of two epistemological problems. They are the problem concerning the possibility of meaningful falsity (of false *logos*) and the problem of distinguishing knowledge from true belief. These two problems are related to each other very closely by Plato. For instance, in the *Theaetetus* the discussion of the relationship of knowledge and true belief leads at once to the question of the possibility of false belief (187B–D). With the former of these two problems Plato also connects a number of further questions (the existence of not-being, the impossibility of contradiction, etc.).

Especially in connection with the former problem, it has frequently been assumed that Plato's discussion was not prompted by any systematic problems intrinsic to his own thought, but rather by his desire to refute sophistical paradoxes. Since my thesis implies that this assumption is incorrect, a brief discussion of Plato's motivation is in order.

I think that all an open-minded historian has to do to arrive at the same conclusion as I is to review the different statements and arguments Plato devotes to the problem of meaningful falsity – in other words, to arrive at the conclusion that this was a serious problem for Plato himself. Plato takes up this problem repeatedly on several different occasions and discusses it sometimes at some length. Most of the end of the *Sophistes* is devoted to it after it has played an important role throughout the same dialogue (*Sophistes* 236E ff., 240B ff., 241D, etc.) and in the *Theaetetus* (183E, 188C–189B, 190E, etc.). In addition to these extended discussions, the same problem is the subject of a shorter or longer discussion in the *Euthydemus* (283E–284C, 285D–286E), in the *Cratylus* (429D ff.), and in the *Parmenides* (160C–E).

No philosopher has ever spent as much time and labour as this on straightening out other people's mistakes, except when these mistakes were for some reason or other tempting, puzzling, or otherwise bothersome from his own point of view – or, rather, on the basis of his conceptual assumptions. And even if other philosophers should have done so, Plato is about the least likely thinker to whom such 'disinterestedly' polemical motives can plausibly be attributed. The impatience of his whole intellectual temperament at once belies such an attribution.

If the hypothesis of the sophistical origin of Plato's problems is a priori as implausible as this, why has it nevertheless gained the wide circulation that it has enjoyed and still does? The primary reason for this seems to be that Plato himself attributes the problem to earlier thinkers, writing at one point as follows:

I have heard this particular argument from many persons and at many times, and it never ceases to amaze me. The followers of Protagoras made considerable use of it and so did some still earlier (*Euthydemus* 286C).

These 'still earlier' thinkers include in any case some Eleatic philosophers, for Plato indicates elsewhere that there is a close relation between his problems and certain arguments and ideas in Parmenides. This prevalence of the problem among earlier thinkers has undoubtedly prompted the idea that Plato's interest in it is derivative. This is not the only possible way of looking at the evidence, however. The ubiquity of the problem might instead be an indication of its being due to deep conceptual assumptions that were shared by as dissimilar thinkers as the Eleatics and some of the Sophists – and presumably also Plato. It seems to me that the facts we know suggest this latter view. In the very passage quoted, Plato records his 'amazement' at it. In any case, from this point of view we can appreciate Plato's ambivalent attitude to it. Parmenides had used (I suggest) arguments closely connected with it to support his own philosophy, which had deeply impressed Plato. Plato himself resorted to the ideas which form the conceptual background of 'the argument against false speaking' for some of the most important explicit arguments for his theory of Forms. Hence there is much here that he found attractive. At the same time, he could not accept some of the skeptical and sophistical uses of arguments of a closely similar type. This posed a striking problem for him to which he felt impelled to devote a major philosophical effort.

3. PLATO'S ATTITUDE TO 'FALLACIES'. THEIR EVIDENTIAL VALUE

Plato's ambivalence vis-à-vis certain types of arguments makes it a questionable procedure to approach his argumentation by asking whether

Plato was 'aware' of the fallacies which apparently led to the denial of meaningful falsity. What precisely can be meant by 'awareness' here? Since the conclusions of these arguments are in so many words rejected by Plato (while he apparently accepts at least some of their premisses), he must have been 'aware' that there is something in them that contradicted his own assumptions. This is rather trivial, however. What is not trivial is to ask whether Plato located the fallacies to his satisfaction – and to ours. However, the criteria of success in this enterprise of Plato's are not absolute, but relative to *his* conceptual assumptions, or more generally relative to the common Greek assumptions, which are likely to be different from ours. This makes an approach to Platonic 'fallacies' in terms of our own classifications of dubitable value. Instead of asking whether Plato was 'aware' of what to us appears as fallacious in these arguments (or in certain variants of these arguments) or whether he 'on purpose' included fallacious arguments in some of the dialogues, it is probably more fruitful to ask how Plato came to use for his own constructive purposes arguments which may appear not much less fallacious than those whose context makes us suspect that Plato was aware of their fallaciousness but which are in fact sometimes closely related to the arguments he accepts. For Plato these fallacies thus might not serve as plain examples of fallacies as much as misuses – even very subtle misuses – of acceptable and important modes of argument. We might be well advised to focus on these acceptable or near-acceptable assumptions rather than the degree of success Plato had in recognizing the mechanics of their misuse. (It is often far from clear just how far he succeeded in becoming aware of the reasons for the fallaciousness of these fallacies, even when he saw that something was wrong about them. Also it is not always clear whether the arguments he accepted are any less fallacious than those he seems to have accepted.) Hence these alleged fallacies might be highly suggestive of Plato's constructive assumptions, too. It is in this context worth noting that Plato seldom labels an argument fallacious and that he but very rarely uses explicitly the notion of ambiguity. (Of course he did not have much ready-made terminology for either purpose.) Probably the clearest example of the rejection of a fallacious argument in Plato is offered by the *Protagoras* (350C–351B), and it is interesting to note that there the fallacious argument (invalid conversion of the universal affirmative premise) is put forward by Socrates in support of a position which he goes on to argue for in other ways with complete seriousness of purpose.

In saying these things I have especially in mind Rosamond Sprague's interesting and valuable study of Plato's attitude to logical fallacies (*Plato's Use of Fallacy*, Routledge and Kegan Paul, London, 1962). Mrs. Sprague points out clearly that Plato consciously uses sophistical and Eleatic materials for his own purposes. Precisely how this happens is not spelled out, however, and some aspects of the main question of Mrs. Sprague's monograph remain in the dark. In particular, Mrs. Sprague's discussion (which includes the attribution of full awareness of most of the fallacies involved to Plato) leaves it completely mysterious how Plato could use for his own systematic purposes arguments closely reminiscent of the 'fallacies' of which Plato was supposed to have been aware. Nor is the precise relation of fallacious and (for Plato) non-fallacious arguments spelled out by Mrs. Sprague.

4. PLATO'S IMPLICIT TELEOLOGY. THE CONCEPT OF 'DYNAMIS'

The presupposition or conceptual preference in the light of which I propose to discuss Plato's views on the relation of knowledge to its objects is the conceptual primacy of the idea of end, aim, goal, or limit (*telos*) in Greek thought. In some earlier papers I have commented on some of the manifestations of this way of thinking in Greek philosophy, including Greek theory of knowledge. In epistemology this way of thinking takes the form of a tendency to handle knowledge, belief, and thinking on the conceptual model of a goal-directed activity, with special emphasis on these goals. It is important to realize that this is but a special case of Plato's and other Greeks' attitudes to all kinds of 'faculties' or 'powers' (*dynameis*). It is therefore also important to examine the peculiarities of the concept of *dynamis* in Greek philosophy.

Plato himself states in so many words that certain theses of his concerning knowledge (ἐπιστήμη) and belief or opinion (δόξα) are special cases of more general doctrines concerning any faculty (*dynamis*). In an interesting passage of the *Republic* (V, 477D–E) knowledge and belief are said to be *dynameis*: "... that by which we are able to opine [or to believe, δοξάζειν] is nothing else than the faculty (*dynamis*) of opinion."

Here and in several similar passages Plato may seem to commit a fallacy or at the very least to include disparate items under one and the same heading. Frequently for Plato *doxa* refers to some particular opinion someone has and *episteme* refers to that item of information which is needed for someone to be in the *state* of knowledge. Now *episteme* and *doxa* are suddenly identified with the faculties of knowledge and opinion. A *faculty* or *power* and its *result* seem to be confused here.

There is nothing surprising about this double meaning, however, for it occurs frequently in Plato and in other Greek thinkers. Here we can utilize the results of the patient examination which J. Souilhé long ago carried out of the meaning of the term *dynamis* in Plato and his predecessors. (See J. Souilhé, *Étude sur le terme Dynamis dans les dialogues de Platon*, Paris, 1919.) He finds that the meaning of the term fluctuates in the way just noted in virtually all writers he studies. For instance, in summing up his discussion of Isocrates Souilhé writes:

Perhaps with less precision than for the physicians [of the Hippocratic school], but yet clearly enough, *dynamis* for Isocrates remained the *characteristic property* of beings, especially the particular *way they act*, the peculiar *effect* which they have and which helps to determine their nature. Occasionally one can also notice that there seems to be a certain confusion between *physis* and *dynamis*. This will explain why things themselves..., for instance arts and sciences, are called *dynameis*. There is no distinction between what things are and what they produce.

The same tendencies, usually in a more pronounced form, are found in Plato's dialogues.

Thus Souilhé finds (and documents) the ambiguity I pointed out in the Hippocratic Corpus, in Isocrates, and in Plato.

Since we are here interested primarily in the history of epistemological concepts, it is especially interesting to note that the same ambiguity has been registered by Snell in connection with the pre-Socratic use of the term γνώμη:

This double meaning of γιγνώσκειν is the basis of that double meaning of γνώμη as 'ability to know' and as 'the result of knowledge' which we find in the literature (*Die Ausdrücke für den Begriff des Wissens in der vorplatonischen Philosophie, Philologische Untersuchungen*, ed. by Werner Jaeger, Vol. 29, Berlin, 1924, p. 33).

In the same connection Snell mentions

'the fact that γνώμη means so different things as the organ (*Organ*) of knowledge and the result (*Resultat*) of knowing' (*op. cit.*, p. 32).

This observation is generalized by Snell in his book *Die Entdeckung des Geistes* (English translation: *The Discovery of the Mind*, Harvard

University Press, Cambridge, Mass., 1953) so as to apply to knowledge and thinking at large:

In the area of thought and knowledge, action and result are at times linked in a peculiar combination. Those nouns which are derived from verbs occasionally denote, at one and the same time, an organ, its function, and its effect (English translation, p. 234).

However, Souilhé's observations show that this tendency is *not* restricted to the 'area of thought and knowledge', as Snell's formulation seems to presuppose. On the contrary, its role in epistemology appears to be but a special case of much more widespread conceptual preferences concerning any *dynamis*.

This general feature of the concept of *dynamis* is in turn a reflection of the focal role of the concept of *telos* in Greek thinking which constitutes the working hypothesis of this paper. If in any event, thing, or phenomenon the essential feature is its end or aim or product or outcome, all talk of it will amount to talking of this end or outcome, this *telos* or *ergon*, and the difference between what is said of the phenomenon itself and what is said of its *telos* or *ergon* tends to be overshadowed. The result in the case of faculties (*dynameis*) is precisely the ambiguity between a faculty and its products that was noted above.

5. SOME PECULIARITIES OF THE NOTION OF 'DYNAMIS'

The crucial role of the results or products of a *dynamis* implied certain further consequences which will turn out to be important in the special cases of the 'faculties' of knowledge and belief. One important consequence that was strongly emphasized by Plato himself was that *different faculties* (different *dynameis*) must have *different results* or objects:

But in the case of a faculty (*dynamis*) I look to one thing only – that to which it is related [i.e. what it is *epi*] and what it effects (*apergazetai*), and it is in this way that I come to call each one of them a faculty, and that which is related to the same thing and accomplishes the same thing I call the same faculty, and that to another I call other (*Republic* V, 477C–D).

We shall later have an occasion to return to this passage. Meanwhile, it is worth noting that the assumption aired by Plato here is a direct consequence of the primacy of the function or work or product (*ergon*) in discussing any faculty (*dynamis*). Hence it is not surprising that it occurs elsewhere in Plato (cf. e.g. *Ion* 537E). It is also worth noting that a similar assumption recurs in other Greek thinkers. For instance, Aristotle writes in the same spirit:

Actions, arts, and sciences are manifold; and their ends must therefore be equally manifold (*Ethica Nicomachea* I, 1, 1094a7–8).

Part of the same syndrome of ideas is Aristotle's repeatedly announced doctrine that each thing is defined by its *ergon*. This is made relevant here by the ambiguity (for us) of the term *ergon* which is usually translated as 'function' but which can also mean 'work' in the sense of the (typical) product of working. (One more instance of the process-product ambiguity.) For other, similar views in Aristotle (one *dynamis* – one product) see *De Anima* II, 4, 415a16–22, III, 2, 426b31–427a16, III, 9, 432a15, and III, 10, 433a13.

The counterpart of this one capacity – one product (or function, *ergon*) assumption in the paradigmatic case of a craftsman is obvious: different trades are distinguished by their respectively different products.

Another indication of the role of telic ways of thought in the concept of *dynamis* is the explicit Platonic assumption that no *dynamis* can lack an object. This assumption is implicit in the passage quoted from the *Republic* V, 477, and Plato applies it repeatedly, especially to the special case of belief or opinion (*doxa*). Since for Plato *doxa* is a *dynamis* it too must have its characteristic 'product' or *ergon*: belief must be belief *about* something. For instance, Plato writes:

Then he who opines opines some one thing? – Yes. (*Republic* V, 478B)
So, then, does he who holds an opinion hold an opinion of some one thing? – He must do so. (*Theaetetus* 189A)

This emphasis – sometimes conscious, often unwitting – on the specificity of the 'products' or *erga* of different kinds of processes, faculties, or men permeates Plato's thinking all the way down to his blueprint of an ideal state. In this ideal state, each citizen has only one function:

... there is no twofold or manifold man among us, since every man does one thing... And is this not the reason why such a city is the only one in which we shall find the cobbler and not a pilot in addition to his cobbling, and the farmer a farmer and not a judge added to his farming, the soldier a soldier and not a moneymaker in addition to his soldiery, and so of all the rest? (*Republic* III, 397D–E)

In the realm of social planning the importance of specific goals thus appears under the guise of an extremely sharp division of labour.

6. KNOWLEDGE AND BELIEF AS 'FACULTIES'.
THEIR OBJECTS MUST BE DIFFERENT

The quotations given above already illustrate a most remarkable aspect of the way in which Plato applies his general ideas concerning *dynameis* to the special case constituted by the faculties of knowledge and belief. In so far as a modern thinker is at all willing to speak of knowledge and opinion as faculties or powers, he might take the 'products' of these faculties to be the particular items of knowledge or of opinions to which these 'faculties' give rise – in other words, to be those *cognitive states* which we mean when we speak of knowing or believing something. Alternatively, he might refuse to speak of products at all and consider instead only the functions performed by our capacities of knowing and of opining. One soon discovers, however, that Plato viewed the situation differently. Those 'functions' or 'ends' of the 'faculties' of knowledge and belief which serve, e.g., to distinguish each faculty from the others and which are somehow analogous to the products of a craftsman's skill were for Plato not just cognitive states in this or that man but sometimes tended to comprise also *those objects which one's knowledge or opinion is about*. In other words, Plato does not always clearly distinguish from each other the *objects* of knowledge and the 'functions' or 'products' of the power to know.

Some of the background of this way of thinking will be sketched later. Meanwhile, it is important to realize how extremely important this view of the objects of knowledge was for Plato's own system. For him it was nothing less than one of the premises of his most explicit proof for the existence of Forms. Plato used the distinction between knowledge and belief to infer that there is a distinction between their respective objects. A vital premise needed in the argument is of course the assumption that a difference between faculties is necessarily reflected by a difference in their *erga*. In order to be able to use this argument in the desired way Plato had to make the further tacit assumption that what the faculties of knowledge and belief 'accomplish and pertain to' are the *objects* of knowledge and belief, respectively, and only by doing so can Plato draw any inference concerning these objects.

He thinks that he can do so, and in fact attaches tremendous importance to this argument. In the *Timaeus* he still writes as follows:

My own verdict, then, is this. If intelligence [or knowledge, *nous*] and true belief (*doxa*) are two different kinds, then these things – Forms that we cannot perceive but only think of [or: have knowledge of] – certainly exist in themselves; but if, as some hold, true belief in no way differs from intelligence [knowledge], then all the things we perceive through the bodily senses must be taken as the most certain reality (*Timaeus* 51D).

The most explicit form of this inference from the difference between knowledge and belief to a difference between their objects occurs in the fifth book of the *Republic* (475–480). This argument is probably Plato's most sustained non-metaphorical line of thought calculated to prove the existence of the Forms.

These arguments hence merit the closest possible attention. We might schematically represent their structure as follows

Step (1): Knowledge and belief are different (proved by earlier arguments).

Step (2): Knowledge and belief are faculties (assumption).

Step (3): Different faculties (*dynameis*) are distinguished from each other by 'what they accomplish and what they pertain to' – in brief, by their respective aims (assumption).

Step (4): The aims of knowledge and belief are different (inference from (1)–(3)).

Step (5): The aims of knowledge and belief are their objects – i.e., the things knowledge or belief is about (assumption).

Step (6): The objects of knowledge and belief are different (inference from (4) and (5)).

This scheme shows how the different assumptions we have found in Plato contribute to the conclusion he reaches at Step (6). All the three unexamined assumptions (2), (3), and (5) are in different ways and to different degrees suggested or made natural by Plato's emphasis on goal-directed (telic) models. Steps (1)–(4) and (6) are all explicit in Plato, while the most striking assumption (5) is largely tacit.

I have formulated (5) in its most explicit and provocative form. It is doubtful, however, to what extent Plato consciously recognized it as a specific assumption (though there are indications in this direction). This premise (5) may have been, rather, a tacit assumption by Plato to the effect that the functions, aims, and objects of each faculty are somehow inter-dependent and therefore go together closely enough for the purposes at hand.

By connecting the conclusion (6) of the above argument with suitable assumptions concerning knowledge, truth, and time, Plato argues further that the different objects mentioned in (6) are the Forms and the objects of the senses, respectively. This part of his attempted proof of the existence of the Forms is not analyzed in the present paper. Some of its presuppositions are discussed in Chapter 3 below, which appeared earlier under the title 'Time, Truth and Knowledge in Ancient Greek Philosophy', *American Philosophical Quarterly* **4** (1967) 1–14.

The first step (1) of the outline argument above was defended by Plato by pointing out that the concepts of knowledge and belief exhibit (as we may put it in contemporary terms) different kinds of logical behavior. Plato emphasizes repeatedly that 'knowledge cannot fail to be true' or, in twentieth-century jargon, that the following implication is valid (true for conceptual reasons):

(*) a knows that $p \to p$,

unlike the analogous implication

(**) a believes that $p \to p$

which is often false. This dissimilarity figures prominently in the proof of the existence of Forms in the *Republic* (V, 476D–E), which was partly analyzed above. Plato calls attention to the same fact elsewhere (see the *Gorgias* 454D, the *Theaetetus* 152C and 186E, and the references to be given later). Because of this logical difference, Plato concludes that the two 'faculties' are different.

Although Aristotle's attitude to the distinction between knowledge and belief is quite different from Plato's, he too ends up saying that knowledge and belief must have different objects – unless we are speaking equivocally. (See the *Analytica Posteriora* I, 33, especially 88b30 ff, and 89a38 ff.) Aristotle agrees with Plato in accepting the validity of (*) and does not hesitate to emphasize it to the point of a paradox:

Moreover, destruction of the knowable carries knowledge (*episteme*) to destruction... For if there is not a knowable, there is not knowledge – there will no longer by anything for knowledge to be of ... (*Categoriae* 7, 7b27ff.).

The paradox here is that according to Aristotle's explicit pronouncements we can only have knowledge of what is indestructible and unchangeable.

7. THE OBJECTS OF KNOWLEDGE AS THE 'AIMS' OF KNOWLEDGE

We have not yet presented anything like a full account of how Plato came to hold his crucial assumption concerning the objects of knowledge and belief – the assumption which identifies these objects with the 'aims' of knowledge and belief when these are conceived of on the goal-directed model and which figures as Step (5) of the above schematized reasoning.

A partial answer is that Plato is here only following an old tradition. Knowledge, thinking, and saying were occasionally thought of as 'aiming' at the things (or facts) they are about and as being 'realized' in them. This tendency is beautifully characterized by Bruno Snell:

In the fragment 34 ... Xenophanes says: occasionally a man may say something that is completely true (literally: 'that has completed itself'), and yet he has no exact knowledge, in contrast to the god. This is Homeric phraseology; a word or thought 'completes itself', i.e., it is concretely realized. The expression is chiefly used of wishes and hopes which look toward the future, but, speaking more generally, it applies to any word that 'comes off' or 'hits the facts'. The godhead always achieves its *telos*, that is its primary characteristic. Instead of deriving divine wisdom from divine omnipotence, Xenophanes has his god proceed from thought to 'completion': knowledge comes first, power is its consequence.

This quotation is from Bruno Snell, *The Discovery of Mind* (Harvard University Press, Cambridge, Mass., 1953), p. 142. (In support of his view, Snell gives the following references: *Iliad* 1.108, 19.90, and H. Gundert, *Pindar und sein Dichterberuf*, p. 113 f., ref. 63.)

Even if Snell had not explicitly mentioned the concept of *telos*, the connection between his observations and the conceptual teleology of the Greeks would have been obvious. Both a modern epistemologist and a half-intuitive pre-Socratic philosopher are likely to emphasize the importance of the relation of knowledge, belief, thinking, and saying to their objects in any theory of knowledge. The implicit teleology of the Greeks led them to conceive of his relation with the help of concepts, images, and locutions drawn from the realm of goal-directed activities – or at least of processes and other phenomena which have a clearly definable end or limit. For this reason, knowledge and thinking are thought of as trying to 'hit' or 'reach' their objects, to 'realize themselves' in these objects. The peculiar way of looking at the relation of knowledge to its objects which is found in Xenophanes and in Plato is thus an immediate corollary of the presuppositions that underlie the conceptual teleology of the Greeks. The apparently surprising tacit near-identification of the objects of knowledge and belief with the *erga* of the 'faculties' of knowledge and belief is just a further consequence of the same assumptions. The fact that Plato was willing to pin the fate of his theory of Forms on this identification is a measure of how deeply ingrained these assumptions were in his way of thinking.

The ultimate, paradoxical consequence of this way of thinking would have been to think of the objects of knowledge as the products of the faculty of knowledge. In Snell, we can see how Xenophanes occasionally yielded to this temptation, and we shall see that Plato skirted at it, albeit jokingly. Moreover, in the case of an *episteme* which is manifested as a practical skill, this identification is not paradoxical at all. However, it is not part and parcel of my thesis that this extreme version of the telic model was accepted by Plato or by anyone else. There are many other ways in which this model can influence a philosopher's thinking. A case in point is the identification Plato needs in his 'epistemological' argument for the existence of Forms.

8. EXAMPLES

An amusing example of Plato's willingness to deal with thinking and speaking as activities that were striving to 'complete themselves' in their objects is offered by the *Euthydemus*:

Well then, when the orators speak to the people, do they do nothing? – No, they do something, he said. – Then if they do something, they also make something? – Yes. – Speaking, then, is doing and making? – He agreed. – Then nobody speaks things that are not, since he would then be making something that is not, and you have admitted that no one is capable of making something that is not. (*Euthydemus* 284 B–C.)

In this exchange speaking is in so many words considered as 'making' the things spoken about.

The argument which Plato here puts forward so playfully may be looked at from different points of view. One of them is the ambiguity of the Greek words for doing (acting) and making (producing). There were several such words (*prattein, poiein,* etc.), but they are all to some degree equivocal in this respect. There was no sharp ready-made distinction which would parallel our doing-making distinction. It is likely – and perhaps even obvious – that this ambiguity contributes to the plausibility of the quoted argument, thus helping to create the paradox it involves.

However, the mere fact that there exists such an ambiguity in Greek vocabulary is not a sufficient explanation for the philosophical interest of the ensuing fallacious inference. There exists a similar ambiguity in some existing languages (e.g., in Finnish *tehdä* is either doing or making) without making it possible so much as to create a philosophical pun in terms of it. Rather, in Plato the ambiguity is made more interesting than a mere homonymy by the much more general phenomenon of conceptual teleology – which also partially helps to understand the survival of the ambiguity.

A fair amount of caution is nevertheless needed here. The *Euthydemus* is full of fallacies, many of them obvious to anyone. The value of the quoted passage for my purpose would not be destroyed, however, even if it could be shown that Plato put forward the argument as an unmistakable fallacy, for even an overt fallacy can throw a great deal of light on what a philosopher thinks of as tempting, interesting, or paradoxical lines of argument in that it illustrates his conceptual preferences and assumptions. Freedom of fallacy is not required for this purpose, although amusement or seductiveness is needed. Perhaps it is not far-fetched to evoke here Wittgenstein's comment on the *depth* of what he called grammatical (=logical) jokes.

It seems to me that arguments like the quoted one offer splendid examples of Plato's ambivalence vis-à-vis arguments (whether fallacious or not) which employed assumptions closely similar to his own but which nevertheless led to conclusions which he could not accept. This ambivalence was mentioned above in Section 3 of this paper; now we can illustrate what was said there.

There are in any case indications that Plato's attitude to the quoted argument in the *Euthydemus* is not without seriousness. The argument prompts a question which exercised Plato repeatedly and at length. This question is the problem of meaningful falsity which was mentioned at the beginning of this paper and which I argued was a very serious problem for Plato himself. In fact, our question goes on as follows:

So according to your own statement, nobody tells lies.

The fact that Plato took seriously the problem which this conclusion of the preceding argument embodies suggests that he took seriously the argument, too.

It may also be relevant to note that the operative admissions are in the quoted exchange made by Ctesippus, who in the words of Mrs. Sprague is one of the 'heroes' of the dialogue (the other 'hero' is of course Socrates), and not by either of its sophistical 'villains'.

In any case, the quoted passage shows that occasionally Plato fully consciously related to each other, however jokingly and experimentally, the two ideas whose close interconnection is according to my suggested interpretation a key to Plato's epistemology – on the one hand, his peculiar idea of the relation of knowledge, thinking, and speaking to their objects, and on the other hand the idea that there is something extremely problematic about meaningful but false statements.

In any case, there are other indications that Plato viewed the relation of knowledge, belief, and saying to their objects in a light different from ours. Perhaps the most straightforward evidence comes from the already quoted and repeatedly discussed passage in the *Republic* V, 477 C–D where Plato speaks of what a faculty 'accomplishes' (*apergazetai*). Subsequently these 'accomplishments' turn out to be in the case of knowledge the *objects* of knowledge.

It may nevertheless look as if Plato were in the *Republic* V, 477 C–D distinguishing the function (or product, *ergon*) of the faculty of knowledge and its object (= what it is related to, i.e. what it is *epi*). However, as I. M. Crombie (among others) has pointed out (in *An Examination of Plato's Doctrines*, Routledge and Kegan Paul, London, 1963, vol. 2, pp. 57–59), Plato's argument is grossly fallacious if a distinction is made between the two. Thus the only hope for Plato to have an acceptable argument is to assimilate the *ergon* of the 'faculty' of knowledge to its objects.

This partial identification was apparently conscious and intentional. This is shown by Plato's formulation when he speaks of 'one thing only' (477D1) which serves to distinguish one *dynamis* from another.

There is no hope to interpret the operative words ἐκεῖνο μόνον so as to escape our conclusion. For instance, it might be suggested that Plato is here including under the heading of 'one thing only' two independent individuating principles for *dynameis*, viz. their functions ('what they accomplish') and their objects (what they are *epi*), either of which could distinguish two *dynameis* from each other. There may be a beginning of a distinction in the text but scarcely a hint of independence, for otherwise the antecedently established difference between knowledge and belief could be accounted for in terms of their different functions (*erga*), invalidating Plato's purported inference to a difference between their respective objects.

9. PLATO'S BACKGROUND. THE 'IDENTITY' OF KNOWLEDGE AND ITS OBJECTS

From the point of view we have reached we can throw light on many different aspects of Plato's epistemology. Among other things, we can see that the requirement 'every *dynamis* must have an object' encouraged his emphasis on the validity of (*). What this implication seems to say is just that the 'propositional attitude' of knowledge cannot fail to have its object. This background is reflected by Plato's and Aristotle's statements quoted above. By the same token, Plato must have been tempted to accept the other implication (**), although he ended up rejecting it. The reason for the temptation is clear. Since belief, too, is according to Plato a *dynamis* it must also have its objects. Belief or opinion that *p* must be belief about something; it must be realized somehow. And what else can this 'belief's being realized' mean but the truth of the belief, i.e., the truth of the implication (**)?

Plato did not accept this paradoxical conclusion although he said in so many words that belief must have its objects. (Cf. the passage quoted above from the *Theaetetus* 189 A.) There are nevertheless strong indications that there in fact existed quite a strong temptation for Plato and for some of his countrymen to accept some principle like (**). At the very least, they found it difficult to see why (**) should be wrong, unlike (*).

In an earlier paper ('Parmenideen peruslause ja kreikkalaisten tiedonkäsitys', *Valvoja* **84** (1966) 138–146) I have indeed suggested that Parmenides virtually yielded to this temptation and accepted a principle that is closely related to (**) and which might be approximately rendered as follows:

(***)   *a* thinks that $p \to p$

I have also indicated how Parmenides was led to this striking assumption by the same sort of 'goal-directed' model of thinking and knowing which I have tried to attribute to Plato. (In addition to this, the ambiguity of the Greek words for knowledge employed by Parmenides also played a role here. The Greek counterparts to 'knows' in (*) and to 'thinks' in (***) are much closer to each other in meaning than these English verbs, in fact almost inseparable.) Insofar as either argument of mine is successful, it supports the other. The affinity of Plato's way of thinking to that of Parmenides is well-known. In the *Theaetetus* (183E) it prompts him to express his great admiration for 'the father of dialectic'. No wonder, for it does not appear too far-fetched to say that Plato's own main proof for the existence of the Forms is forged of precisely the same materials as Parmenides' reasons for announcing his fundamental doctrine that 'one can only think of what is'. In both cases, the starting-point was the validity of (*), and one of the further steps was a comparison of (*) with a closely related implication – with (**) in Plato and with (***) in Parmenides. In both cases, the acceptance of (*) was encouraged by the goal-directed model we have been discussing.

Some manifestations of this model in Greek epistemology have been discussed in the literature. A few commentators have gone as far as to speak of a partial identity between thought and its objects in early Greek thought. A case in point is offered by Bruno Snell's important monograph (*Die Ausdrücke für den Begriff des Wissens in der vorplatonischen Philosophie*, pp. 51–54) which I have already referred to earlier. Snell seeks to relate this phenomenon to certain features of primitive thought. There may be such similarities here, but basically I cannot see anything primitive in the tendency to use goal-directed activities as a general conceptual model, inappropriate though it may often be.

Snell, too, finds the tendency in question in Parmenides (*op. cit.*, p. 53):

Am deutlichsten hat diese Identität von Erkennendem und Erkanntem Parmenides ausgesprochen ... Bei ihm können wir auch nicht unterscheiden, ob die Begriffe ἀλήθεια und δόξα auf die Gegenstände oder auf das Wissen von den Gegenständen bezogen sind ... Stenzel (N.J.XXIV (1021) S. 163) hat diese Erscheinung mit anderen Tatsachen der griechischen Sprache zusammengestellt..., die zeigen, dass das Griechische das verbale Element gegenüber dem logisch Ordnenden, Substantivischen besonders hervorvorhebt.

A little earlier (p. 52) Snell had stated that in pre-Socratic thinkers we often find "die oben geschilderte Einheit von Erkennendem und Erkanntem...''. We may disagree with some of the explanations Snell offers for the curious 'identity of knowledge and the known' he registers, while insisting that this 'identity' is but one extreme form of the goal-directed model as applied to the phenomenon of knowledge.

10. KNOWLEDGE AS ACQUAINTANCE. DIRECT-OBJECT CONSTRUCTIONS WITH 'KNOWS'

In Plato, one form which the close relation between knowledge and its objects takes is a tendency to view knowledge as some sort of direct relation between the knower and the objects of knowledge. For Plato, knowledge was 'a sort of mental seeing or touching', as W. G. Runciman has put it (in *Plato's Later Epistemology*, Cambridge University Press, 1962). Runciman has also convincingly shown that this peculiarity of Plato's does not undergo any modification in the epistemologically central dialogues *Theaetetus* and *Sophistes*. We clearly have here another element of the same conceptual syndrome. By way of a slogan, we might refer to it as 'knowledge as acquaintance'.

The manifestations of this idea are nevertheless subtler than one might first suspect. The natural linguistic counterpart to Plato's idea of knowledge as an immediate perception-like relation to its objects is the use of verbs for knowing together with a direct (grammatical) object in contradistinction to their uses with propositional clauses (knowing that, knowing whether, knowing who, etc.). In most living languages, the former construction seems to be much more common in connection with verbs for perceiving than in connection with verbs for knowing. In some languages, it is even awkward or ungrammatical to use the colloquial equivalent to 'knows' with a direct object. In others, for instance in English, this is possible, but not as common as the corresponding construction with, e.g., 'sees'.

One might be tempted to assume that Plato's idea of knowledge as acquaintance might be betrayed by his frequent use of the direct-object construction. One might also be tempted to surmise that the whole idea of knowledge as acquaintance is due to a fallacious assimilation of all the uses of the Greek verbs for knowing to the direct-object construction. It may be the case that at certain critical junctures (e.g. when he is discussing in the *Charmides* 'knowledge of knowledge') Plato uses direct-object constructions in contexts where we are beginning to find them a little strained. The results of John Lyons' careful study (*Structural Semantics: An Analysis of Part of the Vocabulary of Plato*, Blackwell's, Oxford, 1963, especially p. 182) also show that the direct-object construction (in its several variants and in connection with the different Greek verbs for knowing) was not infrequent in Plato. However, neither peculiarity is very striking, and scarcely conclusive for any philosophical purposes, especially as the propositional constructions are even more frequent in his writings. (In fact, there are according to Lyons more instances of the propositional constructions in Plato than of all the other types of constructions combined.) On the level of quantitative features of overt usage, Plato thus exhibits no preference of the direct-object construction.

This is a salutary fact to recall when one comes upon the claims – made among others by I. M. Crombie and Richard Hare – that Plato's characteristic way of thinking can be explained in terms of an assimilation of the logic of the propositional constructions to that of the direct-object construction. The same explanation could obviously be applied to verbs other than the Greek terms for knowing. Of some of these Crombie writes as follows, apropos the argument we quoted earlier from the *Euthydemus*:

How did we get into this tangle? In something like the following way. 'Report', and certain other verbs of *saying* such as 'mention' or 'recount', can govern either a direct object or a *that*-clause... In the direct-object construction what is reported is a constituent of the world; in the other construction what is reported is a proposition, true or false. The temptation to say that when I make a false statement I say nothing arises from confusing the two objects.... It is in fact by leaving the proposition out of the analysis, and concentrating on the situation, that the trouble arises. (*Plato: The Midwife's Apprentice*, London, 1963, pp. 112–113.)

There is no need to deny that something like this 'confusion' is to be found in Plato. However, there are in most languages any number of similar possibilities of confusion. Some further explanation is needed why this particular possibility was capitalized by Plato or, as I suspect Crombie and Hare would rather say, why Plato fell prey to this particular fallacy. Here, as in almost any other case where it is tempting to attribute a strange argument by a major philosopher to a linguistic confusion, one must look for the deeper reasons why his conceptual preferences made just that particular confusion natural and perhaps almost inevitable.

11. THE DEEPER SOURCES OF THE DIRECT-OBJECT CONSTRUCTION

Instead of saying that Plato's preference of the direct-object construction led him to his view of knowledge as a direct relation between the knower and the known, one should perhaps rather say that both these peculiarities of Plato's can partly be traced back to the same source. Here a logical analysis of perceptual and epistemic concepts may offer us some help. Elsewhere (see 'On the Logic of Perception' in *Perception and Personal Identity,* ed. by N. S. Care and R. Grimm, The Press of Case Western University, Cleveland, Ohio, 1969; 'Objects of Knowledge and Belief', *The Journal of Philosophy* **67** (1970) 869–883; and Chapter 11 of the present volume) I have argued that to use the direct-object construction means to rely on 'methods of individuation' which depend on the personal situation (and personal history) of the knower, or perceiver, or remem-berer, as the case may be. (In the case of perception, the situation in question is the perceptual context of the person in question, and in the case of knowledge it is the cognitive *Lebenswelt* created by one's first-hand acquaintance of persons, things, and facts.) A preference of the direct-object construction with verbs of cognition thus means a tendency to think of cognitive matters from the point of view of someone's personal acquaintance-situation. It is in fact the case, it seems to me, that the Greeks tended to think of epistemic matters in terms of someone's parti-cular vantage-point in space and especially in time. (This I have argued in another context in 'Time, Truth, and Knowledge in Aristotle and Other Greek Philosophers', reprinted as Chapter 3 of this volume.) But if so, Plato's habitual reliance on the direct-object construction as the most appropriate locution in discussing problems of cognition receives at least a partial explanation which is not linguistic in the sense that it would turn on attributing purely linguistic confusion (such as a tacit assimilation of other locutions to the direct-object construction) to him. Rather, the linguistic preference of the direct-object construction is seen as a virtually inevitable consequence of Plato's (and many other Greeks') deeply en-trenched habit of using a context-dependent model in dealing with epistemological matters.

The tacit conceptual assimilation of knowledge to something like direct perception is not a consequence of purely linguistic confusion, either. It seems to be very closely connected with the situational character of Greek epistemology which we have just registered, although there undoubtedly are also other factors which encourage the same idea of knowledge as 'some sort of mental seeing or touching'.

The explanatory value of the claim that Plato overemphasized the perceptual model of knowledge and overlooked other conceptual paradigms for knowing (e.g., true speaking) is likewise very low until and unless we can relate it to deeper conceptual preferences in Plato.

12. PLATO'S CONCEPTION OF KNOWLEDGE IS IN A SENSE 'PROPOSITIONAL'

This is highlighted by the fact that in a certain, not at all negligible sense Plato's idea of knowledge was after all 'propositional', as has been pointed out (among others) by Norman Gulley. (See *Plato's Theory of Knowledge*, Methuen, London, 1962, pp. 94, 165.) The intended sense is one in which knowledge and belief are propositional in that they are analogous to *saying*. (From this kind of propositionality it does not of course follow that the 'propositional' constructions with verbs for knowledge and belief – that is, constructions with 'that', 'whether', etc. – were thought of as primary, as long as Plato was willing to say the same things of saying as of knowledge and belief in this respect. In other senses of the word, knowledge and belief thus need not have been 'propositional' for Plato.)

This shows how very carefully we have to tread here. Richard Hare has claimed (in his article 'Plato and the Mathematicians', in *New Essays on Plato and Aristotle,* ed. by R. Bambrough, London, 1966, p. 23), not unlike Crombie, that Plato's mistake lies in taking sight as the paradigm case of knowing and in forgetting the 'propositional' paradigm. In other words, according to Hare Plato fails to observe a contrast between the idea of knowledge "as if it were something analogous to sight" and the paradigm of 'propositional knowledge' which is "the kind of knowledge that we have when we are able truly and with certainty to *say* that something is the case" (*op. cit.* p. 23, Hare's italics). Hare's diagnosis of Plato's fallacy is a mistaken one, however, for it is conspicuous that Plato typically deals with knowledge and saying as analogous phenomena for the purposes of his epistemological discussion. The same primacy of the

direct-object construction which was noted above in the case of knowledge is in Plato's discussion found also in the case of saying (as is in fact
brought out by our quotation from Crombie). The temptation to assume
the validity of (***), i.e., the temptation to deny the possibility of thinking
what is not the case is paralled by a temptation to deny the possibility of
uttering a meaningful but false sentence. The conceptual model for thinking was for Plato "discourse carried out... not aloud to someone else but
silently to oneself" (see e.g. *Theaetetus* 189E–190B; *Sophistes* 263D–E).
In the sense relevant to Hare's claim, thinking and knowledge were
'propositional' for Plato. The problems which come to a head in connection with the primacy of the direct-object construction with 'knows' in
Plato are even more marked in connection with constructions in terms
of 'saying'. A case in point is once again offered by the quotation from the
Euthydemus given above. We may also recall that for Parmenides, too,
knowledge, thinking, and speaking were on a par as far as their relation to
their objects is concerned. Furthermore, Snell was also seen to emphasize
the role of saying in early Greek thinking. All this is for us welcome evidence to the effect that the telic tendencies manifested here go beyond the
peculiarities to any particular word or expression.

13. The Origins of the Problem of
Meaningful Falsehood

From the vantage point we have reached we can among other things understand why the problem of meaningful falsity (of 'false saying', as Plato
puts it) was as problematic as it in fact seems to have been. What can it
mean to say of an act of saying that it is successful, that it 'comes off', that
one really *says something* (*legein ti*, as Plato repeatedly expresses the
point)? Both from our point of view and from Plato's, this can scarcely
mean anything but that the utterances make sense, that something (some
meaningful proposition) is 'said' or expressed. But in terms of the goal-
directed model this success in 'saying something' will also have to mean
something else or something additional. It will have to mean that the
words uttered 'complete themselves' in their intended objects, that they
'hit the facts' which constitute their aim (to use Snell's locutions once
again). And this kind of success must surely – in the case of a declarative
sentence – amount to the *truth* of the utterance. But if so, an utterance

with a declarative intent can only be *meaningful* if it is *true*. No room will be left for statements which are meaningul but false. No wonder that the problem puzzled Plato intensively and repeatedly.

If I am right, the depth of the problem as to how meaningful falsity is possible is indicated by the fact that Parmenides rejected (for reasons with which Plato expresses some sympathy) the very possibility in question. According to Parmenides, "what can be said and thought of must necessarily exist" (χρὴ τὸ λέγειν τε νοεῖν τ᾽ ἐὸν ἔμμεναι), as fragment 6, line 1, says.

Professor Charles Kahn, who otherwise disagrees with my interpretation, points out (in private communication) that at fragment 8, line 34 ff., Parmenides uses the goal-terminology for the object of νοεῖν, speaking of "the aim [or motive] of cognition".

A somewhat accidental fact of Greek usage helps to strengthen the line of thought which leads to the paradox. The expression which literally means 'to speak what is' was common for 'to speak the truth'. This fact does not by itself 'explain' the problem of meaningful falsehood, however. Rather, it is itself made interesting to Greek philosophers only by the fact that it very nicely reflects a more general way of thinking, some of whose other manifestations we have been charting in this paper.

One symptom of the origin of Plato's problem is his own way of explaining the gist of the difficulty. Unlike Parmenides, Plato accepted the possibility of meaningful falsity. One can *legein ti* without making a true statement. But a mere assertion of this possibility does not solve the problem. Plato still tended to assume that *legein ti* presupposed that the act of saying something hits its objects. If the utterance is false, these objects cannot be the existing ones, for it is its hitting them that would make the statement true. The objects 'hit' must therefore be non-beings, and not-being must therefore exist, too, in some way. Thus Plato can write as follows:

...it is extremely difficult to understand how a man is to say or think that a falsehood really exists and in saying this not be involved in contraction. – Why? – This statement involves the bold assumption that not-being exists (τὸ μὴ ὄν εἶναι) for otherwise falsehood could not come into existence" (*Sophistes* 236E–237A; see also *Sophistes* 237E–239B, 240D–241B, *Euthydemus* 285D ff.).

In his attempted solution to the problem (in the *Sophistes*) Plato still repeatedly expresses himself by saying that in a certain sense not-being has been found out to be. (This sense is based, we shall suggest later, on a re-interpretation of the notion of not-being.)

In a slightly different direction, Plato's difficulty gives rise to the argument which Mrs. Sprague calls "the argument against contradiction". This variant of the problem arises from comparing with each other statement *p* and its negation. They will be realized by different facts, clearly. Hence if these facts are what the statements are about, *p* and ∼*p* will be about different things. Hence we cannot deny or contradict what the other says.

It is often said that this problem – like perhaps other variants of the problem of meaningful falsity – is due to a confusion in Plato between the different senses of 'is'. (See, e.g., Sprague, *op. cit.*, p. 17.) The most direct application of this suggestion is to the problem of non-being. Although a false statement speaks of things that are not (i.e., are not *in the way* stated) it nevertheless does not have to speak of things that are not, i.e., do not exist. In the former, we have a copulative sense of 'are', in the latter, an existential sense. Plato's argument, we are told, turns on a confusion between these two senses.

There is a great deal of truth in this suggestion, but here as in many other cases a purely verbal confusion seems to me woefully inadequate as a full account of Plato's problem. Even though he apparently never distinguished from each other the different senses of 'is', Plato did make distinctions between its several uses, calculated to solve the very problems we found him facing. (See Michael Frede, *Prädikation und Existenzaussage*, Göttingen, 1967.) Furthermore, if the usual dating of the *Timaeus* is accepted, Plato seems to have pinned his hopes to the very end (that is, after having made all sorts of subtle points concerning 'is') on a difference between the objects of knowledge and of belief – which we find, for that matter, still in Aristotle.

It is in fact easy to put forward other partial explanations for those peculiarities in Plato that we have been discussing. One such partial explanation would be to say that Plato had a strong preference for one particular type of theory of (linguistic) meaning – the type of theory which has been called by Moravcsik "the representative theory of meaning" and by Stenius "the name theory of meaning." Again we have a perfectly true – and in fact perceptive – observation. What has been attempted in the present paper is a demonstration that this peculiar preference of Plato's in

the field of semantics is but a special case of much wider conceptual preference which he shared with a number of his compatriots.

14. PLATO'S ATTEMPTED SOLUTION. THE CONCEPT OF DIFFERENCE

Here we cannot hope to discuss fully Plato's attempted solution to the
problem of meaningful falsity (and its variants). We can nevertheless see
how the outlines of his solution fit into the overall picture of his problem
and its background that has been drawn above.

These outlines are determined by the source of Plato's difficulty. Since
the problem was that a false statement seemed to fail to have objects in
which it could 'come about'. Hence what Plato had to do was provide
somehow objects for false sentences, too. Moreover, this is for him *all*
that he had to do. Plato's full and final answer to the crucial questions
(*Sophistes* 262E–263D) has often been said to be crude, oversimplified,
and ambiguous. For instance, Cornford says (*Plato's Theory of Knowledge*,
London, 1935, p. 34) that it is "extremely simple, and consequently vague
and ambiguous." This impression of oversimplification and vagueness is
partly due to a failure to see what Plato is trying to accomplish. It was
axiomatic to him that every statement had to be *about* something (cf.
Sophistes 263C), and all that he wanted to do is show that even a false
statement has its objects, the objects it is about.

The basic idea of his solution is at any rate that thinking, like speaking,
is 'combination'. At 262B–C it is said to be combination of verbs and
nouns. These parts of a sentence refer, according to Plato, to really
existing entities, but it can 'combine' them wrongly. A false sentence
states things other than the existing ones (263B), but this does not mean
that it speaks of non-existing entities.

In this light we can also appreciate the crucial role of the concept of
difference (Plato sometimes calls it the Form of the Other) in his attempted
solution of the problem. It occurs among the 'most general kinds'
(*megista gene*) Plato discusses in the *Sophistes* (254E–259B). If false sentences and false judgements had their objects, it lies close at hand that
they are by and large the same entities that can figure as the objects of
true sentences and true judgements, viz. the actually existing entities. The
explanation of falsehood must then be that in a false sentence one of these

existing entities is mistaken for another. All falsity is thus at bottom mis-identification. Essentially this idea is tentatively presented in the *Theaetetus* (187E–188C, 199A–D), but it is not accepted there and is left in need of further development. This development is accorded to the idea in the *Sophistes*. The outcome of the central discussion of the Forms can be said to be precisely a replacement of the idea of not-being by that of difference:

> We have not only pointed out that things which are not exist, but we have even shown what the form or class of not-being is; for we have pointed out that the nature of the other exists and is distributed in small bits throughout all existing things in their relation to one another, and we have ventured to say that each part of the other which is contrasted with being really is exactly not-being. ... Then let not anyone assert that we declare that not-being is the opposite of being, and hence are so rash to say that not-being exists. (*Sophistes* 258D–E.)

From what has been said it appears why a solution of this sort seemed to serve especially well Plato's purposes: It made it possible for him to find objects for false statements, too, among the actually existing entities. After having re-interpreted not-being as difference Plato could for instance write:

> So the next thing is to inquire whether it [= the idea of not-being] mingles with opinion and speech... If it does not mingle with them, the necessary result is that all things are true, but if if does, then false opinion and false discourse come into being (260B–C).

An affirmative answer is motivated by Plato as follows:

> not-being has been found to partake of being (260D).

The groundwork which is laid by Plato for this view by his interesting discussion of 'the most general kinds' (μέγιστα γένη) earlier in the *Sophistes* makes it a much more sophisticated doctrine than the simple-minded view put forward in the *Theaetetus* that a mistake is always a misidentification. The basic idea nevertheless seems to me to be the same in both cases.

15. The problem of separating the objects of knowledge from those of true belief

We have not yet fathomed the full difficulty of separating the objects of knowledge from those of true belief. Part of the difficulty is seen from our natural tendency to think and to say that one man might have knowledge and another man merely true belief *of the same objects*. A case in point is the difference between the knowledge an eyewitness has (say) of a crime and the true belief someone else might have of the same event on the basis of mere hearsay. Plato's troubles are vividly illustrated by the fact that in the *Theaetetus* (201A–C) Plato used an example of this very sort to demonstrate the difference between knowledge and true belief. This passage has worried several commentators because Plato there seems to be admitting that we can have full knowledge of things he elsewhere seems to deny that we can have true *episteme* about, viz. of sensible particulars. However, this is not the worst puzzle here, and here it in fact lies close at hand to suggest that Plato is not relying on an example but on an analogy: *episteme* is related to true *doxa* in the same way as the information an eyewitness has is related to that based on rumor and hearsay. But this does not absolve Plato of the more serious accusation that his nice explanation is structurally wrong in that in it knowledge and true belief have the same object. It seems to me in fact that there is no way of saving Plato's example in this respect. This insight into its inadequacy ought to discourage attempts to draw any other consequences from it concerning Plato's non-metaphorical views of knowledge and true belief.

Notice how the goal-directed model creates difficulties for Plato at the same time as it enables him to argue for his own conclusions. On one hand it suggests that if knowledge and belief can be distinguished, their objects must be different. On the other hand, it virtually forces Plato to provide different objects for knowledge and belief before he can be as much as satisfied that the two 'faculties' really are different. It seems to me that the only explicit way for Plato to explain the difference between these different objects was to relate the distinction between knowledge and belief to the notions of time, truth, and change. How this could have happened can perhaps be seen from my 'Time, Truth, and Knowledge' already referred to. (See Chapter 3 below.)

In view of the difficulties Plato faced in accounting for the difference between knowledge and true belief, it is interesting to ask whether 'the father of dialectic' distinguished the two. Although no direct answer is contained in the text, there are strong suggestions to the effect that he did not acknowledge such a distinction. One such suggestion is yielded by the proem of Parmenides' main work (fragment 1, line 30) where he lets his goddess to deny that "the opinions of mortals" amount to 'true belief' (... ἠδὲ βροτῶν δόξας, ταῖς οὐκ ἔνι πίστις ἀληθής). Since the 'true belief' of a goddess which the mortals fail to have presumably cannot fall short of real knowledge, Parmenides is in the quoted passage in effect identifying true *pistis* with knowledge.

This is made all the more remarkable by the contrast between Parmenides and Xenophanes who had distinguished between true belief and knowledge, as we saw above in Section 7. Parmenides thus seems to be overlooking a distinction which his predecessors had already made.

Additional evidence is found in fragment 8, line 28, where Parmenides refers as πίστις ἀληθής to the insight which he is announcing and which is said to 'abolish' coming-to-be and corruption, and perhaps also in fragment 8, lines 50–51. The logical situation is not changed by the fact that Parmenides seems to separate *pistis* (belief, faith) from *doxa* (belief, opinion). (Unlike true *pistis*, a true *doxa* apparently does not amount to knowledge for him.)

16. KNOWLEDGE AS PRESUPPOSING TRUTH AND KNOWLEDGE AS 'KNOWHOW'

In view of the importance of the distinction between knowledge and belief for Plato, it is in order to examine more closely the basis of this distinction. The basis Plato offers is, as we have seen, a difference in their logical behavior: (*) is valid although (**) is invalid.

Thus the validity of (*) may be expected to have been of the greatest interest and importance for Plato's system. Its importance is in fact reflected by Plato's faithfulness to it in spite of the wide scope of *episteme* for the Greeks – it included many practical skills in addition to knowledge of propositions – and in spite of the difficulties into which (*) led him as a result of this wide meaning.

In the skills the validity of our implication (*) will mean that whoever possesses a genuine skill (*episteme* as 'knowing how') never fails to use it successfully. It is instructive to note that this conclusion is put forward in the same dialogue as the principle (*), viz. in the *Gorgias*. As a special case, it is concluded there (see 460B) that whoever has learned justice necessarily acts justly. (The reasons why Plato could by locutions of this kind mean *both* 'learned what justice is' *and* 'learned how to practice justice' are discussed elsewhere; see my paper 'Plato on Knowing How, Knowing

That, and Knowing What', reprinted below as Chapter 2 of the present volume.

Here we have in fact one of the most striking features of Plato's conception of *episteme* as skill. Cases in point are offered by *Euthydemus* 280A, *Gorgias* 516E, and by *Republic* I, 340D–E. In the last of these three we read:

Yet that is what we say literally – we say that the physician erred and the calculator and the schoolmaster. But the truth, I take it, is that each of these in so far as he is that which we entitle him never errs: so that, speaking precisely, ... no craftsman errs. For it is when his knowledge abandons him that he who goes wrong goes wrong – when he is not a craftsman.

This quotation already gives us a glimpse of the difficulties into which Plato's views led him and of the manoeuvres which he undertook to disentangle himself from them.

When this idea is applied to the special case of that moral skill which Gould and Snell have argued the Socratic *arete* was, we obtain a fairly strong form of the Socratic paradox. Whoever has learned virtue, cannot fail to practice it. All that is needed for this conclusion is that *arete* can be called an *episteme*.

In this way we can thus understand Plato's view of morality, not just as a skill but indeed as an *unerring* skill. I do not see that those interpreters (Gould, Snell *et al.*) who have emphasized the idea of *arete* as a moral skill have succeeded in accounting for this special feature of the moral 'knowhow' according to Plato.

This special character of moral *episteme* was not without difficulties for Plato, either. It is certainly true that the Socratic paradox of *arete* as *episteme* was for them less paradoxical than it is for us. As it was understood by philosophers like Plato, it nevertheless was not without at least a mild air of a paradox and in any case not without some theoretical difficulties.

One striking peculiarity of the views Plato adopted was apparently discussed at length by him in the *Hippias Minor*. Plato spells out there at some length a difficulty about (*) when applied to most of those skills that a Greek would have been willing to call an *episteme*. Most, if not all, such skills were capable of being used to obtain a result contrary to the usual one. (To be able to hit the aim with certainty is also to be able to shoot so as not to hit it with certainty.) Most kinds of *episteme* may thus give rise to something different from their usual result. Plato seems to have interpreted this to mean that (*) is not valid for such kinds of 'knowhow'. In an important respect, they will thus be like belief rather than full-fledged knowledge. At the end of the *Hippias Minor* he drops a hint that there might perhaps be other types of skills, such as would satisfy (*). This hint is generally taken to be to that particular kind of knowledge which was identified by Plato with virtue. Thus the equation 'virtue is knowledge' takes on a new and sharper meaning. As far as skills are concerned, Plato may be suggesting, *only* virtue is knowledge, for it alone always leads to its typical product – to 'that which it accomplishes and what it pertains to' – i.e., on Plato's interpretation, it alone satisfies (*).

In any case, in this way we can give the *Hippias Minor* an important place in the system of Plato's epistemology and not only in that of his ethics. A. E. Taylor says that the *Hippias Minor* presupposes the Socratic paradox of virtue as knowledge. If what we just said is correct, it is more appropriate so say that this dialogue contributes to one kind of proof of a strong version of the Socratic paradox.

CHAPTER 2

PLATO ON KNOWING HOW, KNOWING THAT, AND KNOWING WHAT

1. WHAT IS 'EPISTEME'? 'EPISTEME' AND 'TEKHNE'

The first and foremost problem of this essay has been debated lively in recent literature. It is the question: how did Plato conceive of the idea of knowledge (ἐπιστήμη, *episteme*, sometimes also translated as 'science')? Similar questions can of course be asked concerning other Greek philosophers, especially concerning Socrates. One reason why this question is important is the paradoxical Socratic identification of virtue with knowledge, ἀρετή (*arete*) with *episteme*. Does the precise meaning of the term *episteme* throw any light on how Socrates (and the young Plato) came to assimilate the two to each other? What kind of knowledge did they have in mind, anyhow?

These questions are not immediately answered by the known facts of Greek usage. Rather, it is this usage that gives rise to the hard problems. It is easily seen that *episteme* meant something not quite identical with our 'knowledge', and the same is true to some extent of the other Greek words for knowledge, such as σοφία (*sophia*), τέχνη (*tekhne*), etc. One of the most important differences was that *episteme* could mean both knowledge and skill, both knowing that and knowing how. "It signifies both knowledge and ability, and is used more particularly to denote experience in manual skills", writes Bruno Snell (*The Discovery of the Mind*, Harvard University Press, Cambridge, Mass., 1953, p. 185). Each of the artisans, a smith, a shoemaker, a sculptor, even a poet exhibited *episteme* in practicing his trade. The word *episteme*, 'knowledge', was thus very close in meaning to the word *tekhne*, 'skill'. The basic use of the corresponding verb ἐπίσταμαι (*epistamai*) is said to be to express, in connection with an infinitive, an ability or a skill, i.e., 'knowing how to do something'. This, we are told, is the only meaning of the verb in the *Iliad*.

In Plato, too, *episteme* is frequently assimilated to *tekhne* or otherwise used in the same sense as the latter term. (See, e.g., *Ion* 537D, 538A ff.; *Charmides* 165D; *Eutyphro* 14C; *Republic* I, 342C, IV, 428B–C; *Euthyde-*

mus 289C). Nor is this due to any accidental ambiguity of the word. No attentive reader of the early Platonic dialogues can doubt that the knowledge so tenaciously sought after by Socrates is there thought of as being in some respects essentially similar to the skills of the craftsmen. In fact, Socrates says of them that "I was conscious that I knew practically nothing, but I knew I should find that they knew many fine things (πολλὰ καὶ καλὰ ἐπισταμένους). And in this I was not deceived; they did know what I did not, and in this way they were wiser than I" (*Apologia* 22D). Nor can this be dismissed as an instance of Socratic irony, for the sequel shows that Socrates' main criticism of craftsmen was not that their *tekhne* was not genuine knowledge, but rather that its applicability was restricted to one field. It is sometimes said that the ideal of knowledge of the Greek philosophers was abstract, impractical, and unrelated to anything like technology. As far as Socrates and the young Plato are concerned, almost the opposite is the case. One of their most important conceptual paradigms was that of a craftsman who is bringing forth a concrete product. (Cf. Snell, *op. cit.*, p. 185.) This is a recurring model in the early Platonic dialogues. The serious limitations of the major Greek philosophers' conception of knowledge cannot be blamed on their alienation from technology. Rather, it seems to me that these very same limitations were shared by the Greek idea of a craftsman or artisan, that is, by the Greek idea of technology.

This makes all the more burning our question of the precise meaning of this Socratic *episteme* which was so closely related to *tekhne*. What kind of knowledge was identified by Socrates with virtue?

2. 'ARETE' AS 'KNOWHOW'

A sweeping answer to this question has been given by John Gould in his interesting book *The Development of Plato's Ethics* (Cambridge University Press, Cambridge, 1955). According to him the moral *episteme* Socrates was talking about was not propositional knowledge, not *knowing that*, but moral skill, *knowing how*. If Gould is right, it is not enough to say that there was an element of skill in addition to an element of knowledge in the Socratic *episteme*; according to him, in the field of morality it is manifested *only* as a skill. "...ἐπιστήμη, as we have seen, is expressed only in action", he writes (*op. cit.*, p. 52). If this is the case, then it follows that the Socratic paradox does not identify virtue with *knowledge* of moral values, but with moral *skill*. To think otherwise is to be seduced by what Gould calls "the intellectualistic legend".

Gould's views have found supporters, and they are worth being discussed with some care. It seems to me that, in their unqualified form, they in any case prove too much. For what was the *arete* which Socrates claimed to amount to *episteme*? It is well known that it was not precisely an ethical 'virtue' in our sense. Tentatively, we might say that it was a configuration of those attributes that commanded the greatest admiration. They included prominently, and sometimes well-nigh exclusively, the attribute of political skill, and more generally the attributes needed for competitive social excellence. (Cf., e.g., Snell, *op. cit.*, ch. 8; Adkins, *Merit and Responsibility*, Clarendon Press, Oxford, 1960, *passim.*) But if so, one cannot maintain that the right-hand side of the *arete* = *episteme* equation simply meant skill without making it into a trivial generalization of that particular skill which the left-hand side denoted. Although we must make a due allowance for the fact that the Socratic paradox was less paradoxical to the Greeks than it is to us, we can scarcely hope to reduce it to the tautology 'moral skill is a skill'.

3. 'ARETE' INVOLVES KNOWING THAT

This general criticism may be slightly unfair to Gould, however, and in any case it has to be supplemented by a more detailed discussion of the evidence. Telling detailed criticisms of Gould's main thesis have in fact been provided among others by Gregory Vlastos. (See *Philosophical Review* **66** (1957) 226–238.) One cannot hope to do better than to quote Vlastos: "Try the 'know how' sense in that sentence and see what you can make of it: 'To fear death is nothing but to think oneself wise while one is not; for it is to think one knows the unknown' (*Apologia* 29A). And there is more at issue here than mere linguistics. Think of the doctrine Socrates is expounding. If 'virtue is knowledge' meant that 'for the achievement of *arete* what is required is a form of ability', Socrates would be saying here that people fear death only because they do not have the ability not to fear it, and what could be more trivial than that? Or, to continue the citation from Gould, 'ability, comparable in some respects to the creative or artistic ability of potters, shoemakers, and the like';

the analogy with these particular acts would imply that the reason we fear death is that we have not acquired skill in meeting it, and what could be further from Socrates' thought? What Socrates wants us to understand is that we fear death because we have mistaken beliefs: we think we know death to be a great evil, greater than disgrace; if we so much as knew our ignorance, our fear of death would leave us. There is no getting away from 'intellectualism' here."

Vlastos goes on to argue that Gould's interpretation misses the whole point of the Socratic art of questioning. The Socratic *elenchus* which clearly "tests statements, not actions", and that this 'intellectualistic' *elenchus* was tied essentially to Socrates' strive to inculcate virtue. "The daily practice of the *elenchus* would have been irrelevant to this aim unless Socrates did not believe that to do the only thing *elenchus* could hope to do – to correct false beliefs, confused ideas, and wrong ways of thinking – was of itself to produce a necessary condition of good moral conduct."

It may be added that long before Plato's time *epistamai* occasionally served to express knowledge of facts, not knowing how. For instance, in the *Odyssey* (δ 730) *epistamai* is used to express Penelope's servant girls' awareness of the fact that her son had gone "on board of the hollow black ship". 'Knowing how' interpretation does not apply here by any stretch of imagination. Hence the general facts about Greek usage do not force us to adopt Gould's interpretation, either.

Gould's thesis is thus wrong. Or, rather, it is oversimplified, for there is no doubt that he is fully right to the extent that there is an element of 'knowhow' in the concept of *episteme* which distinguishes it from our concept of 'knowing that' in the Greek idea.

This does not solve but instead reinforces our problem of the precise nature of *episteme*. Now the problem largely becomes a query as to how the (from our modern point of view) disparate elements of knowledge and skill could coexist in the idea of *episteme* and also how they were related to each other. It is perhaps not so very difficult to see on what kinds of occasions the term *episteme* was used in ancient Greece. The real difficulty is to see what these several occasions had in common, what enabled the Greeks to classify them under the same heading. The problem, we might say, is not in determining the extension of the concept of *episteme*, but rather in determining its intension.

4. 'EPISTEME' VS. 'EMPEIRIA'

A partial answer is obtained by seeing what *episteme* was contrasted with. We have already seen that *episteme* did not exclude practical skill. However, not any human ability, not any manual dexterity could be called *episteme*. Many of them were referred to by the much less honorific title of ἐμπειρία (*empeiria*). The contrast between *episteme* and *empeiria* was not a contrast between knowing that and knowing how. It was a contrast between such skills as are governed by general rational principles and hence could be taught and learned by recipes and rules and those which only could be assimilated by example and rote. *Episteme* could be conceptualized; *empeiria* turned completely on past experiences and training and was therefore comparable to mere habit. Occasionally *empeiria* is translated as 'experience' (a case in point is Sir David Ross' translation of the beginning of Aristotle's *Metaphysics*), which is somewhat misleading because the difference between *episteme* and *empeiria* does not turn on a different origin of the knowledge or skill in question, but rather on the level of conceptualization involved. It even appears that *empeiria*, like *episteme*, could be more like knowing that than knowing how. For a typical move in Greek philosophy was to emphasize the connection between *empeiria* and memory. "From memory *empeiria* is produced in men", Aristotle writes, "for the several memories of the same thing produce finally the capacity for a single *empeiria*. And *empeiria* seems pretty much like *episteme* and *tekhne*, but in truth *episteme* and *tekhne* come to men through *empeiria*... Art arises when from many notions gained by *empeiria* one universal judgement about a class of objects is produced" (*Metaphysics* I, 1980b27–981a7). Plato, too, gives as an example of *empeiria* a mere memory of what has happened. The *episteme-empeiria* distinction thus cuts completely across the *knowing that-knowing how* distinction.

5. 'EPISTEME' PRESUPPOSES AWARENESS OF WHAT ONE IS DOING

Another way of emphasizing the same or closely related point was for the Greek philosophers to say that *episteme*, unlike *empeiria*, presupposed *awareness* of what one was doing and ability to give an account (*logos*) of it. In the *Theaetetus*, *episteme* was even identified tentatively with true belief accompanied by *logos*. (Cf. also *Republic* VII, 533C.) Even though this is in the course of the dialogue rejected as a *sufficient* characterization of knowledge (in the sense of *episteme*), ability to give a rational account of one's beliefs was clearly thought by Plato as a *necessary* condition of knowledge. Nor was this idea a peculiarity of Plato's. In his biting criticism of popular wisdom Xenophanes says that "even if one chanced to say the complete truth, oneself knows it not" (Fragment 34). It seems to me that this is the spirit in which we must also understand Plato's (Socrates') statements that poets, like oracles, say "many fine things, but know none of the things they say" (*Apologia* 22C), not as an expression of mild disapproval, but as a bitter criticism. This bitterness is perhaps more clearly in evidence when the same criticism is applied in the *Meno* (99C–D) to ordinary statesmen: their being "like soothsayers and diviners" is ground for condemning them as having "no knowledge of anything they say". This point is not belied by the fact that later the ageing and increasingly pessimistic Plato came to associate more and more importance to mere true belief and to mere *empeiria* as vehicles of that non-rational persuasion needed to maintain the social order.

The importance of the awareness as a criterion of true *episteme* was for Plato enhanced by the connection of this requirement with the teachability of the knowledge or skill in question. The main problem of the *Meno* thus might almost be 'Is virtue knowledge?' rather than 'Can virtue be taught?'

6. Knowledge of Ends as the Gist of 'Episteme'

Thus we are led to a more specific question in our quest of the meaning of *episteme*. For speaking of awareness or account immediately prompts the question: Awareness of what? Account of what? If even a skill could be *episteme* provided it was accompanied by "one universal judgement about a class of objects", what was this judgement supposed to be about?

Here we come to the main specific suggestion I propose to put forward in this essay. So far my discussion has followed fairly conventional lines; now I shall venture a thesis which obviously needs all kinds of qualifications but which perhaps is understood most easily in a blunt and unqualified form.

We have already noted that the activity of a craftsman was an important conceptual model for the Greeks, especially for Socrates and for the early Plato. What is the knowledge about that enables an artisan to practice his trade? The simple-minded answer is 'knowledge of his own products, of their nature'. A shoemaker's knowledge of shoes is what enables him to produce them, and the same holds for any other craftsman. According to Plato, what makes the activity of a craftsman a real *episteme* is that he is not acting "at random" (οὐκ εἰκῇ), to use Plato's own formulation (*Gorgias* 503D–E), but "with a view to some object", that is, "with the purpose of giving a certain form to whatever he is working upon". Awareness of this form is then thought of as the gist of a craftsman's skill.

Thus the essence of a productive skill and, by a tacit generalization, of any rational skill is seen in the awareness of its end and of the nature of this end. In so far as we can generalize this, we immediately have an answer to our earlier question as to what constitutes the connecting link between 'knowing that' and 'knowing how' in the concept of *episteme*. In any craftsman's activity, *knowing how to produce* (or bring about) x and *knowing what x is* were inseparably connected with each other. (Perhaps it is hopeless in principle to try to separate them sharply in the Greek usage.) We can thus see that typically the 'knowing that' aspect that there is to the *episteme* is of certain very special kind: it is knowledge of essences or definitions, knowing *what* rather than (unspecified) knowing *that*.

7. Examples. knowing what is x and knowing how to bring about x

For instance, the doctor's art, the art of healing, is from this point of view nearly identical with his knowledge of what health is, which of course implies the secondary capacity of telling the healthy from the sick. This somewhat surprising conclusion is in fact explicitly assented to in the Platonic dialogues. In the *Laches* (195C) it is in so many words denied that "doctors know anything more, in treating sick persons, than how to tell what is healthy and what is diseased" and asserted that "this is all that they know". It is worth noticing that what is here identified with 'knowing what' is not any species of abstract, propositional knowledge, but that art or skill which is exhibited by a doctor "in treating sick persons".

One passage is of course not conclusive. Nor do I want to claim that there is a great deal more to be said of the matter. It is clear, nevertheless, that there are many indications in the same direction in the early Platonic dialogues. To catch some of their flavour, we may recall the passage in the *Charmides* (170A) where Plato asks whether "a science of science (i.e., *episteme* of *episteme*), if such exists, be able to do more than determine that one of two things is science (*episteme*), and the other is not science". This question receives an unqualified "no, only that" as an answer. This answer obviously is nothing but another application of the same general principle we found operative also in the *Laches*: Knowledge of *x* equals ability to tell what is *x* and what is not *x*. It is also likely that in the *Laches* practical skills are almost as close to Plato's mind as they are in the *Charmides*: in the very next sentence 'knowledge of health' is explicitly mentioned. Notice also that a little later (170A) the first line of criticism of *sophrosyne* as 'knowledge of knowledge' ends up with the fatal charge that a man with such 'knowledge of knowledge' will not be able to tell knowledge from non-knowledge: "So he will not be able to distinguish neither the man who pretends to be a doctor [i.e., pretends to know medicine], but is none, from the man who really is one, nor any other man who has knowledge from him who has none." (Cf. also 171C.)

The point of view we have reached here seems to me extremely interesting in several respects. I cannot do much more here, however, than to indicate some of the most promising lines of future investigation. Notice, in any case, that my point is not belied by any distinction that might be made between health (ὑγίεια) and the healthy (τὸ ὑγιεινόν) in the examples I have adduced in favor of my interpretation. Whatever distinctions there may be in Plato between the two, they do not affect the fact that Plato speaks of health in terms of the healthy, in the same way as he speaks of goodness in terms of the good and in general of the quality of *x*-ness in terms of the *x*.

My present point is not affected, either, by the kind of *pros hen* ambiguity from which Aristotle finds *to hygieinon* to suffer in *Metaphysics* IV, 2. If anything, it is especially natural to say that a doctor's art consists in knowing what is healthy in the sense of being a means to health. Furthermore, the ambiguity is an ambiguity in the ends of a craft, which does not necessarily affect the relation of each of these several variants of the craft to its respective end.

8. THE IMPORTANCE OF DEFINITIONS

As against Gould, Vlastos was seen to emphasize that if we do not recognize the intellectual, 'knowing that' aspect of Socratic *episteme*, the whole point of the Socratic *elenchus* (ἔλεγχος) is lost sight of. From the point of view we have reached, we can now understand much more than just the intellectualistic overtones of the Socratic *elenchus*: we can understand the specific character it took in Plato's Socratic dialogues, which typically were but as many searches for the *definition* of some philosophically important concept, for instance of this or that virtue. The kind of what-knowledge that the definition of a virtue presumably gives us was seen to be virtually identified by Socrates with a skill in bringing about that virtue in oneself and in others. The definition of a virtue was apparently supposed to present us with a 'form', or a plan, almost a 'blueprint' of that particular virtue, a blueprint that would have enabled us to realize it in the same way a shoemaker's knowledge of the *eidos* of a shoe enables him to work, not at random, but in the way best calculated to bring about a shoe. Small wonder, therefore, that the search for definitions played an overwhelmingly important role in the Socratic method, and small wonder also that this quest turned out to be such a difficult enterprise. Small wonder, for that matter, that Plato could in the *Meno* (99B) infer from the failure of contemporary Athenian statesmen to make their contemporaries or even their own sons virtuous that the virtuous qualities of these statesmen "were not an effect of knowledge" – that is, apparently, not an effect of that definition of *arete* to the search of which much of this dialogue is dedicated.

9. OMNISCIENCE IMPLIES OMNIPOTENCE

It is important to realize that this passage in the *Meno* is much more than a rhetorical or an *ad hominem* argument. It represents a line of thought which is often taken by Plato and which now suddenly becomes understandable. In the *Sophistes* Plato in effect infers from the alleged knowledge of a sophist about all things that the sophist claims to be able to produce everything – "you and me... and the other animals besides, and the trees" (233E). In fact, this alleged omniscience of the sophist is mentioned e.g. in 234A, where a sophist is said to claim that he "knows all things (πάντα οἶδε) and can teach them to another for a small fee", while the consequent alleged omnipotence is mentioned at 233D, 234B, etc. The connection between knowledge and production is again not a rhetorical flourish but part and parcel of Plato's own argument. Just because the sophists' claim to be able to produce anything is false – Plato calls it a "joke" (234A) – their alleged knowledge of all things cannot be genuine, but can only amount to an art of imitation and deception (234B–C).

How deeply ingrained this line of thought was in Plato's philosophy is shown by the fact that in the *Republic* (V, 596–598) essentially the same criticism is levelled at another alleged type of universal knowledge, viz. that of an artist, who is in so many words represented by Plato as being apparently able to "make all the objects produced by individual craftsmen" and also to "create all plants and animals himself included, and, in addition, earth and sky and gods, the heavenly bodies and the underworld." Why should Plato blame a poor artist for such outrageous claims, if all that the artist was trying to do was to imitate these lofty things? Because such claims were according to Plato's lights implied by the artist's alleged knowledge of the things represented.

At an earlier stage of his career Plato had vented his suspicions of universally applicable knowledge in the *Charmides* (170–171). Another aspect of the motivation of these suspicions is discussed in Chapter 1 above (Section 5).

Clearly we are dealing with a most important assumption of Plato's. In the *Laws* (XII, 961E ff.) Plato is still emphasizing that a successful activity presupposes knowing the nature of its end. Similar ideas appear, e.g., in the *Phaedrus* (269E–270A, 270B ff.).

10. VIRTUE AS KNOWLEDGE OF DEFINITIONS

The Socratic assimilation of virtue to knowledge becomes a natural corollary to the general view we have reached. Possessing a virtue, in the normal sense of being able to practice it, will be inseparably tied to knowing the nature and perhaps even the definition of that particular virtue: virtue, indeed, becomes knowledge. But this equation is not a tautology, as it easily was on the interpretation that identified the relevant *episteme* with moral *knowhow*. However unparadoxical the Socratic paradox may become from our point of view, we can see that in any case it presents a mighty challenge to a theoretical thinker to spell out that definitory what-knowledge with which virtue is identified in the 'paradox'.

11. ARISTOTELIAN EVIDENCE

Another doctrine which *prima facie* may appear somewhat far-fetched but which we can now appreciate better is Aristotle's idea of a close connection between knowing the nature of something and being able to bring it about. Or, rather, what may appear far-fetched is not this idea itself but the length to which Aristotle sometimes pushes it. Again a doctor's art of healing serves as an example: "the medical art is in some sense identical with health", Aristotle writes. The context of this kind of statement shows how Aristotle arrived at it and also how he qualified it: "Evidently then there is not necessity, on this ground at least, for the existence of Forms [Ideas]. For man is begotten by man, and a given man by an individual father; and similarly in the arts, for the medical art is the formal cause of health" (*Metaphysics* XII, 3, 1070a28–31). Aristotle's point in the last sentence is that in the same way as each man is begotten by a man, the instances of health that a doctor brings about when he cures his patients are derived from the presence of the form of health (as embodied in its definition) in the doctor's mind. The same point is made by Aristotle in pretty much the same terms in *Metaphysics* XII, 4, especially 1070b33–36, which is the passage I first quoted from.

The familiar Aristotelian theory of a definition as expressing the immediate cause of the thing defined is obviously a part of the same syndrome.

12. CONCEPTUAL TELEOLOGY. THE PARADIGM
OF A CRAFTSMAN

Further examples are easily found. Giving such examples would be a virtually endless task, however, if I am right. For it seems to me that we have much more here than an epistemological peculiarity of the Socratic school. The central role which the concept of an end or limit (*telos*) of an activity plays in the concept of the *episteme* governing this activity in Socrates and Plato seems to me a special case of a much more general tendency of the Socratic philosophers. Not only in their discussions of knowledge, but in discussing almost any phenomenon, they tended to drag in, wittingly or unwittingly, the *telos* of that activity. It is as though they could not conceptually master a situation without subsuming it somehow under the concept of a process with an end, *telos*. We might thus call the tendency in question 'conceptual teleology' and speak of the underlying way of thinking as 'telic'. It is important to realize that explicitly teleological doctrines are not what is meant here. At best, they are particular manifestations of the conceptual or implicit teleology which is being described here.

The prominence of the paradigm of a craftsman which we have already registered is not unconnected with the fact that of all human activities the activity of a craftsman is likely to have the most concrete and clearly definable product.

This general 'telic' tendency has sometimes been noted in the literature, though apparently its different manifestations have never been studied systematically. For instance R. G. Collingwood writes (*Principles of Art*, Clarendon Press, Oxford, 1938, pp. 17–18): "Once the Socratic school had laid down the main lines of a theory of craft, they were bound to look for instances of craft in all sorts of likely and unlikely places. To show how they met this temptation, here yielding to it and there resisting it, or first yielding to it and then laboriously correcting their error, would need a long essay."

Clearly, this is not an occasion for the long essay which Collingwood envisaged but never executed. Elsewhere, I have ventured to offer a few suggestions along similar lines, for instance in Chapter 1 above. A few general comments may nevertheless be in order here in connection with Collingwood's remark. First of all, it seems to me that in one sense Collingwood's suggestion is far too intellectualistic. The temptation to discuss all and sundry phenomena in terms of their outcomes did not arise just from the success of the Socratic school in their conscious attempts to develop "a theory of craft" as Collingwood says. It was deeply ingrained in the very concepts with which the Greeks were wont to operate. The "theory of craft" which the Socratic school elaborated was made an appealing conceptual paradigm by this broader tendency, which largely remained tacit and even unconscious.

On the other hand, Collingwood is entirely right in the idea that conceptual preferences of the kind he describes do not predetermine a philosopher's views. He spoke, as we saw, of the Socratic philosophers as sometimes successfully 'resisting' the temptations of the craftsman-model. I want to emphasize very strongly that even any further claims that the temptations were predominantly unconscious and conceptual does not commit me to what I like to call the Whorfian fallacy, that is to say, to the view that the concepts a thinker inherits and the conceptual preferences he has somehow make it impossible for him to avoid certain views, impossible for him to develop his theories in more than one way. If my suggestion concerning the general nature of the Greek conceptual system is correct, Collingwood's remarks provide us with beautiful counter-examples to the Whorfian fallacy. For Collingwood is certainly right in saying that a large part of the philosophical activity of the Socratic school consisted in attempts, and sometimes not entirely unsuccessful attempts, to free themselves of the implications of their conceptual presuppositions. Understanding these presuppositions nevertheless remains a vital part of the task of a historian, for without appreciating these presuppositions he will never understand why certain problems were so problematic to the old philosophers as they obviously were. However, this appreciation of certain presuppositions does not imply belief in their inevitability.

13. KNOWLEDGE AND ITS OBJECTS IN PLATO

Although I cannot elaborate the point here, it seems to me that this telic way of thinking coloured Plato's concept of knowledge also in other ways than in connection with the relation of knowing how to knowing that. It also coloured his ideas of the relation of knowledge to its objects. These ideas, in turn, were special cases of Plato's general ways of looking at the relation of such 'mental acts' as knowledge and belief (and even saying) to their objects. It seems to me that, in some slightly vague sense, these relations were thought of by Plato in telic terms, somehow as attempts of the knowledge or belief or statement to realise itself in its objects. This is reflected in Plato's classification of knowledge and belief as powers or capacities (*dynameis*) each of which is characterized by its characteristic objects (*Republic* V, 477). One area where this immediately led Plato into trouble was to ask when an act of saying is successful. On one hand, we all agree that this is the case whenever something meaningful is uttered. However, in telic terms a statement is successful only if it 'hits its objects', i.e., reaches the objects which it is about. And what can this mean but that the statement in question is *true*? Thus it becomes a tremendous problem for Plato to account for the possibility of meaningful falsity, of the possibility of 'false saying'. If I am not mistaken, Plato devotes to this subject more space than to the explicit explanation of his theory of forms.

I cannot here go into the details of the solution Plato gave to this problem. (The whole problem was discussed from another angle in Chapter 1 above.) I have mentioned it here only as an illustration of how a historian's awareness of the conceptual presuppositions of some old philosopher enables him, not so much to predict the opinions of this philosopher, but to appreciate the difficulty and depth of some of the problems with which this philosopher was wrestling – appreciate what Collingwood called his "laboriously correcting" his conceptual biases.

Supplementary examples of the implicit teleology that I have mentioned might help to make my suggestion clearer. A nice illustration of my point is the double meaning of that word Werner Jaeger has tried to raise to the status of the key word of the Greek culture, the word *paideia*. Originally, it meant just children's education, but it came to mean the totality of the Greek cultural ideas. What connects the two is just the telic point of view: The ideals of a culture determine the ends of education in that culture. There is of course here a nice connection with the Platonic problem of the teachability of *episteme*.

Likewise, the limitations of Greek technology which were mentioned above and which still must be left largely unexamined here at the very least become more understandable. A Greek engineer needed, like the demiurge of the *Timaeus*, pre-existing models to aim at, and hence could not be a real creative inventor as little as the demiurge could create the world *ex nihilo*. Both were literally *demiourgoi*, craftsmen, in the sense in which we to-day habitually contrast craftsmen to creators or inventors. Not only were the fine arts destined according to Plato and Aristotle to imitate nature (in the sense of imitating nature's ends), but this applied to the art of technology as well. Nature was needed for all the craftsmen to find their paradigms in, for their ends, like the form of the bed in the *Republic*, could not have been created by any human being.

This in any case seems to be the tacitly accepted way of thinking about technology among philosophers like Plato and Aristotle. To what extent it constrained actual technological practice is an extremely complicated problem. It is in any case instructive, it seems to me, to note the frequency of references to the imitation of nature in ancient accounts of technology and its aims.

14. FURTHER EXAMPLES. DOING AS MAKING

Another illustration is even closer to our central topic of Plato's philosophy and the Platonic concept of knowledge. If the end or aims of any activity is the most important aspect of that activity, all activities are assimilated conceptually to the production of certain results, to making. (This is just what is involved in the conceptual preponderance of the craftsman-paradigm.) But if so, the line between *doing* and *making* is apt to remain unclear and unimportant. I cannot here discuss at any great length the intricate problems that arise in connection with the concepts of doing and making in ancient Greece – one is for instance reminded of Hannah Arendt's remarks on the subject. I shall nevertheless register both the general claim that the doing-making distinction was underdeveloped in ancient Greece and also the specific claim that no clear doing-making distinction was ever made by Plato, notwithstanding the claims of many scholars.

The absence of a clear doing-making distinction also helped to emphasize the telic element in *episteme*. We saw that what was characteristic of *episteme* was knowledge (rational awareness) of *what one is doing*, which thus early became *knowledge of what one is making (bringing about)*. One can perhaps say that the generality of my earlier analysis of the relationship of knowing that and knowing how in Socrates and Plato presupposes the assimilation of all kinds of *episteme* to the special kind of *episteme* which pertained to processes with a more or less clearly defined end. Now we can see that this presupposition was fulfilled, if it was fulfilled, in virtue of the implicit teleology of the ancient Greek way of thinking.

15. QUALIFICATIONS: THE PROBLEM OF ACCURACY

I do not think it will be necessary to emphasize that many *caveats* are needed here. Indeed, I believe they come to mind rather more easily than the bold unqualified claims I have made. A few supplementary explanations may nevertheless be in order here.

An apparent counter-example to my main thesis is found in the *Republic*, 472A ff. There Plato seems to be saying that a knowledge of the "perfect patterns" of an ideal state does not give us the power to bring it about. It only shows that the closer we are to the ideals, the better off we are. "That was our purpose, rather than to show that they could be realized in practice, was it not?" – "That is quite true." It also seems to be true that we have here a counterinstance to my thesis of the connection between the knowledge of an end and the ability to realize it in Plato.

This impression is not entirely accurate, however. The main thing that we have to understand here is that in the passage in question Plato is not addressing himself to the problem whether or not the knowledge of an ideal state yields the potentiality to realize it, but rather the question whether such knowledge implies the power to realize the ideal completely, in every detail. What is at issue is not the problem of realization, but the problem of accuracy. As to the question of *approximate* realization, Plato tends to assume that the knowledge of the ideal ensues in the power to bring about such approximation. This is already indicated in 473A, though perhaps not completely conclusively. "Then don't insist on my showing that every detail of our description can be realized in practice, but grant that we shall have met your requirement that the ideal should be realized, if we are able to find the conditions under which a state can approximate most closely to it."

If this quotation is not yet completely categorical as to the connection between knowing what and knowing how to bring it about (in the special case of an ideal *polis*), this is most likely the case merely because at the stage of the passage in question Plato's interlocutors had not yet discussed the nature of his ideal state. For instance, the crucial problem of educating the rules of this state had not yet come up for discussion.

Later, Plato in fact returns to the connection between the knowledge of his ideal and the power to realize it at least approximately. (See *Republic* VI, 499B ff.) There Plato's answer is completely unambiguous. There he is "ready to maintain that ... whenever men knowledgeable of philosophy take part in politics, then the society we have described either exists ... or will exist ...". And this knowledge of philosophy is precisely knowledge about the ends to be brought about. A philosopher's "eyes are turned to contemplate fixed and immutable realities, a realm where there is no injustice but all is reason and order, and which is the model he imitates." Will such a philosopher "lack the skill to produce discipline and justice and all the other ordinary virtues", Plato asks, and answers the question with a resounding "certainly not". Hence we have here further evidence for my thesis rather than a counterexample to it. It is important to realize, it seems to me, that Plato's insistence on the feasibility of his ideal state is not just a piece of persuasive rhetoric but is intimately tied to his central epistemological assumptions.

16. Qualifications: maker's knowledge vs. user's knowledge

The connection which we have found between knowing what x is and being able to bring about x is partially hidden by a distinction which Plato and to some extent also Aristotle superimpose on it. This is a distinction between *maker's* (producer's) *knowledge* and *user's knowledge*. Of these two Plato valued user's knowledge much higher. The distinction is made among other places in the *Republic* (601E–602A), in the *Euthydemus* (289A–D), and in the *Cratylus* (390B). Compare also *Meno* 88E. (In Aristotle it is found, e.g., in *Pol.* II, 6, 1278b37 ff. and 11, 1282a17 ff.)

This contrast marks a definite qualification to my main thesis. How important the qualification appears to one depends on one's view of the contrast maker's knowledge – user's knowledge. It will not be discussed here in any detail beyond noting that it seems to be rather hard to find any purely epistemological motivation for it, even though Plato definitely connects it with his other epistemological doctrines. (Cf. also its relation in Aristotle to the other aspects of the craftsman paradigm, to be mentioned below.) In fact, it lies very close at hand to try to explain this distinction in sociological rather than epistemological terms. If so, its weight as a qualification to Plato's epistemological assumptions is perhaps not very great.

17. QUALIFICATIONS: KNOWLEDGE OF THE MATERIAL FACTOR

Another qualification is found in Aristotle, although it may be said to be implicit in the *Timaeus* and perhaps vaguely already in the very craftsman paradigm for knowledge. According to this qualification, in order to realize a form, say *x*, it is not enough to know this form, although this knowledge is still clearly the most important requisite of realization. What is also needed is knowledge of the material in which *x* is to be realized. This comes up, e.g., in Aristotle's discussion of the Socratic paradox in the *Eudemian Ethics* I, 5, 1216b6 ff. There Aristotle explains that in a productive *episteme* it does not suffice to know the end. One must also know "from what it arises", i.e., the material factor.

In making this point Aristotle incidentally offers striking evidence for the near-identity of knowing what *x* is and knowing how to bring about *x* in his predecessors (see 1216b3–10):

"Socrates... thought the knowledge of virtue to be the end, and used to inquire what is justice, what bravery and each of the parts of virtue; and his conduct was reasonable, for he thought all the virtues to be kinds of knowledge, so that to know justice and to be just came simultaneously.... Therefore he inquired what virtue is...."

It seems to me that this diagnosis of his predecessor's motives by Aristotle is a more accurate one than it is sometimes given credit for.

Likewise, it is said in *Physics* II, 2, 194a22–27 that a doctor knows also "bile and phlegm" and not only (the form of) health, and a builder knows also "bricks and beams" and not just the form of a house. Similar statements are found elsewhere in Aristotle.

It is to be noted that this Aristotelian qualification to the Platonic connection between knowing what and knowing how is a relatively small one. What we have here is another ingredient of the craftsman paradigm rather than a rejection of the paradigm. For obviously a shoemaker needs to know about leather over and above his knowledge of the form of a shoe, and likewise for other craftsmen. Thus this qualification does not change the main connection we have discovered between knowing what and knowing how in Plato and Aristotle.

The *Physics* passage is interesting also because Aristotle there assimilates his distinction between knowing the end-product and knowing its material to the Platonic distinction between user's knowledge and maker's knowledge:

"The arts, therefore, which govern the matter and have knowledge are two, namely the art which uses the product and the art which directs the production of it" (*Physics* II, 2, 194a36–b1).

The qualifications we thus have to make here do not affect my main thesis, but rather tend to reinforce it. It would not be affected by an examination of the main unsolved problem, either, which is constituted by the distinctions Plato makes in his later dialogues between different kinds of knowledge. They nevertheless deserve, and need, a lengthier analysis than can be devoted to them in this essay.

Further circumstantial evidence for my main theses in the present chapter can also be deduced from what was said in Chapter 1 above.

CHAPTER 3

TIME, TRUTH, AND KNOWLEDGE IN ARISTOTLE AND OTHER GREEK PHILOSOPHERS

1. CONCEPTUAL PRESUPPOSITIONS

In this chapter I shall discuss a tacit presupposition, or a group of presuppositions, which seems to lurk behind certain doctrines of Aristotle's and to have been rather widespread in ancient Greece.

A generalization concerning such widespread tacit presuppositions has of necessity something self-defeating about it. If such a generalization is correct, the presuppositions it postulates were shared by the great majority of philosophers and of ordinary people within a culture. If so, there was little occasion for anyone to challenge these presuppositions, to discuss them, or even to bring them out into the open. In such circumstances, not very much direct evidence is likely to be available to show the existence of these presuppositions.

This does not go to show that broad generalizations concerning more or less unconscious ways of thinking within this or that culture are without philosophical interest. In fact, they seem to be worth a great deal more attention than professional philosophers have devoted to them of late. The difficulty I mentioned perhaps explains part of this lack of interest, however. In most cases, it is not very difficult to put forward intriguing suggestions concerning the general features of people's ways of thinking in different cultures or at different periods of intellectual history. The speculative philosophy of history from Hegel onward bristles with such proposals. However, it is usually much more difficult to substantiate them. Often it is rather difficult to connect the more or less implicit *Weltanschauung* that some philosophers of history have thought that they can perceive in the background of the Greek mind with what we actually know about Greek thinkers or of other facets of the Greek civilization.[1] Hence the largely justified qualms of professional philosophers about imputations of implicit general presuppositions to the Greeks.

It seems to me, nevertheless, that a closer study of the most articulate and systematic Greek philosophers may serve a purpose here. Such a philosopher is much more likely to make explicit some of the presuppositions he shares with his countrymen than the majority of these. He may even have to rely on these presuppositions in his philosophical arguments. A careful study of the general presuppositions of an individual Greek philosopher may therefore throw some light on the implicit conceptual presuppositions of the ancient Greeks in general.

We are primarily concerned here with certain general features of Aristotle's philosophical thinking. Some of the assumptions he makes appear to have parallels in other Greek philosophers, and hence occasion the question whether there is something in the common background of all these philosophers to which these assumptions might be related and which might partly explain them. I shall make some suggestions along these lines toward the end of this chapter.

2. THE PREDOMINANCE OF TEMPORALLY INDEFINITE STATEMENTS

The group of presuppositions we deal with here is connected with the notion of time.[2] Many presuppositions in this group seem to stem from a characteristic tendency which permeates many different parts of Aristotelian thought. It is safer to speak of a tendency here than of an assumption, for apparently Aristotle does not consciously choose this way of thought in preference to explicitly formulated alternatives. Rather, he takes this mode of thought as the only natural one, without even becoming quite clear of the alternatives it might have and certainly without ever articulating the alternatives. If we nevertheless want to formulate this tendency as an explicit assumption we may say that for Aristotle the typical sentences used in expressing human knowledge or opinion are not among those Quine calls *eternal sentences* (or, even among *standing sentences*) but among those Quine calls *occasion sentences*.[3] That is to say, they are not sentences to which we assent or from which we dissent once and for all. They are sentences to which we can subscribe or with which we must disagree on the basis of some feature or features of the occasion on which they are uttered (or written). In particular, the sentences Aristotle is apt to have in mind are *temporally indefinite*; they depend on the time of their utterance. They may be said to be relative to the moment at which they are propounded. This relation may be implicit, but it may also be made explicit by the occurrence of such 'token-reflexive' expressions as 'now' or 'at the present moment' in the sentence in question. (Among these we have to count also such expressions as 'yesterday' or 'tomorrow' where another moment or period of time is specified by reference to the present moment.) In a sense they can be fully understood only if we know what moment this 'now' is, i.e., when the sentence in question was uttered or is thought of as being uttered. If Aristotle had been asked to give an example of an arbitrary sentence, he might have chosen something like 'Socrates is awake' or 'Socrates is walking' – and these we may express equally well by 'Socrates is now awake' and 'Socrates is walking at the present moment'.

If Aristotle's tacit assumption is expressed in this way, however, we are already siding with the moderns against him to some extent. What we have said already expresses the spontaneous reaction of almost all modern logicians and philosophers to the sentences of the kind we are discussing. A modern logician is likely to avoid the use (and the mention) of such sentences as much as possible.[4] They are usually thought of by him as incomplete or indefinite sentences whose 'meaning' or 'content' depends on the circumstances in which they are uttered or otherwise propounded. Modern philosophers generally prefer not to deal with such temporally indefinite sentences as 'Socrates is awake' or 'Socrates is walking'; they prefer to discuss and to use instead sentences obtained from these by somehow specifying the time to which they refer independently of the moment of their utterance. The laws of logic are formulated with only or mainly sentences of the latter sort in view, and other procedures are sometimes thought of as being somehow fallacious.

3. STATEMENTS AND THEIR OBJECTS

It is not my purpose here to take sides for or against the Aristotelian assumptions as contrasted with the modern ones. It is important, however, to compare them to see how they differ. How would a modern thinker argue for his view that the 'content' or 'meaning' of a temporally indefinite sentence (say, 'It is now raining') varies? One way of doing so might be as follows. Suppose this sentence is uttered on two different occasions, say yesterday and today. Then the facts that make this sentence true or false are different in the two cases. Yesterday it referred to yesterday's weather; today it refers to today's weather. On one day the sentence is verified or falsified independently of its verification or falsification on the other. It may be true on one day and false on the other. All these things are taken to show that the two utterances of the sentence in question cannot carry the same meaning. Although the sentence in the grammatical sense of the word is one and the same, its content or, as it is often said, the *proposition* it expresses on the two occasions is not the same.[5] Hence if we want to have a satisfactory correspondence between our thought and our language, between the logical and the grammatical form, we really must use a different form of words on the two occasions.

Whether the points I have just made are correct or not, Aristotle would not have accepted them. Aristotle would apparently have accepted the doctrine that the sentence 'It is raining' is made true or false by different sets of facts accordingly as it is uttered today or yesterday. However, he would not have been worried about the consequence that one and the same sentence may be true at one time and false at another. He would have rejected the notion of a proposition and would have stuck instead to the actual thoughts of the people who uttered the sentence on the two occasions. When doing so, he would have been willing to argue that the thought expressed by the sentence today and yesterday is one and the same. And all this he not only would have been willing to say; he as much as said so quite explicitly:

For the same statement (*logos*) seems to be both true and false. Suppose, for example, that the statement that somebody is sitting is true; after he has got up this statement will be false. Similarly with beliefs. Suppose you believe truly that somebody is sitting; after he has got up you will believe falsely if you hold the same belief about him. (*Categories* 5, 4a 23–8)[6]

Statements and beliefs, on the other hand, themselves remain completely unchangeable in every way; it is because the *actual thing* changes that the contrary comes to belong to them. For the statement that somebody is sitting remains the same; it is because of a change in the actual thing that it comes to be true at one time and false at another. Similarly with beliefs. (*Ibid.*, 4a34–4b2)

These quotations show that Aristotle saw no difficulty in combining the two assumptions which to a typical modern thinker are likely to seem incompatible, viz. the assumption that the truth value of a temporally indefinite sentence changes with time, and the assumption that the sentence in question may nevertheless express one and the same content or proposition or, as Aristotle puts it, one and the same belief or opinion (*doxa*) on the different occasions on which it is uttered or otherwise propounded. Apparently, Aristotle did not find anything strange or awkward about his reconciliation of the two assumptions. Later, we shall examine some reasons why he felt this way.

Some comments are in order here. First of all, the authenticity of the *Categories* has sometimes been challenged. Hence the relevance of the passages we just cited is perhaps not beyond doubt. However, even if this work is not by Aristotle himself, it reproduces views current in the Lyceum at a very early date. Hence its testimony can be trusted provided that there are parallel statements in undisputably genuine works of Aristotle's. This is in fact the case. Exactly the same point that was made in the *Categories* recurs in a slightly briefer form in *Metaphysics* IX, 10, 1051b13 ff. Hence it is surely Aristotle's own view. Many of the passages that will be quoted in the sequel constitute evidence to the same effect.

It is also interesting to observe that the view put forward in the *Categories* is not due to Aristotle's desire to rule out recalcitrant facts or to enhance the architectonic neatness of his system. On the contrary, it would have suited the argument of the *Categories* much better if the author could have taken the modern view that the truth value of opinions and full-fledged sentences never changes. For the point made there is that substances are the only entities that can take contrary attributes at different moments of time and nevertheless remain numerically one and the same (*Categories* 5, 4a10 ff.). To this doctrine the changing truth values of opinions and of sentences constituted an unpleasant counter-example. The counter-example was eventually ruled out by means of a rather unsatisfactory manoeuvre. (Substances are the only entities that assume contrary attributes because they themselves change; opinions and sentences do this only because the facts they refer to change.) The fact that the modern view was not even considered by the author of the *Categories* although it would have served his purpose perfectly illustrates the hold of the contrary view of him.

We may also register the fact that the statements we quoted from the *Categories* are completely categorical. A sentence or a belief remains 'completely unchangeable in every way' although the facts it refers to change. Furthermore, nothing is said of beliefs (opinions) and sentences which perhaps never change their truth values. Hence the author is clearly thinking in terms of temporally indefinite sentences. Because of the parallelisms between the *Categories* and other parts of the Aristotelian corpus, we may infer that the same was the case with the Stagirite.

I conclude, then, that Aristotle saw no obvious difficulties in the assumption that a temporally indefinite sentence expresses one and the same thought or opinion on the different occasions of its utterance. My main suggestion is that he tended to take temporally indefinite sentences as paradigms of all informative sentences. This led him, among other things, to define some of his key notions so as to be applicable only or primarily to temporally indefinite sentences or to 'opinions' corresponding to such sentences.

4. FURTHER ARISTOTELIAN EVIDENCE

The fact that Aristotle preferred temporally indefinite sentences is not belied by the fact that in his syllogistic theory, and in his theory of scientific method which was built on his syllogistic theory, he frequently says in so many words that a general premiss has to take in all the different individuals of a certain sort, no matter whether they exist now or at some other moment of time. For instance, 'All men are mortal' is about all men, present, past, or future.[7] That Aristotle had to stress this feature of the syllogistic premisses may equally well indicate that there was a tendency among his audience and perhaps even in himself to understand these premisses in a different way. That such a tendency really existed is betrayed by the fact that Aristotle frequently uses temporally indefinite sentences as putative examples of syllogistic premisses, contrary to his own explanations. In at least one passage he indicates explicitly that his example is of this sort.[8]

A study of Aristotle's usage also tends to support our view of his notion of truth. He often speaks of what was or will be or would be true to say at some particular time. The following are cases in point (the italics are, of course, mine):

For when nothing was separated out, evidently *nothing could be truly asserted* of the substance that then existed. (*Metaphysics* I, 8, 989b6–7)

But there are two senses of the expression 'the primary when in which something has changed'. On the one hand it may mean the primary 'when' containing the completion of the process of change (the moment when *it is true to say* 'it has changed')...(*Physics* VI, 5, 236a7–9)[9]

Notice also the care with which Aristotle habitually qualifies his statements of the law of contradiction: one and the same sentence cannot be
true and false *at the same time*, he says.[10]

Locutions of this sort are by no means infallible evidence. Such locutions could conceivably be used by a philosopher who is not subscribing
to the assumptions I have imputed to Aristotle. In connection with his
explicit pronouncements on the relation of truth to time, however, they
constitute useful circumstantial evidence. Their frequency shows how
deeply engrained the ways of thinking were that we have found in Aristotle.

There are certain passages in Aristotle's works that may seem to call
for a different interpretation. Some passages seem to suggest that in
addition to temporally indefinite sentences, Aristotle sometimes considered sentences containing some kind of more definite time reference.
The evidence is not conclusive, however, but points predominantly in
our direction. When Aristotle says that a sentence includes a time reference, he normally means simply that its verb is in the present, past, or
future tense.[11] Such a sentence normally implies a reference to the moment at which it is uttered. There are also passages in which Aristotle has
in mind some kind of closer specification of the time to which a sentence
refers. But a second look at these passages shows that he is thinking of a
specification (of the time of the occurrence of an event) in terms of "the
measurable stretch of time from now onwards to that, or ... from that on
to now" (*Physics* IV, 13, 222a24–8). For instance, in *Parva Naturalia* (*De
Memoria* 2) 452b17 ff. Aristotle discusses the difference between 'exact'
and 'inexact' estimate of time in connection with memory.[12] One of his
examples is 'the day before yesterday', which is a specification of time in
relation to the present day. In fact, the context makes it quite clear that
what Aristotle is thinking of in this whole passage are exact and inexact
specifications of the length of time that separates the remembered event
from the present moment (cf. e.g., 452b8ff.). Hence we again have an
instance of a temporally indefinite time reference.

5. Propositions, time, and truth in
other Greek thinkers

The same predilection for temporally indefinite sentences is found in other ancient philosophers, although not always in as explicit a form as in Aristotle. Virtually all the examples of singular sentences that were used by the Stoics as examples and are preserved to us seem to be temporally indefinite.[13] What is more important, such temporally indefinite sentences are put forward by the Stoics as examples of sentences that are taken to express a complete λεκτόν (*lekton*). These complete assertoric *lekta* or in short ἀξιώματα (*axiomata*) of the Stoics are in many respects reminiscent of the 'propositions' that many modern philosophers postulate as meanings of eternal assertoric sentences.[14] However, *axiomata* differ from propositions in that they are temporally indefinite in the same way as occasion sentences. By saying 'writes', one does not yet express a complete *lekton*, we are told by the Stoics, because "we want to know *who* [writes]." Nevertheless, a sentence like 'Dion is walking' is said to express a complete *lekton*, in spite of the fact that it leaves room for the analogous question: '*When* is it that Dion is walking?'[15]

From this it followed that the Stoics spoke freely of changes in the truth value of a sentence and also (more properly) in the truth value of *lekta*. As is brought out very clearly by William and Martha Kneale, a *lekton* could change its truth value and even cease to exist.[16] In his list of the different senses of ἀληθής in the Stoics, Benson Mates distinguishes the use of this notion in connection with propositions (Sense I) from its use in connection with sentences that can change their truth value or, as Mates calls them, propositional functions with a time variable (Sense II).[17] The distinction does not seem to be motivated, however. In fact, some of Mates's own examples of Sense I are easily seen to involve sentences (or *lekta*) with changing truth values. Cases in point are found in Diogenes Laertius, *Vitae* VII, 66, where the temporally indefinite sentence "It is day" occurs as an example, as well as in Sextus Empiricus, *Adversus Mathematicos* VIII, 10–13.[18] The latter passage is not unambiguous by itself; however, its import is brought out when Sextus later returns to the same topic (*op. cit.* 85, 88–9), using as an example the same temporally indefinite sentence as Diogenes.

One is also reminded here of the famous Megarian and Stoic controversies concerning the conditions of the validity of implications.[19] This whole controversy is couched in terms of sentences (or *lekta*) with changing truth values. For instance, Diodorus Cronus held that 'if *p*, then *q*' is true if and only if *q* is true whenever *p* is true.[20] If *p* and *q* were temporally definite sentences, this would reduce to our own truth-table definition of material implication. However, the Diodorean doctrine is known to have been directed against Philo's definition which is essentially just our own truth-table definition. Hence Diodorus is clearly presupposing that *p* and *q* are temporally indefinite sentences.

Mates explains the Diodorean definition in terms of quantication over a time variable.[21] This is justified and illuminating, provided that we realize that there is no trace whatever of such a treatment in the Stoics themselves.[22]

6. KNOWLEDGE, TIME, AND IMMUTABILITY

One of the most interesting things about the assumption we are dealing with is that it helps us to understand some of the most characteristic features of the Greek epistemology. Since these features are found not only in Aristotle but also in many other Greek philosophers, the existence of this connection suggests that we are really dealing with a common tendency of many Greek thinkers.

The most important feature I have in mind is the widespread Greek doctrine that we can have genuine knowledge only of what is eternal or at the very least forever changeless.[23] This doctrine becomes very natural if we consider it as the outcome of two tendencies: (1) A tendency to think of temporally indefinite sentences as typical vehicles of communication; (2) A tendency to think of knowledge in terms of some sort of direct acquaintance with the objects of knowledge, e.g., in terms of seeing or of otherwise witnessing them.

I cannot here document the second tendency as fully as it deserves. That there is something here worth being documented is already shown by the facts of the Greek language. One of the common Greek ways to claim that I know was to use the verb οἶδα which, literally taken, amounts to saying that I *have seen* the thing in question. If we are to believe Bruno Snell, this was not a mere piece of etymology but a fact the speakers of the language were aware of. According to him, "in the Greek language we can frequently discern that the verb εἰδέναι means, to know on the basis of one's own observation".[24] The same applies also to the important word γιγνώσκω , especially in Homer, and to other verbs, too, as pointed out by Snell.[25]

Similar observations have often been made. W. G. Runciman sums up his patient examination of the relevant aspects of Plato's *Theaetetus* as follows: "The general impression left by the *Theaetetus* is that Plato continued to think of knowledge as a sort of mental seeing or touching".[26] This impression is not changed by Runciman's scrutiny of the *Sophistes*: "Although Plato says that all statements are either true or false and that all judgments are merely unspoken statements, he does not thereby... commit himself to any modification of what we have seen to be his earlier position on the nature and objects of knowledge."[27]

For our purposes it is especially relevant that there was a marked tendency to conceive of the highest forms of knowledge as being somehow analogous to immediate observation as distinguished from mere hearsay. In short, the highest form of knowledge was thought of as being comparable to that of an eyewitness. In the introduction to his edition of Plato's *Meno*, R. S. Bluck says that "the inferiority of ὀρθὴ δόξα to ἐπιστήμη as a state of awareness of the a priori is analogous to the inferiority of second-hand information about empirical matters to the certainty of one who has learnt from personal experience".[28] It is also instructive to note that the kind of universal knowledge that Plato ascribes to the soul in his famous doctrine of recollection is explained by Plato (whether metaphorically or not is not at issue here) as being due to earlier personal experience: "The soul, then, as being immortal, and having been born again many times, and having seen all things that exist, whether in this world or in the world below, has knowledge of them all" (*Meno* 81C).

As pointed out by Snell, there is a striking example of this way of thinking in Homer.[29] When he appeals to his omniscient Muses to help him, he does not represent their omniscience as a consequence of superhuman intelligence or of more insight into the laws that govern the events than the humans possess. In Homer's own words,

> Tell me now, Muses that dwell in the palace of Olympus –
> For you are goddesses, you are at hand and know all things,
> But we hear only a rumour and know nothing –
> Who were the captains and lords of the Danaans.[30]

As Snell puts it, "the goddesses are superior to man for the simple reason that they are always at hand, and have seen everything, and know it now...." In fact, their having seen it was for the Greeks almost a prerequisite for their knowing it. Perhaps more significant than this old testimony is the fact that almost exactly the same view is echoed by Plato and Aristotle: "You both admit, to begin with, that the gods perceive, see, and hear everything, that nothing within the compass of sense or know-ledge [therefore?] falls outside their cognizance" (*Laws* X, 901 D; tr. by A. E. Taylor; cf. Aristotle, *Poetics* 15, 1454b2–6, and Empedocles, fragment 129 (Diels)).

What happens now if this idea of genuine knowledge as an eyewitness's knowledge is applied to the kind of knowledge that can be expressed by means of temporally indefinite sentences? One case seems to be clear: We know the things that are at the present moment within our sphere of perception. But what about things that are not under our present observa-tion? Take, for instance, the piece of putative knowledge expressed by the sentence 'There is snow on Mount Olympus' as uttered by somebody who is not within the sight of the famous mountain. On what conditions is a man right who claims to know what this sentence asserts? The Greeks had, if I am right, a tendency to take this question as being equivalent to the question: When does his claim, 'I have seen it', amount to a conclusive evidence that the things are now as he says they are? The obvious answer is: Only if the thing in question never changes. Only on this condition does it follow from his earlier observation that things are still as they were at the time of the observation. If the purported object of his knowledge changes, it may have changed in the interval between his seeing it and his making the statement. If the snow sometimes melts from Mount Olym-pus, then the fact that I have seen the snow there does not go to show that there is snow there now. Only if the snow never melts does the 'I have seen it' assertion amount to knowledge concerning the present state of affairs. Hence, the two tendencies I mentioned made it very natural for the Greeks to adopt the view that there can be genuine knowledge only of what is unchangeable (and perhaps also of what is being perceived at the present moment).

This is in fact the way in which Aristotle argues for his doctrine that we have knowledge in the full sense of the word only of what is eternal or forever unchangeable:

Now what scientific knowledge (ἐπιστήμη) is, if we are to speak exactly and not follow mere similarities, is plain from what follows. We all suppose that what we know is not even capable of being otherwise; of things capable of being otherwise we do not know, when they have passed outside our observation, whether they exist or not. Therefore the object of scientific knowledge is of necessity. Therefore it is eternal... (*Ethica Nicomachea* VI, 3, 1139b18–23)

It is worth while noticing Aristotle's locution "We all suppose". It shows that Aristotle thought that what he was saying was not a peculiarity of his but rather a commonplace among the Greeks.

A concurrent reason why it was easy for Aristotle (and for the other Greeks) to accept the doctrine that there can be knowledge only of what is eternally the same is implicit on his view that sentences like 'Socrates sits' express one and the same opinion every time they are asserted. It is natural to say that an opinion of this sort cannot amount to real knowledge if it is sometimes false. For 'false knowledge' – even merely *sometimes* false knowledge – struck the Greeks, as it is likely to strike us today, as a misnomer.[31] Hence opinions that correspond to temporally indefinite sentences can constitute knowledge only if they are always true, i.e., only if they pertain to facts that never change. And if opinions of this kind are thought of as typical, then one may be inclined to say generally that we can have knowledge only of what is indestructible and unchangeable.[32]

If we keep in mind that for Aristotle what is always is necessary and what is merely contingent must sometimes fail to be,[33] we can see that essentially this point is made by Aristotle in *Analytica Posteriora* I, 33, 88b31–4: "... that which is necessary cannot be otherwise; but there are propositions which, though true and real, are also capable of being otherwise. Obviously it is not knowledge that is concerned with these...."

In many pronouncements of Aristotle's, both these reasons appear intertwined. The following seems to be especially worth quoting:

For this reason, also, there is neither definition nor demonstration about individual sensible substances, because they have matter whose nature is such that they are capable both of being and of not being; for which reason all the individual instances of them are destructible. If then demonstration is of necessary truths and definition is a scientific process, and if, just as *knowledge cannot be sometimes knowledge and sometimes ignorance,* but the state which varies thus is opinion, so too demonstration and definition cannot vary thus, but it is opinion that deals with that which can be otherwise than it is, clearly there can neither be definition nor demonstration about sensible individuals. For *perishing things are obscure... when they have passed from our perception*; and though the formulae remain in the soul unchanged, there will no longer be either definition or demonstration (*Metaphysics* VII, 15, 1039b27–40a5; my italics).

This may be compared with *Analytica Posteriora* I, 6, 74b33ff., where a similar point is made. Here we obviously have one of the reasons why, for Aristotle, there could not be any genuine knowledge of sensible particulars, but only of universals. In *De Anima* III, 3, 428b8–9 we similarly read: "But true opinion only becomes false when the fact changes unnoticed."

7. PLATO AND THE THESIS 'KNOWLEDGE IS PERCEPTION'

Similar considerations seem to have been operative in Plato, too. In fact, Aristotle attributes exactly the same mode of argument to Plato:

> Plato accepted his [Socrates'] teaching, but held that the problem [of a universal definition] applied not to sensible things but to entities of another kind – for this reason, that the common definition could not be a definition of any sensible thing, as they were always changing. (*Metaphysics* I, 6, 987b4–7)

A few lines earlier, Aristotle alleges that Plato accepted the Heraclitean doctrine "that all sensible things are ever in a state of flux and that there is no knowledge about them." Whether these attributions are correct or not, similar juxtapositions of doctrines are found in Plato's writing. From our modern point of view, we may be puzzled and surprised by the facility with which Plato connects in the *Theaetetus* the view that 'Knowledge is perception' and the doctrine of Cratylus that all things are constantly changing.[34] This connection is introduced at 152 D, and it is frequently made use of in the argument; witness such passages as the following: "If all things are forever in motion, every answer to any question whatsoever is equally correct" (*Theaetetus* 183 A).

Why should – how could – the constant and universal change postulated by Cratylus make true statements impossible? Clearly only if the statements in question primarily pertain to the moment of their utterance, and to other moments of time only in so far as things remain constant.[35]

The notion of a sentence with a changing truth value may perhaps serve to explain Plato's strange doctrine of degrees of truth which Runciman finds so puzzling.[36] A sentence cannot at any given moment be truer than another true sentence, but it may be truer than another in the sense of being true *more often* than the latter is. Thus the different degrees of truth are in effect different degrees of unchangeability in the objects these truths are about. This connection is explicitly made by Plato in the *Philebus* (58A–59C).

If my interpretation of *De Interpretatione* 9 is correct, Aristotle there in fact uses the expression μᾶλλον ἀληθής meaning 'true *more often*'.[37]

Another form of the same idea is that an opinion (*doxa*) is the better the more permanent it is. Thus in the *Meno* (89C) Socrates says of a certain opinion: "Yes, but not only a moment ago must it seem correct, but now also and hereafter, if it is to be at all sound."

In the *Republic* (see 430A) belief or opinion is in the same spirit compared to "a dye, a dye designed to be as 'fast' as possible". The importance of the immutability of the Forms for Plato also becomes intelligible from this point of view. One of the most important roles of the Forms was just to provide absolutely immutable objects of knowledge and thereby secure the possibility of genuine knowledge.[38]

From this point of view we can also appreciate the firm connection there was in Plato's mind between, on one hand, the distinction between knowledge and true belief and, on the other hand, the distinction between Forms and sensible particulars:

My own verdict, then, is this. If intelligence and true belief are two different kinds, then these things – Forms that we cannot perceive but only think of – certainly exist in themselves; but if, as some hold, true belief in no way differs from intelligence, then all things we perceive through the bodily senses must be taken as the most certain reality. (*Timaeus* 51D)

In general, we can see that there is a close connection between two apparently different and even contradictory preoccupations of Plato and Aristotle. On one hand, they paid a great deal of attention to the idea that 'Knowledge is perception', whether they in the last analysis accepted it or not. On the other hand, they were attracted by the idea that we can have knowledge only of what never changes. We can now see that these two types of knowledge were both assigned a privileged position by the Greek tendencies to conceive of knowledge as a kind of immediate awareness and to think in terms of temporally indefinite sentences. The two preoccupations are really two sides of one and the same coin.

A reference to our quotation from Homer perhaps helps us to appreciate the appeal of the idea that 'Knowledge is perception' to the Greeks. If even the superiority of the divine knowledge was essentially based on the greater share of perceptual evidence that the gods possess, what more could there possibly be to knowledge than perception?

Our observations may also put into an appropriate perspective an argument that Plato's commentators have found puzzling and even mistaken. In *Theaetetus* 201A–C Plato lets Socrates disprove the suggestion that knowledge can be defined as true opinion by drawing a contrast between the correct opinion of a jury which is giving the right verdict, and the knowledge of the event which is possessed by an eyewitness. This may seem puzzling because the objects of which an eyewitness to a crime has knowledge are not the kinds of things of which we can, according to Plato's (or Aristotle's) explicit doctrines, have genuine knowledge; they are not immutable Forms of which alone we can, according to Plato, have knowledge in the full sense of the word.

Now the idea that an eyewitness's knowledge is a paradigm case of genuine knowledge was seen to be one of the motives that led to the doctrine that we can have knowledge in the full sense of the word only of what is eternal. This suffices to explain Plato's apparent use of an eyewitness's knowledge as an example of real knowledge without jumping to the conclusion that we could, according to Plato, have genuine knowledge of sensible reality. The underlying reason why Plato could use the example he mentions is closely connected with the fascination that the idea that 'Knowledge is perception' had for him. Of course, Plato ended up rejecting this idea, but not before conceiving the highest form of knowledge in analogy to perception, as a kind of "mental seeing or touching", to use Runciman's expression.

One could put the point as follows. What Plato wants to establish in *Theaetetus* 201A–C is a distinction between knowledge and true belief. For this purpose it suffices for him to show that genuine knowledge is related to true belief in the same way as an eyewitness's 'knowledge' is related to 'knowledge' by hearsay, the last two being obviously different from one another. Cornford's view that we are here given only an "analogous contrast" has much more to recommend itself than it has recently been given credit for.[39] It is true that Plato does speak of knowledge when he discusses the example, but he seems to restrict the scope of the example in so many words to "matters which one can know only by having seen them and in no other way".

8. 'CHANGING TRUTH' AND HISTORICAL RELATIVITY

The idea of 'changing truth' which we have found in Greek philosophers has to be distinguished from the modern idea of the historical relativity of truth. A historical relativist is apt to argue for an absence of any absolute criteria of truth, which results in an impossibility of obtaining truths that are not liable to be given up when the criteria are changed. What an ancient philosopher like Aristotle had in mind is almost exactly the opposite. He was not concerned with changes in our criteria of truth, but changes in the objects our truths are about. He was not concerned with changes in the opinions we have about reality, but with changes in the reality itself. Aristotle did not think that the discovery of truth is usually very difficult; the difficulty was, rather, that all the truths concerning changing things had to be discovered (as it were) all over again at each new moment.

9. 'CONJUNCTIVE' SENSE OF PRESENT-TENSE STATEMENTS AND THE IDEA OF 'TIMELESS PRESENT'

Our observations concerning the notion of knowledge that naturally results from the Aristotelian presuppositions put these presuppositions themselves into a new perspective. We have so far spoken almost as if a temporally indefinite sentence in the present tense would for Aristotle normally refer merely to the moment at which it is uttered. We can see now that this is not the only way in which Aristotle was willing to understand such sentences and also why he could assume a different interpretation without any compunctions.

The alternative is to understand present-tense sentences in a 'tenseless' or perhaps better 'conjunctive' sense. In this sense, a sentence will mean that things are *always* in the way the sentence states them to be. A number of passages in the Aristotelian corpus seem to rule out such a sense altogether. *De Interpretatione* 3, 16b6–18 and 10, 19b11–18 as well as *De Anima* III, 6, 430a30 ff. are cases in point. However, in other passages the tenseless sense is clearly presupposed (see for instance, *Topics* V, 3, 131b5–18).

The connection between the notions of time and knowledge which we have pointed out enable us to see that the difference between the two senses was much smaller for Aristotle than we might otherwise expect. For even if a present-tense statement appears to refer exclusively to the moment at which it is made, it can embody real knowledge (as we saw) if the same statement would have been true also when made at any other moment of time. In so far as present-tense statements (without explicit temporal specifications or explicit restrictions to the present moment) are taken to represent claims to knowledge, they thus automatically assume a 'tenseless' or 'conjunctive' sense.

The conjunctive sense of present-tense statements might also be called their 'omnitemporal' sense. Recognizing its compatibility with the assumptions I have ascribed to the Greeks enables us to approach those utterances of Greek philosophers on the subject of time that prima facie might seem to go against my interpretation. There is no need for us to try to deny that Greek thinkers gradually developed doctrines of 'timeless present', as they have been called – doctrines, that is to say, according to which certain present-tense statements do not really contain any reference to time at all. Once a development into this direction got squarely under way, a sufficiently strong and independent thinker might very well have ended up with an outright denial of what I have – perhaps a shade too facilely – called tacit Greek presuppositions. It has sometimes been suggested that there in fact was in Greek philosophy a tradition essentially different in emphasis from what I have been describing – a tradition within which the idea of non-temporal existence and non-temporal predication slowly evolved.

As I have just indicated, there is nothing in the account I have given that rules out such a tradition. What my thesis implies is the direction from which this Greek tradition must be expected to approach the idea of an atemporal sense of present-tense statements. If what gave rise to the conjunctive ('tenseless') sense was a tacit (or explicit) knowledge-claim and if this amounted to a claim of permanence, then it is to be expected that the idea of 'timeless present' was first developed by discussing 'real' knowledge as distinguished from mere belief and by postulating immutable objects of (real) knowledge. In short, we may expect to find a connection between the ideas of timelessness, knowledge, and permanence. Only secondarily, if at all, can we expect to find ideas about existence and predication that have no relation at all to time and change.

It seems to me unmistakable that, no matter precisely where we locate the different steps in this train of thought, this prediction or, rather, 'retrodiction' concerning its direction squares very well with what we find in the works of the proponents of this 'tenseless' tradition. The most important of them were undoubtedly Parmenides and Plato. In both, the marriage of the tenseless use of verbs with strong knowledge-claims and immutability is conspicuous. One piece of evidence will have to do duty for many here. G. E. L. Owen sums up his examination of 'Plato and Parmenides on the Timeless Present'[40] by saying that "it is part of the originality of Plato to have grasped, or half-grasped, an important fact about certain kinds of statements, namely that they are tenseless whereas others are tensed. *But he tries to bring this contrast under his familiar distinction between the changeless and the changing*" (my italics).

10. The idea of atemporal being is still under-developed by Plato and Aristotle

Some sort of tenseless sense seems to be present already when Parmenides says of what is (fragment 8, line 5): "Nor was it ever not will it be; for it is now, all together, single, continuous." Hermann Fränkel has argued[41] that even here Parmenides is in effect comparing different moments of time with each other. This has provoked a sharp counter-argument from G. E. L. Owen.[42] I do not have to take sides in this controversy, however, for it concerns merely the stage reached by Parmenides in his groping toward the idea of an atemporal being.[43] The *direction* of Parmenides' approach is what is relevant to my thesis here, and this point is clearly common ground for Fränkel and Owen. Parmenides' starting-point is clearly the idea of immutability, and equally clearly he is led to emphasize immutability because of his quest for knowledge as distinguished from illusory belief.

Whether and how a completely atemporal sense of present-tense statements was reached among the Greeks of course needs a careful separate investigation. One index of such a sense is a clear separation between *omnitemporality* and *eternity*. In Greek they would presumably be expressed by the adjectives ἀΐδιον (*aïdion*, everlasting) and αἰώνιον (*aionion*, eternal). However, the mere presence of this pair of words is not conclusive. For one thing, Plato still uses *aionion* of the "regular motions of the astronomical clock" (as Owen puts it – see *Timaeus* 37D). Even when he seems to have reached an explicitly atemporal concept, Plato cannot but betray the source of his idea. Thus we read (*Timaeus* 37E–38A): "Days, nights, months, years, ... are all parts of time, and 'was' and 'will be' have come about as forms of time. We are wrong to apply them unthinkingly to what is eternal. Of this we say that it was and is and will be, but strictly only 'is' belongs to it." This sounds atemporal enough. But Plato continues: " 'Was' and 'will be' should be spoken of the process that goes on in time, *for they are changes*" (my italics, of course). Plato's posture in the *Timaeus vis-à-vis* 'timeless present' has been described by Owen by saying that Plato "is apparently ready to drop the word 'now' from timeless propositions, but he imports 'always' in its place (38A)".[44] If so, there can scarcely be said to be much of a sharp distinction between the omnitemporal and eternal in the *Timaeus*.

In the *De Caelo* Aristotle likewise uses "the word 'eternity' (αἰών) to describe... never-ending and never-changing existence", i.e., omni-temporality rather than atemporal eternity.[45]

Elsewhere, Aristotle speaks in so many words of things that are not *in time* (see *Physics* IV, 12, 220b32 ff.). It quickly turns out, however, that what he really means by this is that their existence has no bounds in time. 'Things which are always are not, as such, in time, for they are not contained in time' (*Physics* IV, 12, 221b3–5). 'Not being in time' is thus not sharply distinguished – in fact, not distinguished at all – from omnitemporality by Aristotle.

From such indications one may thus plausibly infer that the explicitly atemporal sense of being that Owen almost ascribes to Aristotle in his essay 'Aristotle on the Snares of Ontology'[46] (Owen's *is**) is a radical anachronism. Even when employed merely as an analytical tool, this concept seems to be so foreign to Aristotle as to be useless.

It might perhaps seem that I am watering down my thesis to a near-tautology by admitting a gradual development of the idea of atemporal existence among the Greeks. Surely such a sophisticated idea must in any case have developed by stages from something more concrete, such as the idea of omnitemporal existence, a reader might object. In order to counteract this impression of vacuity, it is in order to indicate what sorts of ideas would tell against my thesis. Conceptually, the most telling counterexamples would not be among the entities that spring to our minds when we think of 'things eternal'. Such metaphysical entities as eternal Forms and everlasting gods often still bear marked traces of their conceptual dependence on the plain notion of omnitemporality. Concep-tually, a philosopher is much further removed from the boundaries of *our* succession of actual nows when he considers *à la* Leibniz altogether different possible histories of the world than when he contemplates exotic actors – even backstage *artistes* – on the stage of *our* world history. Of this idea of possible world in the sense of succession of times altogether separate from ours it is very hard to find traces in Greek thinkers, however. On the contrary, there are indications that it was not taken into account by Aristotle at least.

11. THE SEMANTIC BACKGROUND OF THE IDEA OF CHANGING TRUTH

The features of Aristotle's thinking that we have noted are related in more than one way to his other logical, semantic, and psychological doctrines. The idea that a temporally indefinite sentence may express one and the same opinion or belief when uttered at different moments of time is encouraged by Aristotle's idea that "spoken sounds are symbols of affections in the soul" (*De Interpretatione* I, 16a3–4). It is obvious that the sentence, 'It is raining', as uttered by me today, is made true or false by a set of facts different from those that verified or falsified my utterance yesterday, 'It is raining'. But it is very natural to say that in some sense the state of mind or attitude toward my environment that is expressed by the two utterances is the same. The facts to which yesterday's utterance refers are referred to today by the sentence, 'It was raining yesterday.' But the 'state of mind' that this utterance appears to express seems to be entirely different from that expressed by yesterday's present-tense utterance, 'It is raining'. For instance, the former involves a thought about a temporal difference between the time the sentence refers to and the time of the utterance of the sentence, whereas the latter presupposes no awareness of such a difference.[47] Hence the idea that spoken words are symbols for unspoken thoughts encourages the idea that one and the same temporally indefinite form of words expresses one and the same belief or opinion at the different times when it is uttered.

It is tempting to express this point by saying that Aristotle presupposed a principle of individuation for propositions different from ours. This way of putting my point turns out to need qualifications, but it is nevertheless useful for many purposes. For instance, we can now see that one of my earlier explanations has to be qualified. The typical sentences considered by Aristotle were said to contain, explicitly or implicitly, a token-reflexive expression like 'now' or 'at the present moment'. This makes the sentences in question in a sense token-reflexive from our modern point of view. The proposition such a sentence expresses is different on different occasions. However, the very same sentences were *not* token-reflexive for Aristotle in this sense, for the belief or opinion they express at different times was for him one and the same.

Notice also that a defender of our modern view cannot argue that Aristotle handles temporally indefinite sentences incorrectly because they express a different meaning or thought (Frege's *Gedanke*) in different contexts. Aristotle's procedure implies that we have to individuate thoughts or opinions expressed by temporally indefinite sentences in the same way as these sentences themselves.

In the Aristotelian *Physics* we find a neat metaphysical projection of the semantic idea we have discussed. According to the latter, the belief expressed by a sentence containing the word 'now' remains ordinarily one and the same. In the *Physics*, Aristotle argues that the 'now' is in the actual sense of the word *always the same*. It is what "holds the time together" and makes it continuous (see *Physics* IV, 13, 222a10 ff. and 11, 219b10–20a4). There seems to be an interesting analogy between the way different moments of time are actualized by becoming in turn identified with the eternally identical 'now', and the way in which the content of a known 'now' statement becomes relevant to the world at the different moments of time by becoming utterable at the moment in question. It is thus literally the case that the word 'now' was not token-reflexive for Aristotle, for each actually uttered 'now' referred to the same forever-identical actual 'now' that is postulated in the *Physics*.

12. CULTURAL BACKGROUND

It may be suspected that the peculiarities we have discussed are connected with the general attitudes the Greeks had toward time. It has been suggested that the Greeks 'lived in the present moment' to a larger extent than the members of other cultures.[48] It might seem tempting to see in the Aristotelian way of handling the relations of the concepts of time and truth a reflection of the same attitude. It is as if philosophers were so absorbed in the present moment that they tended to think in terms of sentences that contained a reference to the present moment and therefore dealt primarily with the present state of affairs. It is not easy, however, to find direct evidence for (or against) this suggestion.

There are in any case other general features of the Greek intellectual scene relevant to our subject. Whether or not there was a direct connection between the general Greek attitude toward time and their philosophers' ways of handling this notion, there is the fact that the Greeks were not very succesful with their timekeeping – much less successful than some earlier civilizations, not to speak of the Romans. Different cities could have different calendars to such an extent that the year might begin at different times and that the thirteenth month that periodically had to be added to the year was added at different times.[49] Combined with a general neglect of public timekeeping, it is no wonder that the failure of chronology sometimes amounted to a public scandal, as shown by Aristophanes in the *Clouds*. Because of these failures of chronology, there simply was no handy way for the Greeks to take the course modern philosophers generally assume to be the only satisfactory one, viz. to replace all references to the indefinite 'now' in a sentence by references to some chronology independent of the moment at which the sentence is uttered. What point would there have been in replacing the sentence 'It is raining in Athens today' by a sentence in which the day in question is specified by a reference to a calendar of the form 'On such-and-such a day of such-and-such a year it is raining in Athens' if the day and perhaps even the year were different in another city? A reference to the moment of utterance must have been as useful in general as a reference to a badly kept calendar.[50]

It is difficult not to see in this neglect of a systematic calendar a symptom of a general lack of interest in timekeeping and in chronology. It is perhaps not impossible to find some independent evidence of the same attitude. For instance, Hermann Fränkel's study of the early Greek ideas of time has led him to state bluntly that in the *Iliad* "There is virtually no interest in chronology, neither in absolute chronology nor in relative one."[51] He does not find much more interest in later writers, either. This squares rather well with the early Greek ways of expressing temporal relations that Eric Havelock has emphasized. He points out that events were located in time not with reference to any absolute chronology but rather by reference to each other: "The basic grammatical expression which would symbolise the link of event to event would be simply the phrase 'and next'."[52]

13. RELIANCE ON THE SPOKEN WORD

It seems to me, however, that there is another closely related feature in Aristotle's background which was more important or at least easier to document. This is the fact that in some obvious though elusive sense the Greek culture was largely based on the *spoken* and not on the *written* word. In philosophical literature this oral character of the Greek thought is shown, for example, by the importance of dialogue as a method of presenting philosophical ideas. One is also reminded of the origins of logic in the technique of oral argumentation. Every reader of Aristotle's *Topics* knows to what extraordinary extent he was concerned with the tricks and pitfalls of verbal exchange.

From this emphasis on the spoken word it follows that the reasons for replacing temporally indefinite sentences by temporally definite ones which modern philosophers have were to some extent absent. If the spoken word is primary in relation to the written word, one is apt to think of and discuss logical and semantical matters from the vantage point of some situation in which the words in question are actually uttered. Now this situation supplies what is missing from a temporally indefinite sentence itself; it enables us to know what the moment of time actually is to which the spoken word 'now' refers. A logician eliminates the indefiniteness of temporally indefinite sentences by projecting himself, as it were, to the audience of someone actually uttering the sentence in question. In a written text such words as 'now' and 'at the present moment' are indeterminate in a sense in which they are not indeterminate as a part of actual speech. In a written culture the replacement of temporally indefinite sentences by definite ones is more important than in an oral culture – to the extent that it might appear to its philosophers as the only 'correct' course.

The primacy of the spoken word in relation to the written word is not merely an explanatory hypothesis of a historian; it occurs as an explicit doctrine both in Plato and in Aristotle. Plato's rejection of the written word as a mere aid to one's memory and as being dead and helpless as compared with the spoken word is well known and need not be elaborated here.[53] Aristotle expresses himself in different terms but equally clearly; according to him "written marks are symbols of spoken sounds" in the same way as the latter were in turn symbols of 'affections in the soul'.[54]

Eric Havelock has emphasized the same feature in the background of Plato as I am now stressing in the common background of the philosophers of the Socratic school.[55] The use he makes of this idea is different from mine, however. Havelock considers Plato's philosophy as an expression of a transition from a poetic oral tradition to a conceptual culture based on written records. This approach is appealing, but even if the uses Havelock makes of it are fully justified it does not exclude the possibility that many traces of a reliance on the spoken word persisted in Plato's and Aristotle's thinking. If I am right, the heavy reliance on temporally indefinite sentences as a medium of knowledge and of opinion is such a trace.[56]

It is also remarkable that in some unacknowledged sense the spoken word was for Plato and Aristotle even logically prior to the thoughts it expresses. Plato explained the nature of thinking by calling it "the inward dialogue carried on by the mind with itself without spoken sound".[57] This was not merely a metaphor, for Plato felt free to carry out arguments and considerations in terms of spoken sentences and then to transfer the results so as to apply to the corresponding thoughts as well. This is in fact the strategy of Plato's interesting and important discussion at the end of the *Sophistes*.

Aristotle does not formulate the logical primacy of the spoken word as compared with thinking as an explicit doctrine. However, he sometimes does exactly the same as Plato, that is to say, he too sometimes bases his view of what we can say of people's *thoughts* on what can be said of their words. The passages quoted above from *Categories* 5 are instructive cases in point.[58] It may be observed that the word that Aristotle uses in these passages, which was translated by Ackrill as 'statement', viz. *logos*, often refers to *spoken* words and sentences.

It is perhaps not irrelevant to mention that both Aeschylus (*Agamennon*, line 276) and Homer occasionally referred to people's thoughts as "wingless" or unspoken words.

This primacy of concepts applying to spoken words and sentences in relation to concepts referring to thinking must have encouraged the idea that one and the same temporally indefinite sentence expresses one and the same thought (opinion, belief) even when it is uttered on different occasions. If a thought is, logically speaking, nothing but a statement addressed by the 'speaker' to himself without spoken sounds, the question whether a statement specifies a complete thought becomes tantamount to the question whether the speaker has to add something to this statement when he tacitly addresses it to himself in order to make it fully understood by the 'hearer'. The obvious answer is that no expansion is needed as compared with occasions when the same form of words is addressed to someone else, for surely a man understands his own words if they are explicit enough for others to understand them. Hence the grammatical identity of a spoken sentence (form of words) easily becomes a criterion of the identity of the corresponding thoughts, too. Thus a transition from the spoken word to thoughts it expresses does not seem to necessitate any changes in the principle of individuation involved.

The conceptual primacy of the spoken word over thinking is related to the absence of a full-fledged notion of a proposition in Plato and Aristotle. By and large, they tended to discuss logical and semantical matters in terms of actual utterances rather than in terms of the thoughts or beliefs expressed. It is true that in the opening paragraph of *De Interpretatione* which we discussed the order of relative importance seems to be the opposite. Aristotle says there that spoken sounds are symbols of affections of the soul. However, Aristotle seems to have rather limited purposes in mind in this passage. As Ackrill points out, what the reference to the "affections in the soul" is primarily intended to elucidate is the fact that although spoken and written sounds are different in different languages, what the words express may be "the same for all men", as Aristotle himself says.[59] As Ackrill also points out, "the notion that utterances are symbols of affections in the soul does not have a decisive influence on the rest of *De Interpretatione*". Like other Greek philosophers, Aristotle thought of logical and semantical matters primarily in terms of the spoken language.

The same point is applied to Plato by F. M. Cornford.[60]

Logicians... might maintain that there is a false 'proposition'... which has a meaning, though I cannot believe it. With that we are not concerned, but only with judgements and statements that can be actually made and believed by some rational being. Plato never discusses 'propositions' that no one propounds.

Similar remarks can be made of the Stoic concepts of a *lekton* and of an *axioma*, closely though they approximate our notion of a proposition in many other respects. Thus Mrs. Kneale writes as follows:[61]

As a previously quoted passage has shown, the Stoics wished to insist that an *axioma* which is to be described as true or false must somehow be present when it is so described; ... in one place Sextus clearly assumes that *lekta* exist only when they are expressed or meant.

As far as Aristotle is concerned, it would not be strictly true to say he never considers propositions that no one propounds. He comes very close to envisaging one in *De Interpretatione* 9, 18b36. It is no accident, however, that this passage is, if I am right, exactly the passage in which Aristotle came closest to considering statements that refer to a unique singular event and therefore need an objective chronology.[62] The other similar cases that there are in Aristotle of unasserted propositions are much less clear, and probably explainable as mere *façons de parler*.

14. 'THE SENSE OF THE TEMPORAL'

If there is anything to the contention that the Greeks 'lived in the present' to a larger extent than the members of some other tradition, the justification (and perhaps also the import) of this suggestion has to be spelled out in terms of such concrete facts as those that are known about the ways of Greek philosophers with the concepts of time and truth. Whether or not the facts we have pointed out go very far toward establishing any broad generalizations, in any case they show us how the different facets of the Greek way of thinking are related to each other. The suggestion that the Greeks were immersed in the present moment more deeply than we are easily provokes a reply that points to the preoccupation of the Greek philosophers with the eternal and the immutable. We have seen, however, that this preoccupation is closely connected with the reliance of these philosophers on temporally indefinite sentences. Far from being a counter-example to the temporality of Greek thought, this pursuit of the eternal is more of a manifestation of this very temporality – or perhaps rather an attempt to compensate for it. Plato's and Aristotle's ideal of knowledge was knowledge of eternal truths just because the vehicles by means of which truths were thought of by them as being expressed tended to make all other kinds of truths ephemeral. In a sense I am thus led to agreement with the view of R. G. Collingwood that "the Greek pursuit of the eternal was as eager as it was, precisely because the Greeks themselves had an unusually vivid sense of the temporal".[63]

NOTES

[1] These difficulties are illustrated by the scantiness of genuine evidence for those fashionable contrasts between the ancient Greek and the ancient Hebrew *Weltanschauungen* which have been effectively criticized by James Barr in *The Semantics of Biblical Language* (Clarendon Press, Oxford, 1961). The theoretical problems involved in inferences from linguistic to cultural data are also discussed by Joseph Greenberg in 'Concerning Inferences from Linguistic to Nonlinguistic Data', in *Language in Culture*, ed. by H. Hoijer (University of Chicago Press, Chicago, 1956), reprinted in *Psycholinguistics*, ed. by S. Saporta (Holt, Rinehart, and Winston, New York, 1961), and by Max Black in 'Linguistic Relativity', *Philosophical Review* **68** (1959) 228–38, reprinted in Max Black, *Models and Metaphors* (Cornell University Press, Ithaca, 1962), pp. 244–57.

[2] The importance of people's attitudes to the category of time as an indication of their value orientation is brought out clearly by F. R. Kluckhohn and F. L. Strodtbeck in *Varieties in Value Orientation* (Row and Peterson, Evanston, Illinois, 1961).

[3] W. V. Quine, *Word and Object* (MIT Press, Cambridge, Mass., 1960), §9 and §40.

[4] Instances are far too numerous for me to give more than a sprinkling of examples here: Bertrand Russell, *An Inquiry into Meaning and Truth* (London, Allen and Unwin, 1940), p. 113; A. J. Ayer, *Philosophical Essays* (Macmillan, London, 1954), pp. 186–7; Nelson Goodman, *The Structure of Appearance* (Harvard University Press, Cambridge, Mass., 1951), p. 297; Donald C. Williams, 'The Sea Fight Tomorrow', in *Structure, Method and Meaning*, ed. by P. Henle (Liberal Arts Press, New York, 1951), pp. 282–306, especially p. 287. Further examples will be given in the course of the discussion.

My list might give the idea that only fairly recent philosophers of an analytic bend of mind favour eternal sentences over occasion sentences. This impression would be incorrect, as Appendix A to A. N. Prior's *Time and Modality* (Clarendon Press, Oxford, 1957) convincingly shows. In fact, in this respect most of our logical tastes go back to the seventeenth century at least. An early version of the doctrine that eternal sentences are superior to occasion sentences is especially interesting in that it was developed in conscious opposition to Aristotle. For Aristotle, the time relation in a sentence is carried by the verb. This doctrine is closely related to the fact that a typical Aristotelian sentence refers to the moment at which it is uttered or written, for it was the verb that carried the assertoric element in a sentence and was thought of as creating the judgment expressed by the sentence. In contradistinction to this view, it was already held by the authors of the *Port-Royal Logic* that time reference is not logically speaking a part of the verb. For them, the temporal aspect is, as it were, part of the subject matter and not created by creating the judgement.

Only very recently have logicians again begun to question the predominance of temporally definite statements.

[5] See, e.g., G. E. Moore, 'A Defense of Common Sense', in *Philosophical Papers* (George Allen and Unwin, London, 1959), p. 35.

[6] The translation is taken from J. L. Ackrill, *Aristotle's 'Categories' and 'De Interpretatione'* (Clarendon Press, Oxford, 1963).

[7] *Analytica Priora* I, 15, 34b 17–18; *Analytica Posteriora* I, 4, 73a 28–9, and 8, 75b 21–36.

[8] At *Analytica Priora* I, 10, 30b 37–8 Aristotle considers a syllogistic conclusion that is not necessarily true, but is true 'so long as' (ἕως) the premisses are true. These premisses thus cannot refer to individuals existing at all the different times, for if they did, their truth value could not change. An equally revealing example occurs at 31b 8–10, where Aristotle uses the terms 'sleeping' and 'waking' in a counterexample to a syllogism. These are as clear-cut examples as one might wish of terms that apply to an individual *at a time* only. Hence they

contradict Aristotle's own admonitions as to how syllogistic premisses ought to be construed.

⁹ Similar statements are found, e.g., in *Metaphysics* IV, 7, 1012a 27-8, *Metaphysics* V, 30, 1025a 14–15, *Physics* VI, 8, 239a 28–9.

¹⁰ E.g., *Metaphysics* IV, 3, 1005b 19–20, 23–32; 6, 1011b 15–18; *Topics* II, 7, 113a 22–3; *De Interpretatione* 10, 20a 16–18.

¹¹ See *De Interpretatione* 3, 16b 6–18; *De Anima* III, 6, 430a–30 ff.

¹² I am indebted to Professor John W. Lenz for calling my attention to this passage.

¹³ Cf., e.g., Benson Mates, *Stoic Logic* (University of California Press, Berkeley and Los Angeles, 1961, originally published as vol. 26 of the University of California Publications in Philosophy) which contains a full discussion of the Stoic logic and translations of a number of sources. The closest approximations to genuine exceptions from this type of example that I am aware of are found in Cicero (*De Fato*, IX, 19, and XIII, 30).

¹⁴ For examples of this sort, see, e.g., Mates, *op. cit.*, pp. 96, 113, 118, 121, 123, etc.

¹⁵ See Diogenes Laertius, *Vitae* VII, 63; Mates, *op. cit.*, p. 16.

¹⁶ William and Martha Kneale, *The Development of Logic* (Clarendon Press, Oxford, 1962), pp. 144–6, 153–5. Cf. also A. A. Long, 'Language and Thought in Stoicism' in *Problems in Stoicism*, ed. by A. A. Long (Athlone Press, London, 1971), esp. pp. 97 and 101.

¹⁷ Mates, *op. cit.*, p. 132.

¹⁸ See the Loeb Classical Library edition of Sextus, vol. 2, pp. 244–7.

¹⁹ See Mates, *op. cit.*, pp. 42–51; Kneale and Kneale, *op. cit.*, pp. 128–38.

²⁰ See, e.g., Sextus Empiricus, *Adversus Mathematicos* VIII, 112ff.

²¹ Mates, *op. cit.*, p. 45.

²² Cf. P. T. Geach's review of Mates in the *Philosophical Review* **64** (1955) 143–5.

²³ This tendency is one of the most striking characteristics of both Plato and Aristotle, and is found in other ancient philosophers as well. Its role and background in ancient Greek thought does not seem to have been systematically studied however.

²⁴ Bruno Snell, *Die Ausdrücke für den Begriff des Wissens in der vorplatonischen Philosophie* (*Philologische Untersuchungen*, ed. by Werner Jaeger, Vol. 29, Berlin, 1924), p. 25.

²⁵ Bruno Snell, *The Discovery of the Mind* (Harvard University Press, Cambridge, Mass., 1953), p. 13.

²⁶ W. G. Runciman, *Plato's Later Epistemology* (Cambridge University Press, Cambridge, 1962), p. 52.

²⁷ *Ibid.*, p. 121; cf. p. 125.

²⁸ R. S. Bluck, ed., *Plato's 'Meno'* (Cambridge University Press, Cambridge, 1961), p. 33.

²⁹ Snell, *The Discovery of the Mind* (*op. cit.*), Chapter 7, especially p. 136.

³⁰ Homer, *Iliad*, beginning of the 'Catalogue of Ships'.

³¹ That it seemed a misnomer to Plato may be gathered from *Gorgias* 454D, from *Republic* 476 E, and from *Theaetetus* 152C and 186E. Cf. also Parmenides, fragment 2, lines 7–8 (Diels).

³² This is to all intents and purposes the points of Aristotle's remarks in the *Categories* 7, 7b 27–30: "Destruction of the knowable carries knowledge to destruction.... For if there is not a knowable there is not knowledge – there will no longer be anything for knowledge to be of ...."

³³ See Chapter 5 of Jaakko Hintikka, *Time and Necessity* (Clarendon Press, Oxford, 1973).

³⁴ For reasons other than the one we are interested in that Plato may have had for connecting the two doctrines, see Norman Gulley, *Plato's Theory of Knowledge* (Methuen, London, 1962), pp. 78–80.

³⁵ Aristotle, too, assumes that if all things were at rest, "the same things will always be

true and false", and that, conversely, if all things were in motion, "nothing will be true and everything will be false" (*Met.* IV, 8, 1012b 24–8).

[36] Runciman, *op. cit.*, pp. 124–5.

[37] See Chapter 8 of Hintikka, *Time and Necessity* (note 33 above).

[38] Cf. *Parmenides* 135B–C and *Cratylus* 439D–440C.

[39] F. M. Cornford, *Plato's Theory of Knowledge* (Routledge and Kegan Paul, London, 1935), pp. 141–2; cf. Runciman, *op. cit.*, pp. 37–8. It may be instructive to observe that in the passage I quoted from Aristotle's *Categories* in note 32 above, he commits an inconsistency somewhat similar to the one Plato seems to me to commit here. Saying that the 'destruction of the knowable carries knowledge to destruction' is from an Aristotelian point of view a solecism, for of things destructible we cannot have genuine scientific knowledge (Aristotle's word is here *episteme*) in the first place.

[40] The *Monist* **50** (1966) 317–40; see p. 335.

[41] Hermann Fränkel, *Wege und Formen frühgriechischen Denkens* (second edition, C. H. Beck, Munich, 1960), p. 191 (note 1).

[42] *Op. cit.*, pp. 320–1.

[43] It is nevertheless worth emphasizing that one can deny the presence of a fully fledged idea of timeless being in Parmenides (including fr. 8, line 5) even if one rejects the particular arguments Fränkel uses. Cf., e.g., Leonardo Taran, *Parmenides: A Text with Translation, Commentary, and Critical Essays* (Princeton University Press, Princeton, 1965), pp. 176–83.

[44] *Op. cit.*, p. 333.

[45] See Friedrich Solmsen, *Aristotle's System of the Physical World* (Cornell University Press, Ithaca, N.Y., 1960), p. 157.

[46] See *New Essays on Plato and Aristotle*, ed. by R. Bambrough (Routledge and Kegan Paul, London, 1965). (Cf. my review article on this volume, 'New Essays on Old Philosophers', *Inquiry* **10** (1967) 101–13).

[47] This is borne out by Aristotle's comments in *De Memoria*; see, e.g., 449b 24–30. One is here reminded of Russell's paradoxical statement that "'present' and 'past' are *primarily psychological terms*..." (*op. cit.*, p. 113).

[48] Cf., e.g., the hyperbolic statements of Oswald Spengler's in *The Decline of the West*, Vol. 1 (A. Knopf, New York, 1926), p. 131. "Classical man's existence – Euclidean, relationless, point-like – was wholly contained in the instant."

[49] See *A History of Technology*, Vol. 3, ed. by C. Singer, E. J. Holmyard, A. R. Hall, and T. I. Williams (Clarendon Press, Oxford, 1954–8), p. 569.

[50] The connection between the problems of time-measurement and the logic of tenses cuts deeper than modern philosophers sometimes realize. As Y. Bar-Hillel points out in his useful paper, 'Indexical Expressions', *Mind* **63** (1954) 359–79, the problem of converting temporally indefinite sentences into definite ones is not without its presuppositions. To express 'The sun is now shining' in temporally definite terms, I must know what time it is (at the place I am talking about). What comes up in the ancient Greek world is primarily the practical difficulty of setting up a useful frame of temporal references. But when we consider statements made at spatially distant points, even difficulties in principle start cropping up. These are of the well-known relativistic variety. If we want to build up a tense-logic that applies to more than one world-line (as is necessary if we, for example, want to study quantified tense-logic) and is compatible with physical reality, we cannot accept the usual simple tense-logic with a linear structure but must instead have one that has the structure of Lewis's S4. On this point, see my paper 'The Modes of Modality', *Acta Philosophica Fennica* **16** (1963) 65–81, especially p. 76, reprinted in my *Models for Modalities* (D. Reidel, Dordrecht, 1969), Chapter 5.

[51] Hermann Fränkel, *Wege und Formen frühgriechischen Denkens*, 2nd ed. (C. H. Beck, Munich, 1960), p. 2. Cf. Eric Havelock, *Preface to Plato* (Harvard University Press, Cambridge, Mass., 1963), pp. 192–3, notes 22 and 27.

[52] Havelock, *ibid.*, p. 180.

[53] Cf., e.g., *Phaedrus* 275D–276A. A full documentation is given in Paul Friedländer, *Platon*, Vol. 1 (3rd ed., Walter de Gruyter & Co., Berlin, 1964), Chapter 5, especially pp. 116–21.

[54] *De Interpretatione* I, 16a 3–6.

[55] Havelock, *op. cit.*, *passim*.

[56] In fact, I would go further and say that in the particular matter at hand, *pace* Havelock, Plato is an arch-conservative who in his logical semantical doctrines relies entirely on the spoken word, whatever other differences there may be between him and the 'poetic tradition'. The references given in note 53 above show how deeply Plato felt about this matter.

[57] See *Theaetetus* 190A and *Sophistes* 263E.

[58] *Categories* 5, 4a 23–8, 4a 34–b2.

[59] Ackrill, *op. cit.*, pp. 113–14.

[60] *Op. cit.*, p. 113.

[61] W. Kneale and M. Kneale, *op. cit.*, p. 156.

[62] See Chapter 8 of Hintikka, *Time and Necessity* (note 33 above).

[63] R. G. Collingwood, *The Idea of History* (Clarendon Press, Oxford, 1946), p. 22.

CHAPTER 4

PRACTICAL vs. THEORETICAL REASON –
AN AMBIGUOUS LEGACY

1. MAKER'S KNOWLEDGE

The interrelations of theoretical and practical reason pose a multiplicity of problems which are of considerable urgency both for theoretical and for practical purposes. In order to cover as many of these repercussions within the purview of my discussion, I shall keep my definition of 'practical reason' as wide as possible, even at the cost of some vagueness. By practical reason I shall simply mean reason in so far as it is occupied with human action, human doing and making, and with the results of such action. I shall mainly consider certain problems concerning the relationships between practical and theoretical reason from a historical point of view. These historical questions will lead us to important systematical problems. In this paper, I shall touch on these systematical problems only in so far as they arise out of historical material and can be discussed by reference to it. I envisage the task of my paper as providing materials and impulses for deeper systematical discussions.

One of the most striking features of the history of the two types of knowledge (reason), theoretical and practical, is that they are almost inextricably intertwined. This inseparability is the main thesis of my paper. Perhaps the best large-scale example of the inseparability is the tradition which is somewhat in eclipse in these days in philosophy and which may perhaps be called the tradition of genuine knowledge as maker's knowledge.[1] 'Maker's knowledge' is here supposed to cover also 'doer's knowledge', for no distinction between *poiesis* and *praxis* is intended. The underlying idea of this tradition may be said to be the idea that we can obtain and possess certain especially valuable kinds of *theoretical* knowledge only of what we ourselves have brought about, are bringing about, or can bring about. It emphasizes thus certain theoretical uses of practical reason, we may perhaps say. A few quotations illustrate this tradition and its different ramifications. A medieval exponent of this idea of 'genuine knowledge as maker's knowledge' is Maimonides who writes:

There is a great difference between the knowledge which the producer of a thing possesses concerning it, and the knowledge which other persons possess concerning the same thing. Suppose a thing is produced in accordance with the knowledge of the producer, the producer was then guided by his knowledge in the act of producing the thing. Other people, however, who examine this work and acquire a knowledge of the whole of it, depend for that knowledge on the work itself. For instance, an artisan makes a box in which weights move with the running of water, and thus indicate how many hours have passed.... His knowledge is not the result of observing the movements as they are actually going on; but, on the contrary, the movements are produced in accordance with his knowledge. But another person who looks at that instrument will receive fresh knowledge at every movement he perceives. The longer he looks on, the more knowledge does he acquire; he will gradually increase his knowledge till he fully understands the machinery. If an infinite number of movements were assumed for the instrument, he would never be able to complete his knowledge. Besides, he cannot know any of the movements before they take place, since he only knows them from their actual occurrence.[2]

This quotation illustrates several features of the idea of 'maker's knowledge'. First, behind it lurks apparently the idea that only the maker of a complex mechanism knows it because only he can know its purpose. This assumption is among the more dated aspects of the tradition of maker's knowledge. It seems to have as one of its antecedents the Aristotelian idea that the defining characteristic of any entity is its peculiar function or product.[3]

Second, in speaking of an infinite mechanism Maimonides has in mind God's knowledge of the universe, which he moves on to consider after the quoted passage. The idea of genuine knowledge as maker's knowledge is hence here being applied *ad maiorem gloriam Dei*. In fact, Maimonides' explicit conclusion is that "it is impossible for us in contradistinction to God to know that which will take place in future, or that which is infinite."

2. KNOWLEDGE IS POWER – AND VICE VERSA

The ambivalence of the idea is illustrated by its use by Francis Bacon to advertise the importance of human scientific knowledge. "Human knowledge and human power meet in one; for where cause is not known the effect cannot be produced." "The true and lawful goal of sciences is simply this, that human life be endowed with new discoveries and powers." The idea of 'knowledge as power' which is here expressed by Bacon is but a different application of the assumption we found in

Maimonides. What distinguishes the two is mainly Bacon's optimism with respect to human knowledge, that is, human power. It must in fact be admitted that in many respects pessimistic conclusions from the same principle should have been as close at hand in Bacon's time as the optimistic ones. No wonder we find such Renaissance skeptics as Sanchez inferring in so many words the insignificance of human knowledge from the insignificance of human power over nature. It is a sobering thought that the leading idea of the intellectual background of modern applied science and scientific technology can be traced back to skeptical and theological principles calculated to extol the superiority of the Divine practical reason over the human one.

Other ambiguities in the idea of genuine knowledge as maker's knowledge are in evidence within the realm of human knowledge. A glimpse of them is seen in as hardheaded a thinker as Hobbes, for whom the superior knowledge connected with a maker's 'practical reason' is demonstrative knowledge. "The science of every subject is derived from a precognition of the causes, generation, and construction of the same.... Geometry therefore is demonstrable, for the lines and figures from which we reason are drawn and described by ourselves; and civil philosophy is demonstrable, because we make the commonwealth ourselves. But because of natural bodies we do not know the construction, but seek it from the effects, there lies no demonstration of what the causes be we seek for, but only of what they may be." (See *English Works*, Vol. 7, p. 184.) A modern political scientist is undoubtedly envious of Hobbes' conviction that "civil philosophy" can reach the same demonstrative certainty as geometry, in contrast to the non-demonstrative uncertainties of our sciences of nature. Be this as it may, the serious implication of Hobbes' view is that even within the realm of human reason the idea of genuine knowledge as maker's knowledge can be put to uses almost diametrically opposite to those technological ones Francis Bacon was busy propagating. In fact, the most straightforward application of the idea is to use it to argue for the superiority of the knowledge we have in the field of history and other humanities over the knowledge we have of nature. One of the most outspoken defenders of this view was undoubtedly Giambattista Vico according to whom "the rule and criterion of truth is to have made it."[4] From this principle, he concluded that since the world of history and society, "il mondo delle nazioni", is manmade, our knowledge of it is superior to our knowledge of "il mondo della natura." "Whoever reflects on this cannot but marvel that philosophers should have bent all their energies to the study of the world of nature, which, since God made it, He alone knows; and that they should have neglected the study of the world of nations, or civil world, which, since men had made it, men could come to know." [5]

It is important to realize, however, that even in Vico we do not have a distinction between two kinds of knowledge but a difference in degree. Hobbes bracketed political science with geometry, and likewise Vico sought to apply his methodological ideas to the realm of mathematics and natural science. True to his principles, he for instance advocated the synthetic (constructive) methods of traditional geometry and disparaged the analytic (algebraic and non-constructive) methods of Cartesian geometry. [6]

3. THE SCOPE OF MAKER'S KNOWLEDGE

These Vichian ideas provoke several different kinds of comments. First, the absence of a sharp methodological difference between humanistic studies and natural sciences in Vico – however great a difference in degree he may have postulated between them – makes their respective status subject to be influenced by experience, especially by the relative success or failure of man's attempts to control his physical environment or his historical destiny. From this point of view, modern experience may be said to demonstrate how little truly intentional action there is even among the phenomena studied in Vico's 'New Science' – that is, in language, culture, history, literature, and politics. Man's mastery over his physical environment has opened a much larger scope for maker's knowledge than the most rudimentary control he exercises over his society or his culture.

This point is not unrelated to a third ambiguity in the idea of genuine knowledge as maker's knowledge. It concerns the scope of this kind of privileged knowledge. Here the famous contrast between Vico and Descartes may turn out to be a difference of degree rather than a difference in kind – at least when viewed in a suitable light. A. N. Whitehead claimed to have found in Descartes "the implicit assumption that the mind can only know that which it has itself produced and retains in some sense within itself" (*The Concept of Nature*, Ann Arbor ed., p. 32). Sartre's famous essay on Cartesian freedom is predicated on the attribution of essentially the same presupposition to Descartes. It is not easy to see how these claims are to be reconciled with the kind of knowledge which we according to Descartes have of the physical world and which so offended Vico. Albeit, it is hard not to see something of the Whiteheadian assumption operative in Descartes' discussion of those first and foremost sources of certainty which Descartes finds in the operations of the human mind itself. After all, man's conscious thoughts are as fully of his own making and as fully under his own control as anything one can think of – or so it seems. This interpretation of Cartesian man as constituting himself through his thinking is supported by the 'performative' analysis of the Cartesian *cogito* for which I have argued earlier.[7] It can also be supported by a juxtaposition of the Cartesian doctrine that man's essence is thinking with the Aristotelian doctrine, elsewhere appealed to by Descartes in so many words, that each being's essential nature equals its immediate cause.[8]

But if this perspective on Descartes is acceptable, his great antagonist Giambattista Vico is seen to differ from him in the last analysis only by being bolder – or perhaps less critical. For Vico, the scope of epistemologically relevant maker's knowledge is not restricted to human thoughts, plans, decisions, intentions, hopes, and wishes but comprises also their concrete manifestations and results in the realm of culture and society.

4. MAKER'S KNOWLEDGE AND 'KNOWLEDGE WITHOUT OBSERVATION'

Here we may perhaps have a moral for contemporary topical discussions of that paradigm use of practical reason which has sometimes been called 'practical knowledge' or 'intentional knowledge'. This type of knowledge is very closely related to what I have called the idea of maker's knowledge. Miss Anscombe, who has given us some of the most interesting recent discussions of the subject, quotes with approval Aquinas' account of practical knowledge: Practical knowledge is "the cause of what it understands."[9] This is strongly reminiscent of maker's knowledge, especially when contrasted by Aquinas to 'speculative' knowledge which "is derived from the objects known." Christopher Olsen has in fact argued at some length and with some cogency that the characteristic feature of our knowledge of our intentions is that it is a species of maker's knowledge.[10]

This observation alone does not solve the conceptual problems concerning intentional or practical knowledge. It nevertheless helps us to obtain something of a perspective on such knowledge. One thing we can now see especially clearly is the danger of falling into the Cartesian trap. It seems to me that although Miss Anscombe has not fallen prey to this danger, some of her readers have been misled by the fact that she introduces the idea of knowledge of intentions through examples of one's knowledge of the position of one's limbs and of the place of one's pain. (These are not necessarily examples of intentional knowledge, but they are said to be instances of "knowledge without observation" under which knowledge of our intentional actions also falls.) These examples are not very happy samples of practical knowledge (maker's knowledge) for a reason similar to the reason why the Cartesian realm of maker's knowledge was pathologically narrow. One simply has to grant to Vico that an objectively existing painting or poem can be the product of an act which is as truly creative (and as truly free, Sartre would add) as the movements of my arms or legs. Without imputing the mistake to any particular philosopher, I am tempted to suggest that the use of such paradigms reflects either an intellectual timidity or else radical pessimism vis-à-vis philosophers' chances to understand people's creative activities within his own culture (and within other cultures, for that matter).

What is even more important philosophically, the use of one's thoughts or movements of one's limbs as conceptual paradigms of the objects of intentional knowledge would not do justice to the nature of such knowledge. It could easily create the impression that a special kind of direct agency or causation is needed of the objects of intentional knowledge. This is definitely not required, it seems to me. The product of my intentional activity of which I can have 'maker's knowledge' can be connected with my own action by an arbitrarily long causal chain provided that this chain is known to me. On the other hand, a man can play the role of a merely causal factor without thereby gaining practical or intentional knowledge of its outcome, viz. when he is ignorant of the rest of the causal connections. This point was already made vigorously by John Locke in his criticism of Filmer as applied to the socially important case of parenthood. Human race is often perpetrated, Locke observes, "against the

Consent and Will of the Begetter. And indeed even those who desire Children, are but occasions of their being, and...do little more towards their making, than *Ducalion* and his Wife in the Fable did towards the making of Mankind, by throwing Pebbles over their Heads" (*Two Treatises*, §54). In brief, according to Locke, God "is *King* because he is indeed Maker of us all, which no Parents can pretend to be of their Children" (*ibid.*, §§52 and 53).

The movements-of-limbs example is misleading because it does not bring out this important connection between maker's knowledge or practical knowledge and one's theoretical knowledge of causal dependencies. The only processes involved in this misleading example are psychophysical ones whose causal mechanisms are largely unknown, at very least to the great majority of human agents. Hence precisely the wrong impression is easily created by it. At best, it may be used to represent the first minimal step in the chain of events leading to the desired result, for presumably some sort of psychophysical activity is always needed to initiate the chain. But even this statement, though unexceptionable, embodies a wrong emphasis, for a man can start a chain of events of the relevant sort not so much by carrying out certain bodily movements as sending out suitable messages. What is being emitted is then information rather than ordinary physical influence.

Our insight into an essential connection between practical and theoretical knowledge establishes an important link with history. In a historical perspective, Vico is speaking of the same sort of practical knowledge as Francis Bacon. By increasing man's knowledge of causal dependencies Baconian science has increased his chances of obtaining maker's knowledge of nature in a sense which Vico would be hard put to deny. Any concept of 'practical knowledge' which is restricted to culture or society as contrasted to (say) technology is thus historically inaccurate.

I suspect that the recent preoccupation of several philosophers with one's knowledge of such things as one's pain and the position of one's limbs is at least partly due to a truly Cartesian reason, viz. to a quest of certainty, that is, a quest of knowledge in a sufficiently honorific sense of the word. As soon as physical paraphernalia are needed, the possibility of something's going wrong is opened, such philosophers seem to have thought. One of Miss Anscombe's examples of knowledge without observation is knowing what one is writing on a chalkboard with one's eyes closed. As Miss Anscombe herself points out, this knowledge is not certain if it is thought of as knowledge of the actual outcome, for this may fail to match the intention. (I may have mistaken a stone for a piece of chalk.) Thus there is a temptation to try to trace the chain of causes back to those early stages where no unreliable foreign implements were employed and where accordingly nothing could have gone wrong. I do not see, however, that the factual certainty of one's control of one's limbs is any greater than the certainty one can have of suitable purely physical causal connections. If anything, the former certainty can sometimes be smaller than the latter, and is not in any way absolute. The slips between the cup and the lip need not always be more numerous than those between the lip and the intention, one may perhaps say. I cannot unfortunately take time out here and criticize the alleged incorrigibility of our knowledge of the position of our limbs or of our mental states such as pains, as I would have to do in order to defend my position adequately. Suffice it here to evoke such prima facie counter-examples as the proverbial professor who means A but says B (and who writes down C when the answer is D), Freudian as well as non-Freudian slips of tongue, and the difficulty of practising skills of dexterity and co-ordination. (In one sense, it is easy to aim an accurate gun correctly in that there are no external obstacles to doing so, though in another sense it may be a very difficult feat indeed. Perhaps we should take our clue in this matter from the etymology of the verb 'to intend'.)

5. Intentional knowledge as informed maker's knowledge

In order to avoid misunderstanding, it must be emphasized that practical knowledge certainly is not exhausted by that theoretical knowledge of causal connections which lead up to the desired result, although it may comprise such knowledge as an element. Although I cannot here discuss adequately the nature of such practical knowledge or maker's knowledge, it may nevertheless be pointed out that at the very least the co-occurrence of active awareness of the requisite causal connections with a conceptual framework for judging the outcome of action is required. This outcome may or may not be successful, but one of the most characteristic features of intentional action is that the agent must be able to tell ahead of time (among other things) what counts as success and what not. An especially important element here seems to be this double requirement of awareness or knowledge: it has to comprise *both* knowledge of the causal connections *and* the knowledge needed to judge the outcome. The latter is in some cases due to the agent's knowledge of the nature of the outcome, including its mode of operation. In other cases, it may be due to his decision, that is, to his having imposed on himself aims of a certain sort. Typically, both elements are present.

One of the most interesting variants of the tradition of 'maker's knowledge' in effect suggests that we can have a priori knowledge of things only through imposing this kind of anticipatory framework on them.[11] "Reason has insight only into that which it produces after a plan of its own", says Kant (*Critique of Pure Reason*, B xiii, tr. by Kemp Smith).

The role of this double knowledge of awareness is perhaps perceived best in comparison with other accounts of the nature of practical knowledge. Among many other pertinent things, Miss Anscombe says that when "events effected by human beings" are called intentional, a special kind of description of these events is being used. "In fact the term 'intentional' has reference to a *form* of description of events" (*op. cit.*, p. 84). This does not solve our problems, however, but rather poses them in a new form. It is notorious that as long as our language is extensional, the mode of description of individuals, predicates, or events is immaterial. Part of the import of Miss Anscombe's remark therefore is the etymologically unsurprising but nevertheless highly significant point that the language of intentions is intensional: substitutivity on the basis of *de facto* identity does not hold in it. But then so is the language of ordinary 'theoretical' knowledge, belief, and expectation. Hence one is naturally led to ask whether the involvement of these notions in the concept of intention might go some way towards explaining the peculiarities of the idea of intentional knowledge. In an intentional production of an outcome a double creation as it were seems to be taking place. Besides bringing about the result in a purely causal sense (when successful) the agent creates through his knowledge, his beliefs, and his expectations a kind of framework in which the result can be discussed even when the agent is unsuccessful. I do not see why we cannot along these lines try to account for intentional knowledge as a kind of *informed* maker's knowledge. Perhaps – just perhaps – intentional action is to be understood as being nothing more and nothing less than informed action (doubly informed in the sense I explained earlier). I cannot argue for this suggestion here, but I cannot resist the temptation, either, of reminding you that this is precisely what intentional action should mean in the last analysis historically.[12]

It is in any case clear that implicit in the notion of maker's knowledge there is the idea that the causal knowledge of the means to the desired end must somehow be dependent on, and even derived from, the knowledge used to judge the end. One way of trying to understand this idea is to connect it with the historically important method of analysis which originated in Greek geometry and which consisted precisely in starting from the desired result (originally, desired theorem or construction) and then working one's way backwards to means of bringing it about till one comes to an already established result. This method has had other relatives in the course of history which are equally relevant to the interrelations of practical and theoretical reason.

6. PRACTICAL REASONING IN ARISTOTLE

There are indeed other signs pointing to a greater unity of theoretical and practical knowledge than some recent philosophers have acknowledged. An important *focus* of recent discussions of practical reason and practical reasoning has been the concept of practical syllogism which goes back as far as Aristotle. I find this concept one of Aristotle's less happy inventions, and it seems to me that it has recently created a great deal of unfortunate oversimplification.

In Aristotle, the concept of practical syllogism is best considered against the background of his more comprehensive analysis of the genesis of human action which he carries out under the label of a discussion of deliberation. Aristotle's own description of deliberation is as follows:

We deliberate not about ends but about means. For a doctor does not deliberate whether he shall heal, nor an orator whether he shall persuade, nor a statesman whether he shall produce law and order, nor does any one deliberate about his end. They assume the end and consider how and by what means it is to be attained; and if it seems to be produced by several means they consider by which it is most easily and best produced, while if it is achieved by one only they consider how it will be achieved by this and by what means *this* will be achieved, till they come to the first cause, which in the order of discovery is last.... And if we come on an impossibility, we give up the search, e.g. if we need money and this cannot be got; but if a thing appears possible we try to do it. By 'possible' things I mean things that might be brought about by our own efforts; and these in a sense include things that can be brought about by the efforts of our friends, since the moving principle is in ourselves. The subject of investigation is sometimes the instruments, sometimes the use of them; and similarly in the other cases – sometimes the means, sometimes the mode of using it or the means of bringing it about." (*Ethica Nicomachea*, III, 3, 1112b 12–20, 24–31, tr. by W. D. Ross.)

Deliberation thus results in decision which initiates the step-by-step realization of the aim. In this process, the same intermediate steps which were contemplated in the opposite order in the deliberation are put into effect one by one.

Practical syllogism is best seen as the first step in the reverse process. It is a minimal step, and presumably the first step, in putting the decision into effect. In it the contemplation of an end and the realization that it can be reached through something which is in one's power are combined to yield an action as its 'conclusion'. As Aristotle puts it, what happens in a practical syllogism "seems parallel to the case of thinking and inferring about the immovable objects of science. There the end is the truth seen (for, when one conceives the two premises, one at once conceives and comprehends the conclusion), but here the two premises result in a conclusion which is an action – for example, one conceives that every man ought to walk, one is a man oneself: straightaway one walks" (*De Motu Animalium* 7, 701a–15).

An interesting clue to Aristotle's meaning is given by his comparison of the process of deliberation with the kind of geometrical analysis already mentioned: "For the person who deliberates seems to investigate and analyze in the way described as though he were analyzing a geometrical construction [or proof, *diagramma*] ... and what is last in the order of analysis seems to be first in the order of becoming." (*Ethica Nicomachea* III, 3, 1112b21–24.)

If a historical reminder is needed of the inseparability of theoretical and practical reason, it is hard to think of a more ironical one than this Aristotelian analogy. For precisely the same geometrical analysis was to be the main methodological paradigm of the first great modern scientists.[13] In Newton this paradigm is emphasized in so many words, but it is scarcely any less conspicuous in Galileo or in Descartes. It offers in fact a useful but neglected systematic model of scientific explanation. It is thus instructive indeed to find precisely the same conceptual model at the bottom of both the most typical operation of practical reason and one of the first and foremost methodological ideas of modern natural science.

Even apart from this historical perspective, Aristotle's comparison shows that the links between the different successive means to an end are assumed by Aristotle to be of the sort studied in the theoretical sciences. The kind of heuristic primacy of the desired end which the analytical method illustrates thus fails to confer any special status to the resulting knowledge – a point which is amply confirmed by a systematical study of the logic of the analytical method. The undoubted heuristic usefulness of this method may nevertheless have been instrumental in lending an air of higher knowledge to the result established by its means. If so, Vico's historical perspective was rather superficial in this department in that he failed to appreciate the historical connections between the analytical techniques he disparaged and the kind of maker's knowledge he extolled.

7. THE MULTIPLICITY OF ENDS-AND-MEANS SEQUENCES

The crucial oversimplification in Aristotle's account of deliberation, however, is the assumption that we can analyze deliberation in terms of linear (i.e., not branching) sequences of ends-and-means. Some of Aristotle's formulations go even further and envisage only one chain of means (intermediate ends) connecting the ultimate end with what we can ourselves do. This is wildly oversimplified, for normally the desired end can be brought about in several different ways. In one passage Aristotle recognizes the problem and says that "if it [the end] seems to be produced by several means they [the agents] consider by which it is most easily and best produced" (*Ethica Nicomachea* III, 3, 1112b16–17). This innocent-looking admission is in reality extremely damaging for Aristotle's purposes in several respects. First, the 'good and ease' Aristotle mentions do not easily fit into his conceptual framework, for this framework seems to be predicated on the idea that values always enter into it as ends. For instance, values are apparently supposed to enter into his discussion of deliberation through ends and the rest of Aristotle's deliberative paraphernalia is in so many words said to consist of means (presumably a hierarchy of means).[14]

In Aristotle's account of practical syllogism, the same feature is in evidence in his idea that the major premiss of such a syllogism deals with 'the good' while the minor premiss deals with 'the possible.'[15] How differences in value between different competing minor premises could enter into such a picture, remains a mystery.

In his discussion of *akrasia* in the *Ethica Nicomachea* VII, 3, Aristotle seems to assume that only one minor premiss can actualize at a time. This is scarcely compatible with the comparison between different ways of bringing about a desired end which we saw Aristotle mention, and in any case it would 'amount to a serious flaw in Aristotle's account of the genesis of human action into which comparisons between different, equally practicable means to the same end frequently enter.

One can put essentially the same point in slightly different terms. If Aristotle had consistently allowed comparisons between different means to the same end, as he ought to have done and as he at least once did, it would have spoiled the account he in fact gives of a practical syllogism. According to this account, an action results 'immediately' when the major premiss and the minor premiss are at the same time actualized in the soul. This is implausible as soon as a comparison is needed either between different minor premisses or between different longer sequences of means where the realization of sequences is what is involved in the practical syllogism in question.

Modern theorists of practical syllogism have occasionally recognized that something is amiss here. Their remedies have not been very success- ful, however. Some of them have made the minor premiss of a practical syllogism into a *necessary* condition of the end with which the major premiss deals. Then we have a model of human action which is formally unobjectionable. It should be obvious, however, that this course destroys the value of practical syllogism as a model of intentional action, for it should be obvious that the means through which we in fact realize our ends seldom, if ever, embody necessary conditions of these ends. I do not see that any appeal to *ceteris paribus* clauses or to relative necessity is likely to make a difference here, either.

This line of thought is analogous to the mistake of those interpreters of the Greek geometrical analysis who have it consist (in the case of theoretical analysis) of a series of deductive inferences which start from the desidered theorem. A closer examination of both the mathematical practice and the pronouncements of the theorists of the method prove this view to be misleading, however.[16]

Other recent philosophers seem to put down the difficulty I pointed out in Aristotle merely as an indication of a difference between theoretical syllogisms and practical ones, of which the latter are not supposed to be 'apodeictic'.[17] Much more is involved here, however, than just a difference between theoretical and practical syllogisms. Aristotle is overlooking an important structural feature of human decision-making.

In the parallel problems dealt with in Antiquity under the heading of geometrical analysis, the number of solutions (one, more than one, none) and their conditions were studied in the part of a problem which was known in Antiquity as *diorismos*. Neither the theory nor the practice of *diorismos* yields any solution to the problems that beset Aristotelian theory of deliberation, however.

Nor is the presence of several parallel sequences of means to the same end the only respect in which Aristotle's accounts of deliberation and practical syllogism are oversimplified. There is no realistic hope of dealing with deliberation in terms of several linear sequences of means, either. In order to see the difficulties involved here, we may ask: What sorts of entities are the members of these sequences supposed to be? It is clear that we can hope to get away with *linear* sequences only if the members of these sequences are *states of affairs* (specified by propositions). The dependencies between events, processes, particular tools or implements, or other similar entities of a non-propositional type are likely to be too many-faceted to enable us to capture them in linear sequences of means to an end.

It is doubtful whether Aristotle can be said to have held consistently that the different means to an end have to be thought of (at least for the purpose of his account of deliberation) as states of affairs. Some statements of his square quite well with this reading. Others seem to violate it outright. For instance, even in the passage quoted above from *Ethica Nicomachea* III, 3, instruments rather than their use appeared as a class of means.

8. THE MULTIPLICITY OF ENTITIES NEEDED IN DELIBERATION

But even if we can give Aristotle the benefit of doubt and think of the successive means to an end which are involved in deliberation according to Aristotle as states of affairs, his problems are not yet over. For even if we can in principle describe the realization of the end by means of a succession of states, it is obvious that the point of the description remains to spell out the multivariate causal or functional dependencies between different non-propositional factors of the situation. Aristotle's own analogy with geometrical analysis serves us well here. Although superficial analysts of Greek geometrical analysis still often discuss it in terms of a sequence of *propositions* connecting the desired theorem or construction with axioms, postulates, or previously established results, it is amply clear – especially from actual mathematical practice – that the gist of the famous procedure was to study step by step the interdependencies of the different geometrical objects – lines, circles, points, etc. – involved in the figure which represents the desired theorem or construction.[18] When Descartes and others began to represent these interdependencies systematically in algebraic terms, *analytic* geometry came about. (Here we can see where the name came from.) What is being analyzed in geometrical analysis, in brief, is not the inferential step from axioms and earlier theorems to the desired new one, but the figure – better, the geometrical configuration – with which the theorem deals. In such analysis, dependencies between more than two terms are constantly present, hence destroying all hope of handling the situation in terms of linear sequences of dependencies between the different entities considered. By analogy, it is safe to say that the same holds of the analyses involved in Aristotelian deliberation.

It may be objected that this fact does not spoil the Aristotelian idea of deliberation, as little as it spoils Greek geometrical analysis. Of course it does not destroy the idea, but it does two other things. First, it introduces an additional uncertainty into the situation of deliberation. It suggests that deliberation can be successful only if it takes into account enough of the entities relevant to the interdependencies dealt with in deliberation. It has, so to speak, cast its net so wide as to include all the entities through which all the relevant chains of interdependencies, including roundabout ones, pass in the situation in question. This is analogous to the highly interesting fact that a geometrical analysis can be successful only if enough of the relevant geometrical objects are considered, in other words, only if enough 'auxiliary constructions' have been carried out in the figure. I have argued elsewhere that this kind of uncertainty is inevitably present in all applications of non-trivial knowledge even when the laws that govern the situation are known.[19] I have also shown that in a sense there cannot in general be any mechanically applicable (i.e., recursive) criterion as to when enough 'auxiliary constructions' have been carried out, although in certain particular theories (including, as it happens, elementary geometry) there can be. This kind of uncertainty is therefore inevitably present in Aristotelian deliberation in general. It leads to the almost paradoxical and highly significant result that the procedure by means of which we humans according to Aristotle reach our decisions is not itself decidable (i.e., effective or recursive).

For another thing, the presence of ramified dependencies which cannot be summed up in linear sequences of means to an end has striking consequences for the notion of practical syllogism. Practical syllogism was supposed to be an account of how knowledge of an end and awareness of a means to it which is under one's control combine to yield an action calculated to realize that end. If instead of just one means one has to keep an eye on several simultaneously or sequentially existing factors a certain configuration of which is the 'means' dealt with in the minor premiss of the practical syllogism, an Aristotelian practical syllogism loses its plausibility. Aristotle assumes that the presence of the two premisses in the soul is somehow – for what psychological reasons, we shall not examine here – sufficient to bring about the action. If the 'minor premiss' says that the means of the desired end consist of keeping the lever A at a certain position with one's right hand while controlling a factor x by turning a knob with one's left hand at the same time as a friend sees to it that another factor y is not changed by turning another knob, it is not only implausible but ridiculous to say that the agent's mind instantaneously clicks and that he 'straightaway' performs the trick or that he 'straightaway' tries to do it. In general, it seems to me that the whole plausibility of practical syllogism as an account of the actual genesis of human action depends on its being couched in oversimplified terms – to employ logicians' jargon, in terms of propositional logic and/or monadic predicate logic, not even in terms of the full first order logic.

The credentials of the idea of Aristotelian practical syllogism as an embodiment of a special kind of practical cognition are thus seen to rest on oversimplifications. Moreover, there is no reason to think that deliberation in the Aristotelian sense of the word can be disentangled from obviously theoretical uses of reason. On the contrary, those very analogies between geometrical analysis and deliberation which have been brought to light and utilized in the arguments just concluded themselves offer effective illustrations of the inseparability of practical and theoretical reason.

9. THE INSEPARABILITY OF PRACTICAL AND THEORETICAL REASON

Some of the most important conceptualizations which in the past have been employed to support a distinction between practical and theoretical reason are thus seen to be inadequate or else to fail to uphold any sharp distinction. It also seems to me that a different choice of the ideas to be examined would have yielded the same result, although I would not like to claim any sweeping systematical conclusions yet at this stage of discussion concerning the relation of the two. If there is a general moral to be drawn from my discussion, it probably concerns in the first place those *soi-disant* humanists of today who are in effect cutting themselves loose from much of the most truly humanistic heritage in philosophy – especially from the emphasis on man's creative accomplishments and on their connection with his power – by trying to enforce an oversimplified distinction between different kinds or different uses of reason.

NOTES

[1] I have earlier surveyed it briefly in 'Tieto on valtaa', in Jaakko Hintikka, *Tieto on valtaa ja muita aatehistoriallisia esseitä* (WSOY, Porvoo, 1969), pp. 19–34.

[2] *Guide for the Perplexed*, Part III, Chapter 21 (p. 295 of the Friedländer translation, Routledge and Kegan Paul, London, 1904). The passage is also remarkable in that it contains – albeit implicitly – the earliest comparison of the world to a clockwork known to me.

[3] I am not quite sure that this applies to Maimonides, although it certainly applies to many other early versions of the idea of 'maker's knowledge'. In Part III, Chapter 13, Maimonides writes that "it was not a final cause that determined the existence of all things, but only God's will."

[4] *Opere* (Laterza ed.), Vol. 1, p. 136 (quoted by Fisch and Bergin in the introduction of their translation of Vico's *Autobiography*, Cornell University Press, Ithaca, N.Y., 1944), p. 38.

[5] Vico, *Scienza Nuova*, §331, tr. by Bergin and Fisch as *The New Science of Giambattista Vico* (Cornell University Press, Ithaca, N.Y., 1948).

[6] Cf. Giambattista Vico, *On the Study Methods of Our Time*, tr. by E. Gianturco (Bobbs-Merrill Co., Indianapolis, 1965), pp. xxiii–xxvi, 21–30.

[7] '*Cogito Ergo Sum:* Inference or Performance?', *Philosophical Review* **71** (1962) 3–32, reprinted as Chapter 5 below.

[8] 'Reply to the Fourth Set of Objections', Vol. 2, p. 112 of the Haldane and Ross translation (Cambridge University Press, Cambridge, 1931).

[9] G. E. M. Anscombe, *Intention* (Basil Blackwell, Oxford, 1957), p. 87.

[10] *Philosophical Quarterly* **19** (1969) 324–36.

[11] For a partly historical, partly systematic application of this idea, see 'Quantifiers, Language-Games, and Transcendental Arguments', Chapter 5 of Jaakko Hintikka, *Logic, Language-Games, and Information* (Clarendon Press, Oxford, 1973). For further developments of the idea, see Chapters 6 and 8–10 below.

[12] I am told that the term 'intentio' was used for the first time in a theoretical sense in Latin in the translations of Aristotle's writings from Arabic. The two twelfth-century translators, Dominicus Gundisalinus and John of Spain, translated by 'intentio' the Arabic word which apparently had in turn been used to render the original Greek words for form in those cases where this form was present in the soul, that is, literally, where the soul was 'informed'. (I am grateful for this information to Professor Dagfinn Föllesdal.)

[13] See 'Kant and the Tradition of Analysis', Chapter 9 of *Logic, Language-Games, and Information* (note 11 above), and the literature referred to there.

[14] Cf. the first sentence of our first quotation above from *Ethica Nicomachea* III, 3.

[15] *De Motu Animalium* 7, 701a23–30. It is not perhaps immediately obvious that the 'two kinds of premisses' Aristotle mentions here are the major and the minor premiss. That they are can nevertheless be seen in two ways: (i) A comparison with *Ethica Nicomachea* III, 3, 1112b27 strongly suggests that the premisses 'of the possible' are minor premisses. (ii) Otherwise, there is no continuity in Aristotle's argument in *De Motu Animalium* 7. Aristotle wants to say that we occasionally suppress the *minor* premiss of a practical syllogism. "What we do without reflection, we do quickly." For this purpose, he needs precisely the distinction between the major and the minor premiss, not any old distinction between different kinds of premisses. On my interpretation, the former is just what is made at the crucial passage in terms of 'the good' and 'the possible'.

[16] See my forthcoming work (with Unto Remes) on the Greek concept of geometrical analysis. Some later aspects of the notions of analysis and analyticity are also touched in Chapter 7 below.

[17] Cf. Anscombe, *Intention* (note 9 above), pp. 58–9.

[18] See notes 16 and 13 above.

[19] See 'Kant Vindicated', Chapter 8 of *Logic, Language-Games, and Information* (note 11 above).

CHAPTER 5

COGITO, ERGO SUM:
INFERENCE OR PERFORMANCE?

1. 'COGITO, ERGO SUM' AS A PROBLEM

The fame (some would say the notoriety) of the adage *cogito, ergo sum* makes one expect that scholarly industry has long since exhausted whatever interest it may have historically or topically. A perusal of the relevant literature fails to satisfy this expectation, however. After hundreds of discussions of Descartes's famed principle we still do not seem to have any way of expressing his alleged insight in terms which would be general and precise enough to enable us to judge its validity or its relevance to the consequences he claimed to draw from it. Forty years ago Heinrich Scholz wrote that there not only remain many important questions concerning the Cartesian dictum unanswered but that there also remain important questions unasked.[1] Several illuminating papers later, the situation still seems essentially the same today.

2. SOME HISTORICAL ASPECTS OF THE PROBLEM

This uncertainty of the topical significance of Descartes's dictum cannot but reflect on the discussions of its historical status. The contemporaries were not slow to point out that Descartes's principle had been strikingly anticipated by St. Augustine. Although later studies have unearthed other anticipations,[2] notably in Campanella and in the Schoolmen, scholars still seem to be especially impressed by Descartes's affinity with St. Augustine, in spite of his unmistakable attempts to minimize the significance of Augustine's anticipation. It cannot be denied, of course, that the similarities are striking. One may wonder, however, whether they are all there is to the matter. Perhaps there are also dissimilarities between Descartes and Augustine important enough to justify or at least to explain the one's reluctance to acknowledge the extent of the other's anticipation. But we cannot tell whether there is more to Descartes's *cogito, ergo sum* than there is to St. Augustine's similar argument before we can tell exactly what there is to the *cogito* argument.

If there are important differences between Descartes and his predecessors, the question will also arise whether some of the anticipations are
closer than others. For instance, Descartes could have found the principle
in St. Thomas Aquinas as well as in St. Augustine. Which of the two
saints comes closer to the *cogito, ergo sum*?

3. WHAT IS THE RELATION OF 'COGITO' TO 'SUM'?

What kind of topical questions does *cogito, ergo sum* give rise to? One of
the most important questions is undoubtedly that of the logical form of
Descartes's inference. Is it a formally valid inference? If not, what is
logically wrong about it?

But there is an even more fundamental question than these. Does
Descartes's dictum really express an inference? That it does is suggested
by the particle *ergo*. According to Descartes, however, by saying *cogito,
ergo sum* he does not logically (syllogistically) deduce *sum* from *cogito* but
rather perceives intuitively ('by a simple act of mental vision') the self-
evidence of *sum*.[3] Similarly, Descartes occasionally says that one's own
existence is intuitively obvious without bringing in *cogito* as a premiss.[4]
Sometimes he intimates that his "first principle" is really the existence of
his mind – and not the principle *cogito, ergo sum*, by means of which this
existence is apparently deduced.[5] Once he formulates the *cogito* principle
as *ego cogitans existo* without using the word *ergo* at all.[6]

But if it is true that the Cartesian dictum does not express an inference,
equally perplexing questions are bound to arise. Not only is the particle
ergo then misplaced; the word *cogito* is likewise out of place in a sentence
which only serves to call attention to the self-evidence of *sum*.

But is the word *cogito* perhaps calculated to express the fact that
thought is needed for grasping that *sum* is intuitively evident? Was it
perhaps an indication of the fact that intuition was not for Descartes an
irrational event but an act of the thinking mind, an 'intellectual intuition',
as it has been aptly expressed?[7] Even if this is part of the meaning of
the word, the question will remain why Descartes wanted to stress the
fact in connection with this particular insight. The same point would
equally well apply to most of the other propositions of the Cartesian
system; and yet Descartes does not say, for example, *cogito, ergo Deus est*
in the way he says *cogito, ergo sum*.

Clearly the word *cogito* must have some further function in Descartes's sentence. Even if the sentence did not express a syllogistic inference, it expressed something sufficiently like an inference to make Descartes call his sentence a reasoning (*ratiocinium*),[8] refer to expressing it as inferring (*inferre*),[9] and call *sum* a conclusion (*conclusio*).[10] As Martial Gueroult has trenchantly summed up the problem: "(1) Descartes se refuse à considérer le *Cogito* comme un raisonnement.... (2) Pourquoi s'obstine-t-il alors au moins à trois reprises (*Inquisitio veritatis, Discours, Principes*) à présenter le *Cogito* sous la forme qu'il lui dénie?"[11]

Since the word *cogito* is not dispensable and since it is not just a premise from which the conclusion *sum* is deduced, the relation of the two becomes a problem. One of the main objectives of this essay is to clear up their relation.

4. 'COGITO, ERGO SUM' AS A LOGICAL INFERENCE

But can we be sure that Descartes's dictum does not express a logical inference? In many respects it seems plausible to think that it does. Its logical form seems quite easy to define. In the sentence 'I think' an individual receives an attribute; for a modern logician it is therefore of the form '$B(a)$'. In the sentence 'I am', or 'I exist', this same individual is said to exist. How can one represent such a sentence formally? If Quine is right in claiming that 'to be is to be a value of a bound variable', the formula '$(Ex)\,(x=a)$' serves the purpose. And even if he is not right in general, in this particular case his claim is obviously justified: 'a exists' and 'there exists at least one individual identical with a' are clearly synonymous. Descartes's dictum therefore seems to be concerned with an implication of the form

$$(1) \qquad B(a) \supset (Ex)\,(x=a).$$

Descartes perceives that he thinks; hence he obtains the premiss $B(a)$. If (1) is true, he can use *modus ponens* to conclude that he exists. Those who want to interpret the *Cogito* as a logical inference may now claim that (1) is in fact true, and even logically provable; for is not

$$B(a) \supset (Ex)\,(x=a \,\, \Phi \,\, B(x))$$

a provable formula of our lower functional calculi? And does not this formula entail (1) in virtue of completely unproblematic principles? It may seem that an affirmative answer must be given to these questions, and that Descartes's argument is thus easily construed as a valid logical inference.

Views of this general type have a long ancestry. Gassendi already claimed that *ambulo, ergo sum*, 'I walk, therefore I am', is as good an inference as *cogito, ergo sum*.[12] It is obvious that on the interpretation just suggested, Gassendi will be right. The alleged provability of (1) does not depend on the attribute '*B*' at all. The gist of Descartes's argument is on the present view expressible by saying that one cannot think without existing; and if (1) is an adequate representation of the logical form of this principle, one can indeed equally well say that one cannot walk without existing.

This already makes the interpretation (1) suspect. In his reply to Gassendi, Descartes denies that *ambulo, ergo sum* is comparable with *cogito, ergo sum*.[13] The reasons he gave are not very clear, however. A part of the burden of his remarks is perhaps that although the inferences *ambulo, ergo sum* and *cogito, ergo sum* are parallel – as being both of the form (1) – their premisses are essentially different. *Ambulo* is not an indubitable premiss in the way *cogito* may be claimed to be.

But even if we make this allowance, there remain plenty of difficulties. As we saw, Descartes sometimes denies that in the *cogito* argument *sum* is deduced from *cogito*. But on the view we are criticizing the argument is a deduction. The view is therefore unsatisfactory.

It is also unsatisfactory because it does not help us to understand the role of the *cogito* argument in the Cartesian system. In so far as I can see, it does not, for example, help us to appreciate the consequences Descartes wanted to draw from his first and foremost insight.

The gravest objection, however, still remains to be made. It may be shown that the provability of (1) in the usual systems of functional calculus (quantification theory) has nothing to do with the question whether thinking entails existence. An attempt to interpret Descartes's argument in terms of the provability of (1) is therefore bound to remain fruitless.

By this I mean the following: if we have a closer look at the systems of logic in which (1) can be proved, we soon discover that they are based on important *existential presuppositions*, as I have elsewhere called them.[14] They make more or less tacit use of the assumption that all the singular terms with which we have to deal really refer to (designate) some actually existing individual.[15] In our example this amounts to assuming that the term which replaces *a* in (1) must not be empty. But since the term in question is 'I', this is just another way of saying that I exist. It turns out, therefore, that we in fact decided that the sentence 'I exist' is true when we decided that the sentence 'I think' is of the form $B(a)$ (for the purposes of the usual systems of functional logic).[16] That we were then able to infer $(Ex)(x=a)$ from $B(a)$ is undoubtedly true, but completely beside the point.

It is possible to develop a system of logic which dispenses with the existential presuppositions.[17] If in such a system we could infer 'I exist' from 'I think' – i.e., $(Ex)(x=a)$ from $B(a)$ – it would be highly relevant to the question whether thinking implies existence in Descartes's sense. But this we cannot do. The truth of a sentence of the form (1) turns entirely on existential presuppositions. If they are given up, the provability of (1) goes by the board.

My point may perhaps be illustrated by means of an example constructed for us by Shakespeare. Hamlet did think a great many things; does it follow that he existed?

5. DESCARTES'S TEMPTATION

In spite of all this, there are passages in Descartes which seem to support the interpretation under criticism. I do not want to deny that it expresses *one* of the things Descartes had more or less confusedly in mind when he formulated his famous dictum. But it is important to realize that this interpretation is defective in important respects. It does not help to elucidate in any way some of Descartes's most explicit and most careful formulations. It is at best a partial interpretation.

One can see why some interpretation like the one we have been criticizing attracted Descartes. It gave him what must have seemed a very useful way of defending his own doctrines and of silencing criticism. He could always ask: How can it possibly be true of someone that he thinks unless he exists? And if you challenge the premiss that he is thinking (why cannot the all-powerful *malin génie* make it appear to him that he is thinking?), Descartes could have replied that in a sense the premiss is redundant. He could have resorted to some such argument as the following: If I am right in thinking that I exist, then of course I exist. If I err in thinking that I exist or if I as much as doubt whether I exist, then I must likewise exist, for no one can err or doubt without existing. In any case I must therefore exist: *ergo sum*.

This neat argument is a *petitio principii*, however, as you may perhaps see by comparing it with the following similar argument: Homer was either a Greek or a barbarian. If he was a Greek, he must have existed; for how could one be a Greek without existing? But if he was a barbarian, he likewise must have existed. Hence he must have existed in any case.

The latter argument is obviously fallacious; the celebrated Homeric question cannot be solved on paper. By the same token, the former argument is also fallacious.[18]

Did Descartes realize that it is misguided to represent his insight in the way we have been discussing? It is very difficult to tell. Certainly he never realized it fully. He seems to have realized, however, that on this interpretation the validity of his argument depends essentially on existential presuppositions. For when he tried to present his fundamental doctrines in a deductive or 'geometrical' form, he tried to formulate these presuppositions in so many words by saying that "we can conceive nothing except as existent (*nisi sub ratione existentis*)" (AT VII, 166; HR II, 57). This statement is all the more remarkable since it prima facie contradicts what Descartes says in the *Third Meditation* about "ideas ... considered only in themselves, and not as referred to some other thing," namely that "they cannot, strictly speaking, be false." It also contradicts the plain fact that we can think of (mentally consider) unicorns, or Prince Hamlet, without thereby committing ourselves to maintaining that they exist.

The fact also remains that Descartes resorted to the interpretation we have been criticizing mainly in his more popular writings. As Gueroult noticed, he does not resort to it in the *Meditationes*. His most explicit use of it occurs in *Recherche de la vérité*, in a dialogue whose didactic character has been particularly emphasized by Ernst Cassirer.[19] Descartes's most careful formulations of the *cogito* argument, notably those in the *Meditationes de prima philosophia*, seem to presuppose a different interpretation of the argument.

6. EXISTENTIAL INCONSISTENCY

In order to understand this second interpretation of the *Cogito* we have to have a closer look at the logic of Descartes's famed argument. Descartes's formulations in the *Meditationes* and elsewhere suggest that his result may be expressed by saying that it was impossible for him to deny his existence. One way in which Descartes could have tried to (but did not) deny this would have been to say, 'Descartes does not exist'. As a preliminary to our study of Descartes's first-person sentence *cogito, ergo sum* we shall inquire into the character of this third-person sentence. The reasons why Descartes could not have maintained the latter will turn out to be closely related to the reasons why he asserted the former, if I am right.

What, then, are these reasons? What general characteristic of the sentence 'De Gaulle does not exist' makes it awkward for De Gaulle to assert it?[20] I shall try to formulate this general characteristic by saying that it is *existentially inconsistent* for De Gaulle to assert (to utter) this sentence. The notion of existential inconsistency may be defined as follows. Let *p* be a sentence and *a* a singular term (e.g., a name, a pronoun, or a definite description). We shall say that *p* is *existentially inconsistent for the person referred to by a to utter* if and only if the longer sentence

(2)   *p*; and *a* exists

is inconsistent (in the ordinary sense of the word). In order to avoid our own objections we must of course require that the notion of ordinary inconsistency which is used in the definition involves no existential presuppositions. Provided that this is the case, we may write (2) more formally as

(2)' $p \,\&\, (Ex)\,(x=a)$.

(As the informed reader has no doubt already noticed, we should really use quasi quotes in (2) and (2)'.)

A trivial reformulation of the definition shows that the notion of existential inconsistency really formulates a general reason why certain statements are impossible to defend although the sentences by means of which they are made may be consistent and intelligible. Instead of saying that (2) is inconsistent, we could have said that *p* entails '*a* does not exist' (without the use of any existential presuppositions but otherwise in the ordinary sense of entailment). Uttering such a sentence, p, will be very awkward for the bearer of a: it means making a statement which, if true, entails that its maker does not exist.

It is important to realize that the ills of such *statements* cannot be blamed on the *sentences* by means of which they are made.[21] In fact, the notion of existential inconsistency cannot be applied at all to sentences. As we defined the notion, it is a relation between a sentence and a singular term rather than a property of sentences. The notion of existential inconsistency, however, can often be applied to statements in a fairly natural sense. In order to specify a statement we have to specify (*inter alia*) the sentence uttered (say, q) and its utterer. If the latter refers to himself by means of the singular term b when he makes his statement, we may say that the notion applies to the statement if and only if it applies to q in relation to b.

A simple example will make the situation clear. The *sentences* 'De Gaulle does not exist' and 'Descartes does not exist' are not inconsistent or otherwise objectionable any more than the moot sentence 'Homer does not exist'. None of them is false for logical reasons alone. What would be (existentially) inconsistent would be the attempt of a certain man (De Gaulle, Descartes, or Homer, respectively) to use one of these sentences to make a statement. Uttered by somebody else, the sentences in question need not have anything wrong or even strange about them.

It lies close at hand to express this important feature of the notion of existential inconsistency by means of a term which has recently enjoyed wide currency. The inconsistency (absurdity) of an existentially inconsistent statement can in a sense be said to be of *performatory* (performative) character. It depends on an act or 'performance', namely on a certain person's act of uttering a sentence (or of otherwise making a statement); it does not depend solely on the means used for the purpose, that is, on the sentence which is being uttered. The sentence is perfectly correct as a sentence, but the attempt of a certain man to utter it assertively is curiously pointless. If one of these days I should read in the morning paper, 'There is no De Gaulle any more', I could understand what is being said. But no one who knows Charles de Gaulle could help being puzzled by these words if they were uttered by De Gaulle himself; the only way of making sense of them would be to give them a nonliteral meaning.

We can here see how the existential inconsistency of De Gaulle's fictional utterance (as well as the inconsistency of other existentially inconsistent statements) manifests itself. Normally a speaker wants his hearer to believe what he says. The whole 'language-game' of fact-stating discourse is based on the assumption that this is normally the case. But nobody can make his hearer believe that he does not exist by telling him so; such an attempt is likely to have the opposite result. The pointlessness of existentially inconsistent statements is therefore due to the fact that they automatically destroy one of the major purposes which the act of uttering a declarative sentence normally has. ('Automatically' means here something like 'for merely logical reasons'.) This destructive effect is of course conditional on the fact that the hearer knows who the maker of the statement is, that is, that he identifies the speaker as the same man the uttered sentence is about.

In a special case a self-defeating attempt of this kind can be made without saying or writing anything or doing anything comparable. In trying to make *others* believe something I must normally do something which can be heard or seen or felt. But in trying to make *myself* believe something there is no need to say anything aloud or to write anything on paper. The performance through which existential inconsistency arises can in this case be merely an attempt to think – more accurately, an attempt to make oneself believe – that one does not exist.[22]

This transition from 'public' speech-acts to 'private' thought-acts, however, does not affect the essential features of their logic. The reason why Descartes's attempt to *think* that he does not exist necessarily fails is for a logician exactly the same as the reason why his attempt to tell one of his contemporaries that Descartes did not exist would have been bound to fail as soon as the hearer realized who the speaker was.

7. EXISTENTIALLY INCONSISTENT SENTENCES

It can be seen that we are approaching Descartes's famous dictum. In order to reach it we have to take one more step. We have found that the notion of existential inconsistency is primarily applicable to statements (e.g., declarative utterances) rather than to sentences. In a sense, it may of course be defined for sentences, too, namely by making it relative to a term (name, pronoun, or definite description) occurring therein. This is in fact what we did when we first introduced the notion; we said *inter alia* that the *sentence* 'De Gaulle does not exist' is existentially inconsistent for De Gaulle (i.e., for the person referred to by 'De Gaulle') to utter. Sometimes it may even be possible to omit the specification 'for... to utter', namely when the intended speaker can be gathered from the context.

In a frequently occurring special case such an omission is not only natural but almost inevitable. It is the case in which the speaker refers to himself by means of the first-person singular pronoun 'I'. This pronoun inevitably refers to whoever happens to be speaking. The specification 'inconsistent for... to utter' therefore reduces to the tautology 'inconsistent for whoever happens to be speaking to utter', and may therefore be omitted almost always. In a special case, the notion of existential inconsistency may therefore be defined for sentences *simpliciter* and not only for sentences thought of as being uttered by some particular speaker. These are the sentences which contain a first-person singular pronoun. The existential inconsistency of such a sentence will mean that its utterer cannot add 'and I exist' without contradicting himself implicitly or explicitly.

There are purposes, however, for which it may be misleading to forget the specification. Forgetting it may be dangerous since it leads one to overlook the important similarities which obtain between existentially inconsistent *sentences* and existentially inconsistent *statements*. In a perfectly good sense, existentially inconsistent sentences are all right as sentences. They may be said to be consistent and sometimes even significant (e.g., when they occur as parts of more complicated sentences). According to their very definition, existentially inconsistent sentences are not so much inconsistent as such as absurd for anyone to utter. Their (existential) inconsistency is therefore of performatory character exactly in the same sense as that of the existentially inconsistent statements. The only difference between the two lies in the fact that the latter are inconsistent for some particular man to make while the former are inconsistent for anyone to utter. The inconsistency of existentially inconsistent sentences means that whoever tries to make somebody (anybody) believe them, by so doing, helps to defeat his own purpose.[23] Such an attempt may take the form of uttering the sentence assertively; or it may take the form of trying to persuade oneself of the truth of the sentence in question.

In the same way as existentially inconsistent sentences defeat themselves when they are uttered or thought of, their negations verify themselves when they are expressly uttered or otherwise professed. Such sentences may therefore be called existentially self-verifying. The simplest example of a sentence of this kind is 'I am', in Descartes's Latin *ego sum, ego existo*.

8. DESCARTES'S INSIGHT

Now we have reached a point where we can express precisely the import of Descartes's insight (or at least one of its most important aspects). It seems to me that the most interesting interpretation one can give to it is to say that Descartes realized, however dimly, the existential inconsistency of the sentence 'I don't exist' and therefore the existential self-verifiability of 'I exist'. *Cogito, ergo sum* is only one possible way of expressing this insight. Another way actually employed by Descartes is to say that the sentence *ego sum* is intuitively self-evident.

We can now understand the relation of the two parts of the *cogito, ergo sum* and appreciate the reasons why it cannot be a logical inference in the ordinary sense of the word. What is at stake in Descartes's dictum is the status (the indubitability) of the sentence 'I am'. (This is shown particularly clearly by the formulations of the *Second Meditation*.) Contrary appearances notwithstanding, Descartes does not demonstrate this indubitability by deducing *sum* from *cogito*. On the other hand the sentence 'I am' ('I exist') is not by itself logically true, either. Descartes realizes that its indubitability results from an act of thinking, namely from an attempt to think the contrary. The function of the word *cogito* in Descartes's dictum is to refer to the thought-act through which the existential self-verifiability of 'I exist' manifests itself. Hence the indubitability of this sentence is not strictly speaking perceived *by means* of thinking (in the way the indubitability of a demonstrable truth may be said to be); rather, it is indubitable *because* and *in so far as* it is actively thought of. In Descartes's argument the relation of *cogito* to *sum* is not that of a premiss to a conclusion. Their relation is rather comparable with that of a *process* to its *product*. The indubitability of my own existence results from my thinking of it almost as the sound of music results from playing it or (to use Descartes's own metaphor [24]) light in the sense of illumination (*lux*) results from the presence of a source of light (*lumen*).

The relation which the particle *ergo* serves to express in Descartes's sentence is therefore rather peculiar.[25] Perhaps it would have been less misleading for Descartes to say, 'I am in that I think', or 'By thinking I perceive my existence', than to say, 'I think, therefore I am'. It may be worth noting that one of our formulations was closely anticipated by St. Thomas Aquinas when he wrote: "Nullus potest cogitare se non esse cum assensu: in hoc enim quod cogitat aliquid, percipit se esse" (*De veritate*, X, 12, *ad* 7). The peculiarity of this relation explains Descartes's vacillation in expressing it in that he sometimes speaks of the *Cogito* as an inference and sometimes as a realization of the intuitive self-evidence of its later half.

Similarly we may now appreciate the function of the word *cogito* in Descartes's sentence as well as his motives in employing it. It serves to express the performatory character of Descartes's insight; it refers to the 'performance' (to the act of thinking) through which the sentence 'I exist' may be said to verify itself. For this reason, it has a. most important function in Descartes's sentence. It cannot be replaced by any arbitrary verb. The performance (act) through which the existential self-verifiability is manifested cannot be any arbitrary human activity, contrary to what Gassendi claimed. It cannot be an instance of arbitrary mental activity, say of willing or of feeling. It must be just what we said it is: an attempt to think in the sense of making myself believe (an attempt to think *cum assensu*, as Aquinas put it) that I do not exist. Hence Descartes's choice of the word *cogito*. This particular word is not absolutely indispensable, however, for the act of thinking to which if refers could also be called an act of doubting; and Descartes does admit that his insight is also expressible by *dubito, ergo sum* (in *Recherche de la vérité*, AT X, 523; HR I, 324; cf. also *Principia philosophiae*, I, 7).

But did I not say that the performance through which an existentially self-verifying sentence verifies itself may also be an act of uttering it? Is this not incompatible with Descartes's use of the word *cogito*? There is no incompatibility, for Descartes says exactly the same. In his second meditation on first philosophy he says in so many words that the sentence 'I exist' is necessarily true "whenever I utter it or conceive it in my mind" – "quoties a me profertur, vel mente concipitur" (AT VII, 25; HR I, 150).[26]

The performatory character of Descartes's insight presupposes a characteristic feature of his famous method of doubt which has frequently been commented on in other contexts. Descartes's doubt does not consist in the giving up of all opinions, as a skeptic's doubt might. Nor is it an attempt to remove certain specific sources of mistakes from our thinking, like Francis Bacon's. It amounts to an active attempt to think the contrary of what we usually believe. For this reason Descartes could claim that in an important point this rather doctrinaire doubt of his defeats itself. A skeptic's passive doubt could never do so.

The performatory character of Descartes's insight is in fact part and parcel of the general strategy of his *reductio ad absurdum* (or perhaps rather *projectio ad absurdum*) of skepticism. This strategy is brought out very well by Richard Popkin in his important work *The History of Skepticism from Erasmus to Descartes.*[27] As Popkin writes, "Only by forcing oneself to doubt and negate to the greatest possible degree, can one appreciate the indubitable character of the cogito."

9. The 'cogito' and introspection

The attempt to see the *Cogito* as a logical inference is not the only one-sided interpretation of Descartes's insight. Sometimes it has been understood, on the contrary, as a more or less purely factual statement, as a mere *Tatsachenwahrheit.*[28] This interpretation is often combined with a definite view as to how this particular truth is ascertained, namely by introspection. The function of the *Cogito*, on this view, is to call our attention to something every one of us can ascertain when he 'gazes within himself'.

It is very misleading, however, to appeal to introspection in explaining the meaning of the *Cogito*, although there is likely to be a connection between the notion of introspection and the peculiarities of the Cartesian argument. We have seen that an existentially inconsistent sentence may also defeat itself through an 'external' speech-act. The reason why Descartes could not doubt his own existence is in principle exactly the same as the reason why he could not hope to mislead anybody by saying 'I don't exist'. The one does not presuppose introspection any more than the other. What the philosophers who have spoken of introspection here are likely to have had in mind is often performatoriness rather than introspectiveness.

The independence of Descartes's insight of introspection is illustrated by the fact that there is a peculiarity about certain sentences in the *second* person which is closely related to the peculiarities of Descartes's *ego sum, ego existo*. In the same way as it is self-defeating to say 'I don't exist', it is usually absurd to say 'You don't exist'. If the latter sentence is true, it is *ipso facto* empty in that there is no one to whom it could conceivably be addressed.

What makes us connect the *Cogito* with introspection is the 'spiritualization' which takes place when an 'external' speech-act is replaced by a thought-act and on which we commented above. In the *Cogito* it is presupposed that a man not only can converse with his fellow men but is also able to 'discourse with himself without spoken sound' in a way closely reminiscent of Plato's famous definition of thinking "as a discourse that the mind carries on with itself" (and also reminiscent of Peirce's pertinent remarks on the dialogical character of thought[29]).

Another reason why it is natural to connect the *Cogito* with one's self-knowledge is implicit in what was said above. In order to ascertain that a statement like 'De Gaulle does not exist' (supposing that it is made by De Gaulle himself) is existentially inconsistent, I have to know the speaker; I have to identify him as the selfsame man whom his statement is about. In the same way, appreciating the existential inconsistency of an utterance of the form 'I don't exist' presupposes realizing that the man whom it is about is necessarily the speaker himself. Descartes's *cogito* insight therefore depends on 'knowing oneself' in the same literal sense in which the insight into the self-defeating character of the statement 'De Gaulle does not exist' depends on knowing De Gaulle. Expressed in less paradoxical terms, appreciating the *cogito* argument presupposes an ability to appreciate the logic of the first-person pronoun 'I'. And although mastering the latter is not the same thing as the capacity for introspection, the two are likely to be connected with each other conceptually (logically). The *cogito* insight is essentially connected with one's own case in the same way introspection is, we might say.

10. THE SINGULARITY OF THE 'COGITO'

Descartes realized that his *cogito* argument deals with a particular case, namely with his own. This is in fact typical of his whole procedure; it is typical of a man who asked 'What can *I* know?' rather than 'What can men know?' Descartes denied that his argument is an enthymeme whose suppressed major premiss is 'Everybody who thinks, exists'. He seems to have thought, nevertheless, that this general sentence is a genuine generalization of the insight expressed by his singular sentence.[30]

The general sentence cannot be such a generalization of the *Cogito*, however; it cannot serve as a general truth from which the sentence *cogito, ergo sum* could be inferred, as Descartes seems to have thought. This is perhaps seen most readily by making explicit the existential presuppositions which are implicit in the general sentence. If they are removed, the sentence takes the form 'Every actually existing individual that thinks, exists' and becomes a tautology. This tautology is useless for the purpose Descartes had in mind; it can entail 'I think, therefore I exist' only in conjunction with the further premiss 'I exist'. This further premiss, however, is exactly the conclusion that Descartes ultimately wanted to draw by means of the *cogito* argument. Hence the alleged deduction becomes a *petitio principii*.

Alternatively we might try to interpret the word 'everybody' which occurs in the general sentence as somehow ranging over all *thinkable* individuals rather than all *actually existing* individuals. I am sure that such a procedure is illicit unless further explanations are given. But even if it were legitimate, it would not help us to formulate a true generalization of the Cartesian sentence. For then our generalization would take the form 'Every thinkable individual that thinks, exists' and become false, as witnessed by Shakespeare's meditative Prince of Denmark.

In a sense, therefore, Descartes's insight is not generalizable. This is of course due to its performatory character. Each of us can formulate 'for himself' a sentence in the first person singular that is true and indubitable, namely the Cartesian sentence *ego sum, ego existo*. But since its indubitability is due to a thought-act which each man has to perform himself, there cannot be any general sentence which would be indubitable in the same way without being trivial. The *cogito* insight of each of us is tied to his own case even more closely than Descartes realized.[31]

11. THE ROLE OF THE 'COGITO' IN DESCARTES'S SYSTEM

Our interpretation is supported by the fact that it enables us to appreciate the role of Descartes's first and foremost insight in his system, that is, to understand the conclusions he thought he could draw from the *Cogito*. For one thing, we can now see the reason why Descartes's insight emerges from his own descriptions as a curiously *momentary* affair. It is a consequence of the performatoriness of his insight. Since the certainty of my existence results from my thinking of it in a sense not unlike that in which light results from the presence of a source of light, it is natural to assume (rightly or wrongly) that I can be really sure of my existence only as long as I actively contemplate it. A property which a proposition has *because* and *in so far as* it is actually thought of easily becomes a property which belongs to it only *as long as* it is thought of. In any case, this is what Descartes says of the certainty of his own existence. I can be sure of my existence, he says, 'while' or 'at the same time as' I think of it or 'whenever' or 'as often as' I do so.[32] "Whereas I had only to cease to think for an instant", he says, "and I should then (even although all the other things I had imagined still remained true) have no grounds for believing that I can have existed in that instant" (*Discours*, Part IV; AT VI, 32–33; HR I, 101).

This shows, incidentally, that the sole function of the word *cogito* in Descartes's dictum cannot be to call attention to the fact that this insight is obtained *by means of* thinking. For of an ordinary insight of this kind (e.g., of a demonstrative truth) we may of course continue to be sure once we have gained it.

In the same way we can perhaps see why Descartes's insight *cogito, ergo sum* suggested to him a definite view of the nature of this existing *ego*, namely that its nature consists entirely of thinking. We have seen that Descartes's insight is not comparable with one's becoming aware of the sound of music by pausing to listen to it but rather with making sure that music is to be heard by playing it oneself. Ceasing to play would not only stop one's hearing the music, in the way ceasing to listen could; it would put an end to the music itself. In the same way, it must have seemed to Descartes, his ceasing to think would not only mean ceasing to be aware of his own existence; it would put and end to the particular way in which his existence was found to manifest itself. To change the metaphor, ceasing to think would not be like closing one's eyes but like putting out the lamp. For this reason, thinking was for Descartes something that could not be disentangled from his existence; it was the very essence of his nature. We may thus surmise that the original reason why Descartes made the (illicit but natural) transition from *cogito, ergo sum* to *sum res cogitans* was exactly the same as the reason for the curious momentariness of the former which we noted above, namely the performativeness of the *cogito* insight. In any case, the two ideas were introduced by Descartes in one and the same breath. The passage we just quoted from the *Discours* continues as follows: "From this I knew that I was a substance whose whole essence or nature consists entirely in thinking." In the *Meditationes* Descartes is more reserved. He has already become aware of the difficulty of converting his intuitive idea of the dependence of his existence on his thinking into a genuine proof. The way in which the idea of the dependence is introduced is, nevertheless, exactly the same: "*Ego sum, ego existo*. This is certain. How long? As long as I think. For it might indeed be that if I entirely ceased to think, I should thereupon altogether cease to exist. I am not at present admitting anything which is not necessarily true; and, accurately speaking, I am therefore only a thinking thing" (AT VII, 27; HR I, 151–152).

The transition from *cogito, ergo sum* directly to *sum res cogitans* remains inexplicable as long as we interpret the *Cogito* in terms of the logical truth of (1). For then the blunt objections of Hobbes carry weight: Even if it were true that we can validly infer *ambulo ergo sum* or *video ergo sum*, there would not be the slightest temptation to take this to suggest that one's nature consists entirely of walking or of seeing in the way Descartes thought he could move from *cogito, ergo sum* to *sum res cogitans*. (Cf. AT VII, 172; HR II, 61.)

12. DESCARTES AND HIS PREDECESSORS

It seems to me that Descartes is distinguished from most of his predecessors by his awareness of the performatory character of his first and foremost insight.[33] In spite of all the similarities that there obtain between Descartes and St. Augustine, there are also clear-cut differences. In so far as I know, there is no indication that Augustine was ever alive to the possibility of interpreting his version of the *Cogito* as a performance rather than as an inference or as a factual observation.[34] As far as Augustine is concerned, it would be quite difficult to disprove a 'logical' interpretation such as Gassendi and others have given of the Cartesian *cogito* argument. What he dwells on is merely the 'impossibility of thinking without existing'. I do not see any way in which Augustine could have denied that *ambulo, ergo sum* or *video, ergo sum* are as good inferences as *cogito, ergo sum* and that the sole difference between them lies in the different degree of certainty of their premises.

In this respect, there is an essentially new element present, however implicitly, in Descartes's formulations. This difference also shows in the conclusions which Descartes and Augustine drew from their respective insights. For instance, Augustine used his principle as a part of an argument which was designed to show that the human soul is tripartite, consisting of being, knowing, and willing. We have already seen that Descartes's insight was for him intimately connected with the notion of thinking (rather than, say, of willing or feeling): the performance through which an existentially inconsistent sentence defeats itself can be an act of thinking of it, but it cannot possibly be an act of willing or of feeling. Hence Descartes could use the performatorily interpreted *cogito* insight to argue that the human soul is a *res cogitans*, but not to argue that it is essentially a willing or feeling being. In view of such differences, is it at all surprising that Descartes should have emphasized his independence of Augustine?

If there is a predecessor who comes close to Descartes, he is likelier to be St. Thomas than St. Augustine. We have already quoted a passage in Aquinas which shows much more appreciation of the performatory aspect of the *Cogito* than anything in Augustine. The agreement is not fortuitous; Aquinas' ability to appreciate the performatoriness of the *Cogito* was part and parcel of his more general view that "the intellect knows itself not by its essence but by its act." [35] The significance of this crucial similarity between Aquinas and Descartes is not diminished by the interesting dissimilarities which also obtain between them. For instance, it is not diminished by the fact that for Aquinas the relevant acts of intellect needed an object other than the intellect itself, whereas Descartes denies "that a thinking being needs any object other than itself in order to exercise its activity" (AT IX, 206; HR II, 128). This dissimilarity is smaller than it first appears to be. Descartes did not hold that the thinking mind could apprehend itself directly, but only by means of its activities (see his reply to Hobbes's second objection; also AT VII, 422; HR II, 241; HR II, 343), exactly as Aquinas did. I should go as far as to wonder whether there is more than a coincidence to the fact that Descartes was particularly close to Aquinas (as far as the *cogito* insight is concerned) in that work of his, the *Meditationes*, in which the Thomistic influence on him is in many other respects most conspicuous.

13. SUMMING UP

Some of the main points of our analysis of the *Cogito* may be summed up as follows: Whatever he may have thought himself, Descartes's insight is *clear* but not *distinct*,[36] to use his own terminology. That is to say, there are several different arguments compressed into the apparently simple formulation *cogito, ergo sum* which he does not clearly distinguish from each other.

(i) Sometimes Descartes dealt with the *Cogito* as if it were an expression of the logical truth of sentences of the form (1) or at least of the indubitable truth of a particular sentence of this form. On this interpretation the argument *cogito, ergo sum* is on the same footing with such arguments as *volo, ergo sum*. Arguments like *video, ergo sum* or *ambulo, ergo sum* can be said to be less convincing than the *Cogito* merely because their premises are not as indubitable as that of Descartes's argument. The word *cogito* may thus be replaced by any other word which refers to one of my acts of consciousness.

(ii) Descartes realized, however, that there is more to the *Cogito* than interpretation (*i*). He realized, albeit dimly, that it can also serve to express the existential self-verifiability of the sentence 'I exist' (or the existential inconsistency of 'I don't exist'). On this interpretation the peculiarity of the sentence *ego sum* is of performatory character. The verb *cogitare* now has to be interpreted rather narrowly. The word *cogito* may still be replaced by such 'verbs of intellection' as *dubito* (or *profero*) but not any longer by verbs referring to arbitrary mental acts, such as *volo* or *sentio*. This interpretation, and only this one, makes it possible to understand Descartes's rash transition from *cogito, ergo sum* to *sum res cogitans*.

By comparing the two interpretations we can further elucidate certain peculiarities of Descartes's thought. We shall mainly be concerned with the following two points:

(A) Descartes does not distinguish the two interpretations very clearly. We cannot always expect a clear answer to the question whether a particular instance of the *cogito* argument is for him an inference or a performance. The two types of interpretation merge into each other in his writings in a confusing manner.

(B) Nevertheless, the relation of these two possible interpretations of the Cartesian *Cogito* throws light on the meaning of the critical verb *cogitare* in the different parts of Descartes's philosophy.

14. THE AMBIGUITY OF THE CARTESIAN 'COGITO'

Interpretation (*ii*) easily gives rise to an expectation that is going to be partly disappointed. It easily leads us to expect a definite answer to the question: What was Descartes thinking *of* in that thought-act which to him revealed the indubitability of his own existence? Interpretation (*ii*) suggests that Descartes should have been thinking of *his own existence*. This agrees very well with some of Descartes's most explicit pronouncements. One of them was already quoted above (in the penultimate paragraph of Section 8). In the same connection Descartes writes: "Let him [viz. Descartes's *malin génie*] deceive me as much as he will, he can never cause me to be nothing so long as I shall be thinking that I am something." The same point is repeated in the *Third Meditation* (AT VII, 36; HR I, 158–159).

Elsewhere, however, Descartes often uses formulations which clearly presuppose that his crucial thought-act pertains to something different from his mere existence. These formulations can be understood, it seems to me, as hybrids between the two arguments (*i*) and (*ii*). This hybridization was undoubtedly encouraged by the following (correct) observation: If the sentence 'I don't exist' is existentially self-defeating, then so are a fortiori such sentences as 'I think, but I don't exist' or 'I doubt, but I don't exist'. In other words, there are no objections in principle to saying that what is at stake in the *Cogito* is the status of these latter sentences rather than that of the sentence 'I don't exist'.

On this intermediate interpretation the word *cogito* has a curious double role in Descartes's dictum. On one hand, it is a part of the proposition whose status (indubitability) is at stake. On the other hand, it refers to the performance through which the indubitability of this proposition is revealed. If we are on the right track, we may expect that this duality of functions will sometimes be betrayed by Descartes's formulations, that is, that he will sometimes use two 'verbs of intellection' (such as *think*, *doubt, conceive,* and the like) where on interpretation (*i*) there should be only one. This expectation turns out to be justified: "... from this very circumstance that I *thought to doubt* [*je pensais à douter*] the truth of those other things, it very evidently and very certainly followed that I was..." (*Discours*, Part IV; my italics); "... but we cannot in the same way *conceive* that we who *doubt* these things are not..." (*Principia philosophiae* I, 7; my italics).

This duplication of verbs of intellection [37] shows that we still have to do with a performatory insight. Where Augustine would have said that nobody can doubt anything without existing, Descartes in effect says that one cannot think that one doubts anything without thereby demonstrating to oneself that one exists. But he does not clearly distinguish the two arguments from each other. He thinks that interpretation (*ii*), thus expanded, is tantamount to interpretation (*i*). For instance, the passage which we just quoted from the *Principia* continues as follows: "... for there is a contradiction in conceiving that what thinks does not, at the same time as it thinks, exist." The change may seem small, but it makes all the difference. In the first passage Descartes is saying that it is impossible for him to think that *he himself* should not exist while he doubts something. In the second passage he says that it is impossible for him to think that *anybody else* should not exist while he (the other man) doubts something. The former passage expresses a performatory insight, whereas the latter cannot do so. We have moved from the ambit of interpretation (*ii*) to that of interpretation (*i*).[38]

15. The ambiguity of the cartesian 'cogitatio'

To tell what Descartes meant by the verb *cogitare* is largely tantamount to telling what is meant by his dictum: *sum res cogitans.* We saw that this dictum originally was for Descartes a consequence (a fallacious, albeit natural one) of the principle *cogito, ergo sum,* which for this purpose had to be given interpretation (*ii*). From this it follows that the word *cogitans* has to be interpreted as referring to thinking in the ordinary sense of the word. It is not surprising, however, that Descartes should have included more in his alleged conclusion *sum res cogitans* than it would have contained on the basis of the way in which he arrived at it even if this way had amounted to a demonstration.

Descartes had to reconcile his 'conclusion' that the essence of a human being consists entirely of thinking (in the ordinary sense of the word) and the obvious fact that there are genuine acts of consciousness other than those of thinking, for example those of willing, sensing, feeling, and the like. This he sought to accomplish by extending the meaning of the verb *cogitare*. He tried to interpret all the other acts of consciousness as so many modes of thinking.[39] In this attempt he was helped by the following two facts:

(a) The meaning of the verb *cogitare* was traditionally very wide. According to Alexandre Koyré, "it embraced not only 'thought' as it is now understood, but all mental acts and data: will, feeling, judgment, perception, and so on."[40] Because of this traditionally wide range of senses of the word Descartes was able to smuggle more content into his 'result' *sum res cogitans* than the way in which he reached it would, in any case, have justified.

It is significant that nonintellectual acts of consciousness enter into the argument of the *Meditationes* at the moment when Descartes pauses to ask what a *res cogitans* really is, that is, what is meant by the *cogitatio* of a *res cogitans*:

What then am I? A thinking thing [*res cogitans.*] What is a thinking thing? It is a thing that doubts, understands, asserts, denies, wills, abstains from willing, that also has sense and imagination. These are a good many properties – if only they all belong to me. But how could they fail to? [AT VII, 28; HR I, 153]

Descartes is not here simply stating what is meant by a *res cogitans*. He is not merely formulating the conclusion of an argument; he is proceeding to interpret it.[41] This is shown by the last two quoted sentences. For if willing and sensation were included in Descartes's thinking *ego* already in virtue of the argument which led him to conclude *sum res cogitans*, there would not be any point in asking whether they really belong to his nature.

(b) However, the wide range of senses of the verb *cogitare* in Descartes is not all due to external influence. There are factors in his own thinking which tend in the same direction. Among other things, the confusion between the two interpretations is operative here. Descartes can hope (as we saw) to be able to jump from *cogito, ergo sum* to *sum res cogitans* only if interpretation (*ii*) is presupposed. This interpretation in turn presupposes a narrowly 'intellectual' meaning of the verb *cogitare* in that it cannot be replaced by any arbitrary verb which refers to some act of one's immediate consciousness. In contrast, on interpretation (*i*) the verb *cogitare* could be understood in this wide sense. The confusion between the two interpretations made it possible for Descartes to deal with the 'conclusion' *sum res cogitans* as if it were based on a *cogito* argument in which *cogitatio* covers all one's acts of consciousness – as he strictly speaking is not justified in doing.

This explains Descartes's apparent inconsistency in using the verb *cogitare*. It is interesting to note that some of the critics (e.g., Anscombe and Geach; see *op. cit.*, p. xlvii) who have most strongly stressed the wide extent of this verb in Descartes have nevertheless been forced to say that in the *cogito* argument the verb is used in a rather narrow sense to refer to what we nowadays call thinking. This may seem paradoxical in view of the fact that the broad interpretation is applied in the first place to the sentence *sum res cogitans* to which Descartes moved directly from the *cogito* argument. In our view, this prima-facie paradox disappears if we realize the ambiguity of the *cogito* argument.

The close connection between this argument and the notion of *cogitatio* in Descartes is amply demonstrated by his formulations. In our last quotation Descartes was left asking whether doubt, understanding, will, sense, imagination, and the like belong to his nature. He reformulates this question successively as follows: "... how can any of these things be less true than my existence? Is any of these something distinct from my thinking [*cogitatione*]? Can any of them be called a separate thing from myself?" Only such things could belong to Descartes's nature as were as certain as his existence. Why? The reason is seen from the context of the quotation. Descartes had already pronounced his *Cogito*; he had already ascertained the indubitability of his existence. He held that nothing he did not have to know in order to ascertain this could, in the objective order of things, constitute a necessary condition of his existence.[42] Such things could not belong to his essence, for "nothing without which a thing can still exist is comprised in its essence."[43] Hence nothing could belong to his essence or nature that he could not be sure of already at the present stage of his argument, that is, nothing that he could not ascertain in the same way and at the same time as he ascertained his own existence. For this reason, nothing that belonged to his nature could be 'less true than his existence'.

What this requirement amounts to is that everything that Descartes was willing to accept as a part of his nature (even in the sense of being a mere mode of his basic nature of thinking) had to be shown to belong to him by means of the *cogito* argument in the same way in which he 'demonstrated' that thinking belonged to him by 'deducing' *sum res cogitans* from *cogito, ergo sum*. A mental activity was for Descartes a part of his nature if and only if the corresponding verb could function as the premise of a variant of the *cogito* argument. For instance, the sense in which apparent sensation can be said to belong to his nature (as a mode of thinking) is for Descartes exactly the same as the sense in which he could infer *sentio, ergo sum*. The former is explained by Descartes as follows:

Finally, it is I who have sensations, or who perceive corporeal objects as it were by the senses. Thus, I am now seeing light, hearing a noise, feeling heat. These things are false [it may be said], for I am asleep; but at least I seem to see, to hear, to be warmed. This cannot be false and this is what is properly called my sensation; further, sensation, precisely so regarded, is nothing but thinking [*cogitare*]. [AT VII, 29; HR I, 153]

The latter is explained in a strikingly similar way:

Suppose I say *I see or I am walking, therefore I exist*. If I take this to refer to vision or walking as corporeal action, the conclusion is not absolutely certain; for, as often happens during sleep, I may think I am seeing though I do not open my eyes, or think that I am walking although I do not change my place; and it may even be that I have no body. But if I take it to refer to the actual sensation or awareness [*sensu sive conscientia*] of seeing or walking, then it is quite certain; for in that case it has regard to the mind, and it is the mind alone that has sense or thought [*sentit sive cogitat*] of itself seeing or walking [*Principia* I, 9; cf. Descartes's similar reply to Gassendi's objections to the *Cogito*.]

In short, the reason why sensation belonged to Descartes's nature was for him exactly the same as the reason why he could argue *sentio, ergo sum*. For him, doubting, willing, and seeing were modes of his basic nature of thinking exactly in the same sense in which the arguments *dubito ergo sum, volo ergo sum*, and *video ergo sum* were variants or 'modes' of the argument *cogito ergo sum*.

Why, then, is one of these arguments a privileged one? If Descartes could argue *volo, ergo sum* and *sentio, ergo sum* as well as *cogito, ergo sum*, why did he refuse to infer that his nature consists of 'Wille und Vorstellung', claiming as he did that it consists entirely of thinking? The answer is again implicit in the ambiguity of the *cogito* argument. Such parallel arguments as *volo, ergo sum* presuppose interpretation (*i*). Now there was more to the Cartesian *Cogito* than this interpretation; Descartes was also aware of the 'performatory' interpretation (*ii*). It is the latter interpretation that gives the verb *cogitare* a privileged position vis-à-vis such verbs as *velle* or *videre*. Descartes could replace the word *cogito* by other words in the *cogito, ergo sum*; but he could not replace the performance which for him revealed the indubitability of any such sentence. This performance could be described only by a 'verb of intellection' like *cogitare*. For this reason, the verb *cogitare* was for Descartes a privileged one; for this reason nothing could for him belong to his nature that was "something distinct from his thinking".

This special role of the verb *cogitare* seems to me difficult to explain otherwise. If I am right, the conspicuous privileges of this verb in Descartes therefore constitute one more piece of evidence to show that he was aware of interpretation (*ii*).

There is a further point worth making here. We have already pointed out that the verb *cogitare* is not the most accurate one for the purpose of describing the performance which for Descartes revealed the certainty of his existence (see note 26). This inaccuracy led Descartes to assimilate the peculiarities of the existentially self-defeating sentence 'I do not exist' to the peculiarities of such sentences as 'I doubt everything' or 'I am not thinking anything'. There is an important difference here, however. The latter sentences are not instances of existential inconsistency. They are instances of certain related notions; they are literally impossible to believe or to think in a sense in which 'I do not exist' is not. I have studied the peculiarities of some such sentences elsewhere (in *Knowledge and Belief, An Introduction to the Logic of the Two Notions* (Cornell University Press, Ithaca, N.Y., 1962). In many respects, their properties are analogous to those of existentially self-defeating sentences.[44]

NOTES

[1] Heinrich Scholz, 'Über das Cogito, ergo sum', *Kant-Studien* **36** (1931) 126–147.
[2] See, e.g., L. Blanchet, *Les antécédents du 'Je pense, donc je suis'* (Paris, 1920); Étienne Gilson, *Études sur le rôle de la pensée médiévale dans la formation du système cartésien* (*Études de philosophie médiévale*, Vol. 13) (Paris, 1930), Part II, Chapter 2 and the first appendix; Heinrich Scholz, 'Augustinus und Descartes', *Blätter für deutsche Philosophie* **5** (1932) 406–423.
[3] *Œuvres de Descartes*, published by C. Adam and P. Tannery (Léopold Cerf, Paris, 1897–1913), Vol. 7, p. 140; *The Philosophical Works of Descartes*, tr. by E. S. Haldane and

G. R. T. Ross (Cambridge University Press, Cambridge, 1931), II, 38. In the sequal, these editions will be referred to as AT and HR, respectively, with Roman numerals referring to volumes. Normally I shall not follow Haldane and Ross's translation, however; I shall make use of the existing translations (notably of those by N. Kemp Smith and by Anscombe and Geach) rather eclectically.

[4] AT X, 368; HR I, 7.

[5] AT IV, 444; AT VII, 12; HR I, 140.

[6] AT VII, 481; HR II, 282.

[7] L. J. Beck, *The Method of Descartes* (Clarendon Press, Oxford, 1952), Chapter 4.

[8] AT X, 523; HR I, 324.

[9] AT VII, 352; HR II, 207; cf. AT III, 248.

[10] *Principia philosophiae* I, 9; AT VIII, 7; HR I, 222; cf. AT II, 37, and AT V, 147.

[11] Martial Gueroult, 'Le *Cogito* et la notion "pour penser il faut être"', *Travaux du IXe Congrès International de philosophie* (*Congrès Descartes*) (Paris, 1937; reprinted as the first appendix to Gueroult's *Descartes selon l'ordre des raisons*, Aubier, Paris, 1953) Vol. 2, pp. 307–312, see p. 308.

[12] In his objections to the *Second Meditation* (AT VII, 258–259; HR II, 137).

[13] AT VII, 352; HR II, 207.

[14] In 'Existential Presuppositions and Existential Commitment', *Journal of Philosophy* **56** (1959) 125–137.

[15] All the singular terms (e.g. names or pronouns) which in an application may be substituted for a free individual variable are assumed to do so; and as a consequence all the free individual variables have to behave like singular terms which really possess a reference (or 'bearer', vulgarly 'referent').

[16] Cf. Leibniz' incisive remark: "And to say *I think, therefore I am*, is not properly to prove existence by thought, since to think and to be thinking is the same thing; and to say, I am thinking, is already to say, *I am*" (*Nouveaux Essais*, tr. by A. G. Langley (Open Court, La Salle, Ill., 1949), IV, 7, Sec. 7).

[17] Such a system was outlined in the paper referred to in note 14. Essentially the same system was developed independently by Hugues Leblanc and Theodore Hailperin in 'Nondesignating Singular Terms,' *Philosophical Review* **68** (1959) 239–243.

[18] But maybe you are not convinced; maybe you feel that the question of Descartes's own existence is essentially different from the question of Homer's existence. If so, you are right. I have not wanted to deny that there is a difference, and an important one. All I am saying is that the reconstruction we are considering does not bring out this difference.

[19] *Descartes: Lehre, Persönlichkeit, Wirkung* (Stockholm, 1939), p. 126.

[20] My example is inspired by his predilection for referring to himself in the third person. (Added in 1973: note that this paper was written in 1961 when the general was still alive.)

[21] It may be worth while to recall here the distinction between a sentence, an utterance, and a statement. A sentence is of course a grammatical entity that involves no reference to any particular utterer or any particular time of utterance. An utterance is an event (a speech-act) that may be specified by specifying the uttered sentence, the speaker, and the occasion on which he makes his utterance.

Utterances of declarative sentences (with prima-facie fact-stating intent) are typical examples of *statements*. (The term does not seem especially happy, but I shall retain it because it appears to be rather widespread.) A statement is an event (an act) occurring in some particular context. Usually it is a speech-act of a certain kind, but we shall not insist on that. For our purposes a statement may equally well be made, e.g., by writing a sentence. *Any* act will do which is prima facie designed to serve the same purposes as the act of

uttering a declarative sentence with the intention of conveying bona fide information.
²² This means, in effect, that Descartes arrives at his first and foremost insight by playing for a moment a double role: he appears as his own audience. It is interesting and significant that Balz, who for his own purposes represents Descartes's quest as a dialogue between "Cartesius, who voices Reason itself'", and "René Descartes the Everyman", finds that they both 'conspire in effecting this renowned utterance', the *cogito ergo sum*, wherefore 'in some sense, its meaning is referable both to Cartesius and René Descartes'. See Albert G. A. Balz, *Descartes and the Modern Mind* (Yale University Press, New Haven, 1952), pp. 89–90.
²³ For this reason it might be more appropriate to call them (existentially) *self-defeating* than (existentially) *inconsistent*.
²⁴ See his letter to Morin, dated July 13, 1638 (AT II, 209).
²⁵ Martial Gueroult has again neatly located the source of trouble by calling our attention to the peculiarities of this relation. He has realized that Descartes's dictum does not (merely) express a logical relation between thinking and existing but that it is concerned with an additional 'fact' or 'act' ('le fait ou l'acte', 'le fait brut de l'existence donnée') which is just what is needed to show the certainty of my existence. However, his explanations leave the status of this fact or act (which cannot be an ordinary fact given to us by our senses or by introspection) rather vague. Nor does Gueroult realize that the logical aspect of Descartes's insight is in principle completely dispensable. See Gueroult's *Descartes*, Vol. 2, p. 310.
²⁶ What we have said shows that Descartes's verbs *cogitare* and *dubitare* are not, in the last analysis, the most accurate ones for describing the act through which the sentence 'I don't exist' defeats itself. It is not strictly true to say that an inconsistency arises from Descartes's attempt to *think* that he does not exist or to *doubt* that he does. Somebody else may think so; why not Descartes himself? He can certainly think so in the sense of contemplating a 'mere possibility'. What he cannot do is to *persuade* anybody (including himself) that he does not exist; wherefore he cannot try to *profess* (to others or to himself) that he does not exist without defeating his own attempt. In fact, Descartes himself resorts to explanations of this kind when he gives his most explicit explanation of the moves which made him recognize the self-evidence of his own existence. For instance, just before the passage quoted he uses the Latin verb *persuadere* for the purpose.
²⁷ *The History of Skepticism from Erasmus to Descartes* (Wijsgerige Teksten en Studies IV, Van Gorcum & Co., Assen, 1960) Chapter 9, especially pp. 185–187. See also Henri Gouhier. 'Doute méthodique ou négation méthodique?', *Études Philosophiques* **9** (1954) 135–162.
²⁸ For the history of this view as well as for an interesting argument for its importance, see P. Schrecker, 'La méthode cartésienne et la logique,' *Revue philosophique* **123** (1937) 336–367, especially pp. 353–354.
²⁹ *Collected Papers* (Harvard University Press. Cambridge, Mass., 1931–1958). Vol. 6, Sec. 338; Vol. 5, Sec. 421.
³⁰ See AT IX, 205–206; HR II, 127; cf. AT VII, 140–141; HR II, 38.
³¹ As Popkin aptly observes (*op. cit.*, p. 187), "the method of doubt is the *cause* rather than the *occasion* of the acquisition of new knowledge" (my italics).
³² See, e.g., *Principia philosophiae* I, 7; I, 8; I, 49.
³³ The difference is marked even though Descartes himself was not fully aware in all respects of the nature of his insight.
³⁴ To some extent this may be merely an indication that the *cogito* insight was in Augustine less fully developed than it is in Descartes.
³⁵ *Summa theologica*, I, Q.87, art. 1.
³⁶ For the relation of the two notions in Descartes, see N. Kemp Smith, *New Studies in the*

Philosophy of Descartes (Macmillan, London, 1952), pp. 52ff.

[37] That a verb of intellection should in Descartes serve to describe the object of another thought-act is all the more remarkable as it is virtually inconsistent with his explicit doctrines. For Descartes held that "one thought [conscious act, *cogitationem*] cannot be the object of another" (Reply to Hobbes's second objection; cf. AT VII, 422; HR II, 241).

[38] This is not strictly true, for the second passage is concerned with the alleged inconsistency of sentences of the form '*b* thinks that *a* does not exist while *a* doubts something', whereas interpretation (*i*) was concerned with the alleged inconsistency of sentences of the form '*a* does not exist while he doubts something'. The difference is immaterial for our purposes, however, and was obviously neglected by Descartes.

[39] Cf. N. Kemp Smith, *op. cit.*, pp. 324–331.

[40] See his introduction to *Descartes, Philosophical Writings*, ed. and trans. by E. Anscombe and P. Geach (Thomas Nelson & Sons, Edinburgh, 1954), p. xxxvii.

[41] A little earlier Descartes had written: "I am, then, a real thing. ... What thing? I have said it, a thinking thing. And *what more* am I?" (my italics; AT VII, 27; HR I, 152).

[42] This part of his doctrine was criticized by Arnauld and others. In the preface to the *Meditationes* and in his replies to objections Descartes sought to defend himself. The question whether he succeeded is not relevant here.

[43] AT VII, 219; HR II, 97.

[44] I am indebted to Professors Norman Malcolm and G. H. von Wright for several useful suggestions in connection with the present chapter.

CHAPTER 6

KANT'S 'NEW METHOD OF THOUGHT' AND HIS THEORY OF MATHEMATICS

1. KANT'S 'COPERNICAN REVOLUTION'

It is instructive and frequently amusing to try to place philosophers into broad categories. There are, as Coleridge said, born Platonists and born Aristotelians. There are, according to Sir Isaiah Berlin, foxes and hedgehogs and foxes who want to be hedgehogs. Perhaps the broadest classification one can use is to divide philosophers according to their main interest, the main direction of their thought. There are thinkers like Albert Einstein for whom the world of nature with its immutable laws has promised an escape from the limitations of human life, and there are philosophers like G. E. Moore who have been less concerned with nature or man than with the views which other philosophers have held concerning nature or man.

In this broad classification the place of Immanuel Kant is clear enough. His dominating interest was neither God nor nature, but man. In his theory of knowledge, Kant stressed the elements we have ourselves contributed to what we know of mathematics or of the physical world, and in his ethics he wanted to see the humanity of human beings as an end in itself. The meager events of Kant's life also illustrate this preoccupation. One of the very few things that ever upset the daily routine of this fastidious bachelor was his reading of Rousseau's *Émile*.[1] What fascinated this dry-as-dust professional philosopher in Rousseau's educational romance? The answer is that in Rousseau Kant thought that he had found the beginnings of a general study of human nature comparable to Newton's studies of the physical world which had so impressed Kant's contemporaries.[2]

This does not yet fully distinguish the direction of Kant's thought from that of his predecessors some of whom were already trying to put into effect the slogan, 'the proper study of mankind is man'. In so far as one can make a clear distinction here, one can perhaps say that Kant was more interested in the active and constructive aspects of human mind than a Hume or a Locke. This appears, albeit somewhat obliquely, from the famous comparison by means of which Kant illustrated his 'new method of thought'. Rather self-consciously, Kant compared his new approach to philosophy to the new point of view which Copernicus had introduced into astronomy.[3] Accordingly, Kant's shift of emphasis is often referred to as his 'Copernican revolution'. The nature of this analogy has sometimes been misunderstood, and at first sight it may seem quite inappropriate. After all, Copernicus had deprived man of his privileged position in the centre of the mediaeval universe, whereas Kant wanted to make man the focal point of his philosophical theories.

Actually Kant himself makes the application of the analogy fairly clear. What Copernicus had done, Kant says, was to "seek the observed movements [of the heavenly bodies], not in the heavenly bodies [themselves], but in the spectator." In a similar way, Kant wanted to explain the applicability of certain fundamental concepts not in terms of the constitution of the objects to which they are applied but rather in terms of what we ourselves have to do in order to come to know these objects. Kant's basic assumption was that human reason "has insight only into that which it produces itself after a plan of its own" or that human reason "must adopt as its guide... that which it has itself put into nature."[4]

2. KANT AND THE TRADITION OF 'MAKER'S KNOWLEDGE'

This basic idea places Kant squarely within a long philosophical tradition. According to this tradition we can have full-fledged knowledge or in some sense higher knowledge only of what we have ourselves made or brought about.[5] In a way, Kant's 'Copernican revolution' was merely a new way of applying this old idea. The nature of the 'higher' knowledge with which this tradition is concerned is different for its different representatives. For Kant, it was the kind of knowledge he called synthetic knowledge a priori. An earlier proponent of the same basic idea was Hobbes, for whom this 'higher' knowledge was demonstrative knowledge. Hobbes anticipated some salient aspects of Kant's philosophy of mathematics when he said that in geometry we can have demonstrative knowledge because geometrical demonstrations are about figures which we have ourselves drawn and constructed.[6] For this reason we can have demonstrative knowledge about them, as long as we merely use those properties of theirs which we have ourselves put into them, and not any chance properties which they may happen to have. Hobbes' point is echoed very closely by Kant according to whom the true mathematical method does not consist in inspecting the mere geometrical figure, but rather in bringing out what is necessarily implied in the properties which we have ourselves put into the figure in constructing it so as to exemplify certain general geometrical concepts. "If he is to know anything with a priori certainty," Kant says of a geometer, "he must not ascribe to the figure anything save what necessarily follows from what he has himself set into it in accordance with his concept [of it]." [7]

This passage is interesting because it suggests that a widespread interpretation of Kant's theory of mathematics is mistaken. Kant is not saying, as he is often made to say, that in addition to drawing logical inferences we must in a geometrical argument inspect a figure in order to perceive further facts in it by means of our geometrical imagination. [8] On the contrary, Kant is in so many words forbidding such an appeal to geometrical intuition when he says that we must not ascribe to the figure anything more than what we have put into it in order to make it to exemplify certain geometrical concepts. I shall soon return to this point.

3. DIVINE 'SENSORIUM' REPLACED BY HUMAN 'SENSORIUM'

Another partial anticipation of Kant's theory illustrates neatly the direction of his interests as compared with many other thinkers. One of the main aims of Kant's theory of space and time was to give a philosophical foundation to the concepts of absolute space and absolute time which Newton had used in his physical theory. It has been argued that no such foundation was really needed. [9] But even if this is so, the historical fact remains that Newton and many of his successors thought that a deeper justification was called for. Newton himself attempted such a justification in philosophical and theological terms. He suggested that space and time are the medium in which God beholds all things. [10] In the same way as we humans consider before our mind's eye images of objects conveyed to us by our senses, in the same way God is aware of all the objects themselves in space and time. Space and time are thus, as it were, God's *sensorium* or perceptual space.

It has been pointed out repeatedly, and forgotten almost as often, that this strange doctrine of Newton's anticipates strikingly some aspects of Kant's theory of space and time. All Kant had to do in order to arrive at his own doctrine, it has been said, was to replace God by man; a change which was very much in accordance with the general trend of his thought.[11]

For Kant, space and time were thus the forms into which the activity of our senses forces all the reports which they receive from the outside world. For Newton, space and time were the forms of God's immediate awareness of objects; for Kant, they are the two forms of man's immediate sensory awareness of individual objects. According to Kant, spatial and temporal relations do not belong to objects as they are in themselves; they are put into objects by ourselves in the process of sensation. Hence we can speak of space and of extended objects "solely from the human standpoint," Kant says.[12] In this way he also strives to explain the applicability of spatial and temporal concepts to all our experience. Since all our experience is derived from the reports of our senses, the framework into which our senses force all the incoming reports must necessarily apply to all experience. To use an illustration which is in this context almost unavoidable: We experience everything in space and time for a reason similar to the reason why a man with blue spectacles on experiences everything as blue. If such a man realizes his condition, he will also know that he must necessarily continue to see everything as blue as long as he has his spectacles on.

4. KANTIAN INTUITIONS

Kant's theory of space, time, and mathematics is frequently presented as if there were little more to it than this set of ideas. This is misleading, however, for it overlooks the role of the premises from which Kant argued for his doctrine of space and time. These premises were given to Kant by his theory of the mathematical method.[13] And the reason why this theory is generally neglected is that it is generally misunderstood.

The blame for this misunderstanding is partly due to Kant's own terminology. He says that the characteristic feature of the mathematical method is the use of intuitions. Now this term 'intuition' (in German: *Anschauung*) is very easy to misunderstand. Usually Kant is taken to mean that mathematical reasoning depends on an appeal to our spatial or temporal imagination or to some similar immediate non-logical evidence.[14] This interpretation appears attractive because it seems to explain why Kant came to connect mathematics with the form of our faculty of sensible perception. If this interpretation of Kant's theory of the mathematical method is correct, then we must say that this theory has largely been refuted by subsequent developments in logic and in mathematics which have shown that all mathematical arguments can in principle be represented in the form of strictly logical reasoning, completely free from all appeal to our mathematical imagination.[15]

I have already suggested that this interpretation is incorrect. It simply misconstrues the force of the term 'intuition' in this part of Kant's philosophy. In Kant and in his immediate predecessors, the term 'intuition' did not necessarily have anything to do with appeal to imagination or to direct perceptual evidence. In the form of a paradox, we may perhaps say that the 'intuitions' Kant contemplated were not necessarily very 'intuitive'. For Kant, an intuition is simply anything which represents or stands for an individual object as distinguished from general concepts.[16] For instance, the use of variables in algebra was for him an 'intuitive' method because these variables were thought of as standing for (unspecified) individual numbers.[17]

5. MATHEMATICAL METHOD AS INSTANTIATION METHOD

When Kant says that mathematics is based on the use of intuitions he therefore does not mean in the first place that it is based on evidence more immediate than a logical argument. He is saying that in a mathematical argument general concepts are considered by means of their individual representatives. One of the things Kant has in mind here is likely to be familiar to everyone who has read Euclid's *Elements* or any of the traditional textbooks based on it. Euclid never starts his proof from the general enunciation of the theorem he wants to prove. For instance, after having stated the general theorem that in every triangle the sum of the three angles equals two right angles, Euclid does not proceed directly to the proof but says first something like this: "Let *ABC* be a triangle. I say, in the triangle *ABC* the sum of the angles *CAB*, *ABC*, and *BCA* is equal to two right angles." The proof Euclid gives is carried out in terms of this particular triangle which is usually assumed to be drawn. Whether we actually draw a triangle or even imagine one is not essential, however; what is essential is to consider what the general statement amounts to in a particular case. When Kant says that the mathematical method turns on the use of individual representatives of general concepts, he is generalizing upon this feature of Euclid's presentation.[18]

This generalization is much wider and much more flexible than Kant's better known doctrines. What Kant's theory of the mathematical method will say on this view is little more than that in a mathematical argument one is dealing with the existence and non-existence of individual objects having different properties and different relations to each other. This characterization is so very wide that it would include a great deal of modern symbolic logic within its scope.[19] Indeed, it is so wide that you may very well doubt whether Kant ever really accepted it.

6. ARE PARTICULARS 'GIVEN TO US' IN SENSE-PERCEPTION?

It is true that Kant tried to say much more about mathematical knowledge than this. Nevertheless the view I just sketched was held by him in the sense that it was one of the premises from which he argued for his further doctrines. This part of his theory is not disproved simply by showing that mathematical arguments can be presented as chains of strictly logical inferences. Whatever weaknesses Kant's theory of space, time, and mathematics may have are only brought out by considering the further arguments by means of which Kant tried to relate the use of individual representatives of general concepts in mathematics to our faculty of sensation. Why did Kant think that the representatives of individual mathematical objects which a mathematician like Euclid uses are in any way connected with the operation of our senses? Because he thought that it is the only way of explaining why the knowledge which we can obtain by means of such 'intuitions' is applicable to all experience.[20] Starting from his fundamental assumptions, Kant seems to have argued somewhat as follows: The only satisfactory explanation of the applicability of our mathematical arguments to all experience is to assume that we have ourselves put into objects the properties and relations with which these arguments deal. Now these arguments deal with the properties and relations of individual objects. But there is only one way in which we can put the requisite mathematical properties and relations into all the individual objects which are known to us. For the only way in which we can come to know individual objects is through our senses. As Aristotle had already said, "it is sense-perception alone which is capable of grasping the particulars." [21] It follows, Kant seems to have thought, that all our knowledge of individual objects which applies to them universally and necessarily is really about properties and relations which we have ourselves put into objects in the act of sensation. As we have seen, this is just Kant's main conclusion concerning mathematical knowledge.

Is this conclusion justified? It seems to me that the weakest link in Kant's argument is the Aristotelian assumption that we can have knowledge of particulars only in sense-perception. This is a natural thing to assume only as long as we think of our knowledge as a rather passive affair, as a registration of the information which we receive from the outside. This Aristotelian assumption overlooks entirely the activities which we in fact perform in order to gain knowledge about individual objects. It seems to me that Kant ought to have focused on these activities rather than on the mere registration of sensations. It is instructive to note that Kant actually spoke of objects as "given to us in sensation." [22] I would like to submit that only very rarely can we passively wait until the objects we are interested in are *given* to us. Usually we have to go out and look for them ourselves. Thus the Aristotelian assumption fails, and together with it Kant's main conclusion concerning mathematics. [23]

If this is so, then Kant's real failure in his theory of mathematics is due, ironically enough, to his unfaithfulness to his own principles. For we saw that he generally wanted to emphasize the active and constructive aspects of our knowledge; and in a way this is just what he neglected to do here. [24] It may seem a back-handed compliment to say that Kant failed in his theory of mathematics in so far as his point of view was un-Kantian; but to me this seems a perfectly genuine compliment.

NOTES

[1] L. E. Borowski, *Darstellung des Lebens und Charakters Immanuel Kants* (Nicolovius, Königsberg, 1804), p. 79.
[2] Ernst Cassirer, *Rousseau – Kant – Goethe* (Princeton University Press, Princeton, 1945), p. 18.

³ Immanuel Kant's *Critique of Pure Reason*, translated by Norman Kemp Smith (Macmillan, London, 1933), p. 22; second edition of the original (B̄), pp. xvi–xvii.

⁴ Kemp Smith, p. 20; original, B xiii–xiv. Cf. also Kemp Smith, p. 23 (B xviii): "... we are adopting as our new method of thought ... that we can know a priori of things only what we ourselves put into them."

⁵ I have tried to sketch the outlines of this tradition in my article, 'Tieto on valtaa' ('Knowledge is Power'), *Valvoja* 1964, pp. 185–195. Concerning Kant's relation to it, cf. his *Critique of Judgement*, Book II, Part 1, end of §68: "... denn nur so viel sieht man vollständig ein, als man nach Begriffen selbst machen und zustande bringen kann." (I am indebted to Professor W. H. Walsh for this reference.) See also the preceding footnote and Chapter 4 above.

⁶ "Of arts, some are demonstrable, others indemonstrable; and demonstrable are those the construction of the subject whereof is in the power of the artist himself, who, in his demonstration, does no more but deduce consequences of his own operation.... Geometry therefore is demonstrable, for the lines and figures from which we reason are drawn and described by ourselves..." (*English Works*, Vol. 7, pp. 183–184). See also *De Homine*, Chapter 10, v; *De Corpore*, Chapter 3, ix; *Leviathan*, beginning of Chapter 46. A somewhat different anticipation of Kant's theory of space occurs in *De Corpore*, Chapter 7, ii. Of this part of Hobbes' doctrines Kant was fully aware; see e.g. Vaihinger, *Commentar*, Vol. 2, p. 133.

⁷ Kemp Smith, p. 19 (B xii).

⁸ A classical statement of this mistaken interpretation is due to Betrand Russell: "Kant, having observed that the geometers of his day could not prove their theorems by unaided argument, but required an appeal to the figure, invented a theory of mathematical reasoning according to which the inference is never strictly logical, but always requires the support of what is called 'intuition'." (See *Introduction to Mathematical Philosophy*, George Allen and Unwin, London, 1919, p. 145.) I am not claiming, however, that Kant is completely free of confusion on this point.

⁹ S. Toulmin, 'Criticism in the History of Science: Newton on Absolute Space, Time, and Motion', *Philosophical Review* **68** (1957) 1–29, 203–227.

¹⁰ Isaac Newton, *Opticks* (Dover, New York, 1952), p. 403. Cf. also H. G. Alexander, *The Leibniz – Clarke Correspondence* (Manchester University Press, Manchester, 1956), pp. xv–xvi, 13, 22, 181.

¹¹ Vaihinger, *Commentar*, Vol. 2, p. 426, supplies further references. Cf. also H. Höffding, *History of Modern Philosophy*, Vol. 2, p. 569, where Höffding also refers to his own monograph on the development of Kant's thought.

¹² Kemp Smith, p. 71. (Original, A 26 = B 42.)

¹³ This theory is expounded mainly in the section of the *Critique of Pure Reason* entitled 'The Discipline of Pure Reason in its Dogmatic Employment' (Kemp Smith, pp. 576–593; A 713–738; B 741–766). The dependence of Kant's arguments in the Transcendental Aesthetic (concerning space, time, and mathematics) on this theory of mathematics (the mathematical method) is brought out by Kant's discussion in the *Prolegomena*, where he refers repeatedly to this very theory in support of his assertions before he has carried out the arguments which in the *Prolegomena* correspond to the Transcendental Aesthetic of the *Critique of Pure Reason*. (See *Prolegomena*, end of §1; §2, 2); §7.) It may be pointed out that many of the views Kant puts forward in his theory of the mathematical method are precritical, and hence prior to the Transcendental Aesthetic also historically.

¹⁴ See, e.g., the quotation from Russell in note 8 above.

¹⁵ Cf. Russell, *loc. cit.* "The whole trend of modern mathematics, with its increased pursuit

of rigour, has been against this Kantian theory" – i.e., what Russell takes to be the Kantian theory. Russell's interpretation of Kant also underlies his claim that a reduction of mathematics to logic would disprove Kant's theory of mathematics.

[16] Cf. "Knowledge... is either intuition (*Anschauung*) or concept (*Begriff*). The former relates immediately to the object and is single, the latter refers to it mediately by means of a feature which several things may have in common" (Kemp Smith p. 314; original, A 320 = B 376–377); "Intuition is a representation, such as would depend directly on the presence of the object" (*Prolegomena* §7); see also Kant's *Logik*, §1, and Vaihinger, *Commentar*, Vol. 2, pp. 3 and 24. In E. Schmid's *Wörterbuch zum leichteren Gebrauch der Kantischen Schriften* (Cröker, Jena, 1798) we read: "Anschauung. ... Im engern, eigentlichen Sinne: nicht bloss eine Gesichtsvorstellung, sondern eine jede unmittelbare Vorstellung von dem Einzelnen; eine einzelne Vorstellung, die sich unmittelbar an einen Gegenstand bezieht; Vorstellung eines Individuum...." The contrast is thus simply between intuitions (which represent individuals) and (general) concepts. In his *Logik* Kant writes: "Es its eine blosse Tautologie, von allgemeinen oder gemeinsamen Begriffen zu reden" (§1).

[17] This observation goes a long way towards solving some of the problems which C. D. Broad discusses lucidly in his paper on 'Kant's Theory of Mathematical and Philosophical Reasoning', *Proceedings of the Aristotelian Society* **42** (1941–42) 1–24. Broad goes as far as to say that Kant has provided no theory whatsoever of the algebraic method of reasoning. This may be true in the sense that Kant's remarks on algebra are incompatible with his full-fledged theory of space and time, developed in the Transcendental Aesthetic. Kant's theory of algebra is nevertheless only a special case of his broader theory of the mathematical method. See also Kant's *Werke* (Academy Edition), Vol. 2, p. 278.

[18] Euclid's *Elementa* is explicitly referred to by Kant; see *Werke* (Academy Edition), Vol. 2, p. 307. The structure of a proposition in Euclid is explained by T. L. Heath in his introduction to *The Thirteen Books of Euclid's Elements* (Cambridge University Press, Cambridge, 1926), Vol. 1, pp. 129–131.

[19] This is almost exactly what Broad (*op. cit.*) says of Kant's remarks on algebra.

[20] Kant's arguments to this effect are perhaps seen best from the *Prolegomena*, §§7–10.

[21] *Analytica Posteriora* I, 18, 81b6.

[22] E.g., Kemp Smith, p. 65; original, A 19 = B 33.

[23] But do not similar conclusions still follow if we replace the passive process of sensation by the activities which we in fact use when coming to know individual objects? I think that this is in fact the case, i.e., that a modified and qualified form of Kantian arguments can be carried out even if we discard Kant's mistaken emphasis on sensation. It would take us too far, however, to investigate these restored Kantian arguments here.

[24] To some extent, Ernst Cassirer already tried to shift the emphasis from sensation to (constructive) thinking in Kant's philosophy of mathematics. See his paper on 'Kant und die moderne Mathematik', *Kant-Studien* **12** (1907) 1–49, especially pp. 32–35. Cassirer refers in particular to *Prolegomena* §38.

CHAPTER 7

ARE LOGICAL TRUTHS ANALYTIC?

1. VARIETIES OF ANALYTICITY

The title of this paper may seem pointless. Nowadays the concept of analyticity is usually so characterized as to make all logical truths analytic by definition.[1] Hence, why the question?

The purpose of the title is not only to ask a question but also to challenge the ways in which the concept of the analytic is currently defined. This concept was brought into philosophical prominence by Kant;[2] I shall therefore examine some characterizations of this concept against the background of his use of it. It seems to me that the concept of analyticity as actually employed by philosophers like Kant is highly ambiguous and that most current definitions catch only one of the term's possible meanings.

I shall begin by listing a few of the ways in which the concept of the analytic (and, by implication, the concept of the synthetic) has been understood. The following explicit or implicit assertions have been made concerning analytic (analytically true) sentences:

(I). They are true by sole virtue of the meanings of the terms they contain (analytic truth as conceptual truth).

(II). They do not convey any factual information (analytic truth as tautological truth).

(III). They can be shown to be true by strictly analytic methods.

2. ANALYTIC TRUTH AS CONCEPTUAL TRUTH

The first interpretation of the concept of the analytic is often elaborated by remarking that truths of logic are as clear-cut examples of truths based solely on meanings as we are likely to have. This has inspired attempts to obtain all analytic truths by starting from the truths of logic and suitably extending their range. The following definition is probably the best-known attempt of this sort:

I(a). Analytically true sentences comprise the truths of logic together with all sentences reducible to them by substituting synonyms for synonyms.[3]

In this paper I shall disregard definitions of type I or I (a). Recent discussion has demonstrated, it seems to me, that they are unsatisfactory as they stand.[4] Moreover, they make logical truths trivially analytic, and are therefore beside my present purpose.

But are there relevant senses of analyticity different from the one defined by I? I shall try to discover such senses by analyzing characterizations II and III. I shall first try to see somewhat more carefully what is implied by formulation III. Then I shall try to develop further characterization II so as to show that certain important truths of logic are analytic according to it. And finally I shall apply certain insights gained during the discussion to point out that the same truths are synthetic according to III, at least on one very natural interpretation of this characterization.

3. ANALYTIC TRUTH AND ANALYTIC METHODS

Let us therefore ask what can be said of sense III (that is, of the sense of analyticity defined by III). Here it is advisable to consider first the concept of an analytical argument-step instead of the concept of an analytic sentence. What can be said of the former can be subsequently extended to apply to the latter as well.

The basic idea of sense III seems to be expressible as follows:

III (a). All that is said by the conclusion of an analytic argument-step is already said in the premises.

This is admittedly very vague, largely owing to the vagueness of the notion of 'saying' that is used here. For the purpose of definition III (a), this notion can be made somewhat clearer. In order to be able to speak of merely repeating or merely analyzing what is already said in the premisses of an argument, we must restrict the sense of 'saying' to what is in some sense actually or explicitly stated or mentioned in the premises. A traditional formulation of this idea was to say that the conclusion of an analytical argument-step merely repeats something already thought in the premises, although perhaps not yet with the same clarity and consciousness.[5] Part of our task here is to see what objective explications such psychological or quasi-psychological formulations might have.

In spite of the vagueness which still remains in III (a), we can draw conclusions from it. The following criterion of analyticity will in any case follow from it:

III (b). In the conclusion of an analytic argument-step no more individuals are considered together at one and the same time than were already considered together in the premisses.

For if more individuals are considered together in the conclusion than in the premisses, some of them or some of their interrelations were not considered in the premisses. Hence the conclusion does not consist in merely repeating what was already said in the premisses, and the argument-step in question could not count as a case of 'mere analysis'.

Principle III (b) follows from III (a) no matter how the notion of 'number of individuals considered together in a sentence' is to be understood. In the sequel I shall show how this notion can be clarified in the case of quantificational sentences.

A closely related consequence of criterion III (a) seems to be that the conclusion of an analytic argument cannot consider any individuals not already considered in the premisses. Kant took this to imply the following principle:

III (c). An analytic argument never carries us from the existence of an object to the existence of a different object.

In short, according to Kant interindividual inferences concerning existence are impossible by analytic means.[6]

It is not difficult to see how similar considerations might be applied to longer arguments, and hence to sentences established by means of such arguments. There is even more than one way of doing so. We might call a proof of q from p analytic if all its steps are analytic in one of the senses just indicated. This approach does not appear to be as interesting, however, as a slightly different one in which the proof in question is considered not only from the point of view of the premiss p but also from that of the conclusion q. Then a proof of q from p is analytic in sense III (b) if no more individuals are considered at any of the intermediate stages than are already considered either in p or in q. This is the sense of analyticity as applied to proofs which I shall be using in what follows. A logically true sentence p of quantification theory may then be called analytic if it can be proved analytically, in the sense just explained, from a propositional tautology in which no more individuals are considered together than in p. A sentence will be called analytically inconsistent if a propositional contradiction in which no more individuals are considered together can be derived from it analytically.

4. ANALYTIC TRUTHS AS TAUTOLOGIES

I shall return to these senses of analyticity later. Meanwhile, I shall stage my first main attack on analyticity in the direction of sense II. About forty years ago, a notion very much like this one was prominent. This was the notion of tautology of Wittgenstein's *Tractatus*. Unfortunately, the original form of this notion was satisfactorily defined only for propositional logic. Certain important generalizations have been suggested since, but for one reason or another they seem to have less philosophical interest than Wittgenstein's original notion.

I want to argue, nevertheless, that something like Wittgenstein's notion of tautology can be generalized in a natural and informative way so as to be applicable in quantification theory. In order to see what the generalization is, we have to see what makes his original notion so appealing.

It is made so, I think, by the fact that in propositional logic one can actually list all the 'possible worlds' that we can describe by means of a given supply of atomic sentences.

If we are given the atomic sentences p_i $(i = 1, 2, ..., k)$, the descriptions of the possible worlds are conjunctions which for each i contain either p_i or its negation $\sim p_i$ (but not both) but which do not contain any other members. Following a time-honoured precedent established by Boole, I shall call these conjunctions the *constituents* of propositional logic, and I shall designate an arbitrary constituent by $\prod_{i=1}^{i=k} p_i$, or, more simply, by $\prod_{i=1} p_i$. Different constituents may be distinguished from each other by attaching subscripts to $\prod$. These subscripts are assumed to run consecutively from one onward, so that the same notation can be applied repeatedly.

An arbitrary constituent $\prod_{i=1} p_i$ may also be said to be of the form

$$(\pm) p_1 \mathbin{\&} (\pm) p_2 \mathbin{\&} ... \mathbin{\&} (\pm) p_k .$$

Here each symbol $(\pm)$ stands either for a negation sign or for nothing at all. For different patterns of negation signs a different subscript j is chosen.

Why does the existence of the constituents make the notion of tautology appealing? Because each consistent sentence of propositional logic has a normal form which is a disjunction of some (perhaps all) of the constituents. In an obvious sense, every sentence considered in propositional logic thus admits some of the possibilities listed by the constituents but excludes the rest. In an equally obvious sense, the more possibilities it excludes, the more informative it is.[7]

A limiting case is that of a sentence admitting all the possibilities listed by the constituents, but excluding none of them. Such a sentence is empty in a very obvious sense of the word: it cannot convey any genuine information. And this limiting case is just that of the logically true sentences of propositional logic. They are undoubtedly true, but in the striking sense just explained they do not carry any information concerning the subject matter of which they apparently speak.

These are the facts, it seems to me, that make Wittgenstein's notion of tautology so very appealing.

They immediately suggest a more general sense in which we may ask whether the truths of other parts of logic are also tautological. This sense is not quite sharply defined yet, but we can nevertheless understand what is being asked. In any part of logic we may ask: is it always possible to list all the alternatives concerning the world in such a way that the truths of this part of logic are just the sentences admitting all these alternatives, but excluding none? If so, the truths of this part of logic are so many tautologies.[8]

Let us study quantification theory as a test case. Can we list all the possibilities concerning the world that can be expressed by means of the resources employed in some given quantificational sentence?

5. THE NOTIONS OF DEPTH AND DEGREE

The answer depends on the meaning we assign to the expression 'by means of the resources employed in some given sentence'. If this is taken to mean 'by means of the predicates occurring in the given sentence' (plus quantifiers and propositional connectives, of course), then in most cases there is no hope of making a finite list of the desired kind.[9]

But if we introduce further limitations, the answer is different. For each sentence which is considered in quantification theory, there is a maximum to the lengths of the sequences of nested quantifiers occurring therein. More popularly expressed, each quantificational sentence is characterized by the number of the layers of quantifiers it contains. This number will be called the *depth* of the sentence in question. In other words, the depth of a sentence is the maximum number of quantifiers whose scopes all overlap in it.[10] Each sentence has, moreover, a finite number of free individual symbols (constants or free variables). The sum of this number and the depth of the sentence in question will be called its *degree*. If we now consider what can be expressed by means of sentences constructed from a given finite supply of predicates and free individual symbols plus quantifiers and having a degree smaller than a given positive integer, there is a way of listing all the different alternatives concerning our universe of discourse that can be expressed by means of these resources.

The limitation on the degree of the sentences is a natural one, for the notion of the degree of a sentence has a very simple intuitive meaning. The degree of a sentence is the maximum number of individuals we are considering at any one time in their relation to each other in the sentence.

Since this intuitive meaning of the notion of degree will be important in what follows, it is worth explaining carefully. For this purpose, we may ask: how are individuals introduced into our arguments? Part of an answer is obvious: individuals are introduced into our reasoning by free individual symbols. This gives us the first of the two addenda whose sum is the degree of a sentence. This answer is only a partial one, however, for individuals are introduced into our propositions also by quantifiers (bound individual variables). In order to see this, it suffices to recall the most accurate translations of quantifiers into more or less ordinary language: '(Ex)' is to be read 'there is at least one individual (let us call it x) such that' and '(x)' is to be read 'for each individual (call it x) it is the case that'. Each quantifier thus invites us to consider exactly one new individual, however indefinite this individual may be. Two quantifiers whose scopes do not overlap cannot both be counted here, however, for there is no way of relating to each other the individuals which such quantifiers invite us to consider. Hence the contribution of quantifiers to the maximal number of individuals we are considering together in a certain sentence is the maximal number of quantifiers whose scopes overlap in it, exactly as was suggested.[11]

Another way of seeing the intuitive meaning of the notion of a degree in quantification theory is to ask the question: what are the individuals whose properties and interrelations you are considering (or may consider) in a given part of a quantificational sentence, say between a certain pair of parentheses? Obviously, they include the individuals referred to by the free individual symbols of the sentence. They also include all the indefinite individuals introduced by the quantifiers within the scope of which we are moving. They do not include any other individuals. The maximum number of these individuals is just the degree of the sentence in question, which is therefore the maximum number of individuals we are considering together in the sentence.

This informal explanation has a neat formal counterpart. If it is required, as is natural, that quantifiers with overlapping scopes must have different variables bound to them, then the depth of a sentence is the least number of different bound variables one needs in order to write it out, and its degree is therefore the least number of different individual symbols (free or bound) one needs in it.

The intuitive meaning of the degree of a sentence is straightforward enough to have already caught the eye of C. S. Peirce, at least in a simple special case. (See his *Collected Papers*, Vol. 3, Sec. 392: "The algebra of Boole affords a language by which anything may be expressed which can be said without speaking of more than one individual at a time.")

But does not a general sentence speak of all the individuals of the domain (universe of discourse)? Is not the number of individuals considered in such a sentence therefore infinite if the domain is infinite? Surely a general sentence does speak in some sense of all the individuals in the domain; but in such a sentence we are not considering all these individuals in their relation to each other. In a sentence like 'All men admire Buddha' we are not considering the interrelations that obtain between any two men. We are, so to speak, considering each man at a time and saying something about *his* relation to the great Gautama. Hence the number of individuals considered in their relation to each other in this sentence is two, which is just its degree. In the first half of the sentence 'John has at least one brother and John has at least one sister' we are considering John in his relation to an arbitrarily chosen brother of his, and in the second half we are considering him in his relation to one of his sisters. Nothing is said, however, of the relations between his brothers and his sisters. Hence the number of individuals considered together at any given time in the sentence is only two, which is again exactly its degree. This illustrates the fact that quantifiers with nonoverlapping scopes do not count in the total. By contrast, in the sentence 'All John's sisters are older than his brothers' an arbitrary brother of John's is compared as to age with an arbitrary sister of John's; hence the number of individuals considered in their relations to each other is three, again equaling the degree of the sentence.

6. DISTRIBUTIVE NORMAL FORMS IN QUANTIFICATION THEORY: THE MONADIC CASE

These examples illustrate the intuitive meaning of our notion of degree. Apart from this intuitive meaning, it plays an interesting role in quantification theory. If a limit is imposed on the degrees of our sentences, we have in quantification theory a situation strongly reminiscent of propositional logic. Given a finite supply of predicates and free individual symbols, there is a finite number of constituents such that every consistent sentence considered has a normal form in which it is a disjunction of some (perhaps all) of the constituents. I shall not prove this result here. I have done so in a number of other papers in which I have also considered these 'distributive normal forms' in certain other respects.[12]

It is not my purpose here to examine the structure of distributive normal forms in any greater detail. There are two questions concerning them which must nevertheless be discussed. First, we want to make sure that the constituents occurring in them really list all the alternatives concerning the world in as clear-cut a sense as do the constituents of propositional logic. Secondly, we have to ask whether the logical truths of quantification theory are related to the constituents in the same way as are the logical truths of propositional logic.

I think that the first point can be sufficiently established by considering, by way of example, some of the simplest kinds of quantificational constituents. If there are no free individual symbols present and if we have merely a number of monadic (one-place) predicates $P_i(x)$ $(i=1, 2, ..., m)$, the constituents will have the following form:

$$(1) \qquad \prod_{k=1}^{k=2^m} (Ex) \prod_{i=1}^{i=m} {}_k P_i(x)$$

This is in a clear-cut sense a description of one kind of a 'possible world'. It is easy to see how this description is accomplished. First, we list all the possible kinds of individuals that can be specified by means of the predicates $P_i(x)$. This is what the conjunctions

$$(2) \qquad \prod_{i=1}^{k} P_i(x) = C_k(x)$$

($k = 1, 2, ..., 2^m$) do. Then we specify, for each such kind of individuals, whether individuals of that kind exist or not. It is perhaps not entirely surprising that everything we can say by using only the predicates $P_i(x)$, quantifiers, and propositional connectives is a disjunction of such descriptions of kinds of possible worlds.

A simple example perhaps makes the situation easier to appreciate. Suppose that $m = 2$, that is to say, suppose that we are given two monadic predicates, say 'red' and 'round'. Then conjunctions (2) are of the form

$$(\pm) (x \text{ is red}) \& (\pm) (x \text{ is round}).$$

They specify all the different kinds of individuals that can be specified by means of the two predicates:

(2)*
> x is red and round;
> x is red but not round;
> x is round but not red;
> x is neither red nor round.

Each constituent of form (1) indicates, for each of the different kinds of individuals (2)*, whether such individuals exist or not. To take a random example of constituents of form (1), one of them will be the following sentence:

> There are individuals which are red and round;
> there are no individuals which are red but not round;
> there are no individuals which are round but not red;
> there are individuals which are neither red nor round.

We can also see an interesting way of rewriting a constituent of form (1). Instead of listing all the different kinds of individuals that exist and also listing the kinds of individuals that do not exist, it suffices to list the kinds of existing individuals and simply to add that they are all the kinds of individuals in existence. This means that each constituent of form (1) can be rewritten so as to be of form

(3)
$$(Ex)\, C_1(x)\, \&\, (Ex)\, C_2(x)\, \&\ldots\&\, (Ex)\, C_n(x)\, \&$$
$$(x)\, (C_1(x)\, \vee\, C_2(x)\, \vee\, \ldots\, \vee\, C_n(x)),$$

where $\{C_i(x)\}$ $(i=1, 2, \ldots, n)$ is some subset of the set of all conjunctions (2). It can be shown that all the constituents of quantification theory may be similarly rewritten.

For instance, the constituent which was formulated in words above could obviously be rewritten as follows:

> There are individuals which are red and round as well as individuals which are neither red nor round; and every individual is either red and round or neither red nor round.

7. DISTRIBUTIVE NORMAL FORMS IN QUANTIFICATION THEORY: THE RELATIONAL CASE

In order to have more insight into the structure of our constituents, let us assume that we are given a number of dyadic (two-place) predicates $R_i(x, y)$ $(i=1, 2, \ldots, r)$ but no other predicates nor any free individual symbols, and that the depth of our sentences is at most two. Then constituents are still of form (3). In fact, (3) may be said to be the general form of those constituents which do not contain free individual symbols. The definition of the conjunctions $C_i(x)$ has to be changed, however, from case to case. In the case at hand, each $C_i(x)$ is rather like (3):

(4)
$$(Ey)\, C_1'(x, y)\, \&\, (Ey)\, C_2'(x, y)\, \&\ldots\&\, (Ey)\, C_s'(x, y)$$
$$\&\, (y)\, (C_1'(x, y)\, \vee\, C_2'(x, y)\, \vee\, \ldots\, \vee\, C_s'(x, y))\, \&$$
$$\prod_{i=1}^{i=r} R_i(x, x)$$

Here each $C'(x, y)$ is of the form

$$\prod_{i=1}^{i=r} R_i(x, y)\, \&\, \prod_{i=1}^{i=r} R_i(y, x)\, \&\, \prod_{i=1}^{i=r} R_i(y, y).$$

The intuitive meaning of (4) is not very difficult to fathom. In effect, we first list all the different ways in which an individual y may be related to a given individual x. Given a fixed x, this list is also a list of different kinds of individuals y (in their relation to x). Then we specify which of these different kinds of y exist for some fixed x. (We specify, furthermore, the ways in which x is or is not related to itself.) What I am saying is that this gives us a list of all the possible kinds of individuals x that we can specify by using only the dyadic predicates $R_i(x, y)$, quantifiers, and propositional connectives, provided we do not make use of sentences of a degree higher than one.

What happens in (4) may also be described as follows. We took a list of all the relations (two-place predicates) which may obtain between two individuals and which can be specified without using quantifiers, and we constructed out of them a list of all the possible complex attributes (one-place predicates) which an individual may have and which may be specified by means of just one layer of quantifiers. It is a straightforward task to generalize this: in the same way we may start from the list of all the possible relations which may obtain between $n+1$ individuals and which can be specified by m layers of quantifiers, and construct out of them a list of all the different relations which can obtain between n individuals and which can be described by means of $m+1$ layers of quantifiers. In this way we may in fact easily obtain an inductive definition of constituents in general, for in the case $m=0$ we have simply constituents in the sense of propositional logic. (Such a definition is of course relative to a given finite list of predicates and free individual symbols.)

These examples and indications perhaps suffice to show that the constituents of quantification theory really give us a systematic list of all the different possibilities concerning reality which can be specified by the means of expression that we have at our disposal, in the same sense in which the constituents of propositional logic do so. We could also use these constituents in the same way as the constituents of propositional logic have sometimes been used, namely to develop measures of the information which a sentence carries. Tautologies would then be sentences with zero information. In other respects, too, the situation is exactly the same in quantification theory as it is in propositional logic, with but one important exception. This one difference between the two cases is that in quantification theory some constituents are inconsistent whereas no constituents of propositional logic are.[13]

8. INCONSISTENT CONSTITUENTS

The question we have to ask is whether this makes the situation essentially different from what it is in propositional logic. It may appear that it does make a difference. The fact that there are inconsistent constituents implies that a sentence may be logically true even though its distributive normal form does not contain all the constituents, provided that the missing constituents are all inconsistent. Thus it may appear that the truths of quantification theory need not be tautologies in the sense of admitting all the alternatives that we can specify with respect to the world. It suffices for them to admit all the alternatives specified by the consistent constituents.

An answer lies close at hand. We suggested defining a tautology as a sentence which admits of all the possibilities that there are with respect to the world. Now it is perfectly natural to say that an inconsistent constituent does not specify a genuine possibility concerning the subject matter it seems to be speaking of, but only appears to describe one. Just because it is inconsistent, the state of affairs it purports to describe can never be realized, so there is no need for any sentence to exclude it. Hence a necessary and sufficient condition for a sentence of quantification theory to admit all the kinds of worlds which are really possible – that is to say, to be a tautology – is that its distributive normal form contains all the *consistent* constituents. And it is readily seen that all the truths of quantification theory really are tautologies in this sense.

This way out of the difficulty may seem far too simple. It can be strengthened, however, by means of further arguments.

9. CONSTITUENTS AND JIGSAW PUZZLES

I shall here give in the form of an analogy an argument which, although merely persuasive, can be converted into a stricter one. If we are given a constituent, we are not yet given a genuine picture of a possible state of affairs. We are given, rather, a way of constructing such a picture – as if we were given a jigsaw puzzle. In fact, (3) shows that being given a constituent is very much like being given an unlimited supply of a finite number of different kinds of pieces of a jigsaw puzzle, with two instructions: (*i*) at least one piece of each kind has to be used; (*ii*) no other kinds of pieces may be used. An attempt to construct 'a picture of a possible state of affairs' in accordance with these instructions may fail. Then the jigsaw puzzle does not give any picture of reality: it cannot be used to convey information concerning the state of the world. We cannot give it to somebody and say 'This is what the world is like' and hope to convey any real information to him as we could have done by giving him a ready-made picture of the world or even a jigsaw puzzle which might yield a genuine picture. Similarly, it may be suggested, an inconsistent constituent does not describe a genuine possibility as to what the world may be like but only appears to do so. Hence its presence or absence makes no difference to the normal forms: no knowledge of the subject matter of which the sentence in question speaks is needed to rule it out.

This analogy can be made stronger in two ways. It may be argued that what most directly specifies the structure of the world (and in this sense gives us the 'real meaning' of a constituent) is not the constituent itself but rather the outcome of those operations that we have compared to the construction of a jigsaw puzzle. Such an argument might take the form of a defense of a rudimentary form of what is known as the picture theory of language. On this view, a constituent or a sentence of some other kind is not itself a 'picture' of a possible state of affairs, but rather gives us a starting point for the construction of a picture or a set of alternative pictures. It would take us too far afield, however, to develop this idea here.

It will have to suffice to give a single reason for the aptness of the jigsaw puzzle analogy. This is the fact that it very well reproduces the reasons why inconsistent constituents are inconsistent. In order to see two such reasons, we may consider sentences (3) and (4) and assume that the latter occurs as a part of the former.[14] Both (3) and (4) are lists of all the kinds of individuals that there are. In the first list these individuals are classified absolutely, in the second with respect to the given individual x. Nevertheless, the two lists have to be compatible for every $C_i(x)$ – that is, for each sentence of the form (4) which occurs in (3). For, clearly, every individual that exists according to the absolute list has to find a place in the relative list of each existing individual, and vice versa. These two requirements are not always met. If they are not, (3) is inconsistent. If the first requirement is violated, (3) may be shown to be inconsistent by essentially one application of the exchange theorem $(Ex)(y)\,P(x,y) \supset (x)(Ey)\,P(y,x)$. If the second is violated, (3) may similarly be shown to be inconsistent by essentially one application of the exchange theorem $(Ex)(Ey)P(x, y) \supset (Ex)(Ey)P(y, x)$.

If I am right, these two are essentially the only ways in which a constituent can turn out to be inconsistent. Of course, this cannot mean that every constituent which is not inconsistent for one of these two reasons is thereby shown to be consistent. Often the failure of a constituent to meet the two requirements is implicit and becomes explicit only when the constituent in question is expanded into a disjunction of several constituents of a greater depth. At some finite depth, each of these deeper constituents will then be inconsistent for one of our two reasons.[15]

Here the jigsaw puzzle analogy serves us remarkably well. I may sum up my explanation of the two reasons why a constituent may be inconsistent by comparing one of my inconsistent constituents to a jigsaw puzzle which can fail to yield a coherent picture, for two reasons. Either there are two pieces (or, rather, kinds of pieces) which are incompatible in the sense that they cannot be fitted into one and the same picture; or else one of the pieces leaves a gap which is such that it cannot be filled by any of the different kinds of pieces that are at our disposal. The former case arises when some member of the absolute list cannot find a niche in the relative list of one of its fellow members; then the two members of the absolute list are incompatible. The latter case arises when some member of the relative list of some fixed $C_i(x)$ does not fit into the absolute list; then this $C_i(x)$ 'leaves a gap' which cannot be completed by any of the members of the absolute list of which we are allowed to make use. The fact that we sometimes have to expand the given constituent into a disjunction of several constituents of a greater depth may be compared to the fact that we sometimes have to carry an attempted construction of a jigsaw puzzle to a certain extent before it can be seen that it is impossible to complete for one of the two reasons mentioned.

This success of the jigsaw puzzle analogy will reinforce the point which I made by its means: knowing that certain constituents are inconsistent does not give us any information concerning the reality which the constituents purport to speak of and hence does not interfere with the tautologicality of the logical truths of quantification theory.

Our observations thus strongly suggest that the truths of quantification theory are really analytic in sense II – that is, tautologies in the sense in which we have decided to use the term.

10. INCONSISTENT CONSTITUENTS
AND INTERINDIVIDUAL INFERENCES

In the course of our discussion, we have already found indications that some of the logical truths of quantification theory are nevertheless *not* analytic in our sense III – that is, not provable by analytic methods. Now I shall argue more fully for this second main point.

For those truths of quantification theory that do not turn on the elimination of any constituents, it may be argued that they are analytic in sense III.[16] But for the rest the situation is entirely different. The briefest glimpse already suggests that the inconsistency of some of the constituents is essentially connected with sense III of the analytic and the synthetic. If a constituent like (3) is inconsistent, then the following implication is provable.[17]

$$(5) \qquad \begin{aligned} &((Ex)\, C_1(x)\, \&\, (Ex)\, C_2(x)\, \&\ldots\&\, (Ex)\, C_n(x)) \supset \\ &(Ex)\, (\sim C_1(x)\, \&\, \sim C_2(x)\, \&\ldots\&\, \sim C_n(x)). \end{aligned}$$

This is clearly an instance of the kind of interindividual existential inference which for Kant constituted the paradigm of synthetic inferences (cf. criterion III (c) formulated above). In this case the difference between the different individuals that Kant speaks of is understood in the strongest possible sense, to wit, in the sense of logically necessary difference. Conversely, it may be argued (with certain qualifications) that in every logically valid inference from the existence of a number of individuals to the existence of another individual which is for logical reasons different from them there is implicit the inconsistency of at least one of our constituents. In short, inconsistencies of constituents would have been for Kant paradigmatic instances of synthetic truths of (modern) logic.

11. INCONSISTENT CONSTITUENTS UNCOVERED BY
INCREASING THE DEGREE OF EXPRESSIONS

There are other ways of arguing that the elimination of the inconsistent constituents is a synthetic procedure in sense III of the analytic and the synthetic. An especially clear-cut one is given by criterion III (b). It was suggested earlier that one way of showing that a constituent is inconsistent is to transform it into a disjunction of constituents of a greater depth and therefore of a higher degree and to show that all of these are inconsistent for one of the two reasons I explained. Now the intuitive meaning of the notion of the degree of a sentence is, as I indicated, that of the maximum number of individuals that we are considering together at one and the same time in the sentence in question. According to criterion III (b), this number must not be greater in any of the sentences by means of which a given sentence p is proved or disproved than it is in p itself, if this proof or disproof is to be analytic. Since the procedure I just mentioned for eliminating an inconsistent constituent makes use of sentences of a degree higher than that of the constituent to be eliminated, it is a synthetic procedure in the sense of criterion III (b).

Is this perhaps an accidental peculiarity of my procedure? I do not think so; on the contrary, I think it an unavoidable feature of every complete proof procedure in quantification theory, in some fairly natural sense of 'proof procedure'. Every such proof procedure must make frequent use of sentences of higher degree than that of the sentence to be proved. This is made inevitable by the fact, noticed earlier, that only a finite number of nonequivalent sentences can be made by means of the predicates and free individual symbols occurring in a given sentence, if a limitation is imposed on the degree of these sentences. If our rules of inference do not affect this degree, they cannot lead us out of this finite set of sentences. If certain fairly natural limitations are imposed on these rules of inference, it will be possible to show that this would give us a decision procedure, which is known to be nonexistent in many cases. In order to give us a complete proof procedure, our rules of inference must therefore allow proofs of sentences by means of sentences of higher degrees. Such a proof procedure will then be synthetic in our sense III (b).

12. NATURAL RULES OF INFERENCE REQUIRE INCREASE IN DEGREE

The limitations that have to be imposed on rules of inference in order for what was just said to be true have some interest in themselves. Sometimes a rule of inference in the most general sense of the word is essentially identified with a two-place recursive predicate of the Gödel numbers of sentences (or formulae, if you prefer). In this wide sense, we can indeed have rules of inference which are analytic in sense III (b) and which nevertheless enable us to prove all (and only all) the logical truths of quantification theory.[18] I think this sense in any case far too broad, however, to constitute a natural explication of what we would naturally mean by a rule of inference. We have to require that the applicability of such a rule depends, intuitively speaking, only on what the sentences in question express or say and not on accidental features of their formulation. This requirement may seem too vague to be useful; nevertheless it has some very definite implications. For instance, it may be taken to imply that a rule of inference must be independent of the way in which truth functions are written out; and it must be independent of the particular free individual symbols which occur in the sentences in question. Hence only such two-place recursive predicates of Gödel numbers of sentences will qualify for a rule of inference as are invariant with respect to arbitrary replacements of truth functions by tautologously equivalent truth functions (of the same arguments) in the sentences in question (or which can be extended so as to become invariant in this sense without affecting provability relations).[19] Such replacements must of course be admissible also inside larger sentences. Moreover, we must require symmetry with respect to the different free individual symbols.

If these natural restrictions are imposed on what we are willing to call a rule of inference, it may be shown that no set of rules of inference analytic in sense III (b) suffices to enable us to prove each logical truth of quantification theory from propositional tautologies of the same degree or to carry out analytically (in sense III (b)) all the proofs from premises which we would like to carry out.[20]

It is easy to verify that most of the familiar proof procedures in quantification theory satisfy the two requirements, and also that they in fact allow proofs of sentences by means of higher-degree sentences, that is to say, proofs synthetic in the sense we are now considering. An innocent exception is constituted by some of the natural deduction methods, where the process known as existential instantiation does not depend solely on the existential quantified sentence to be instantiated.[21] Usually it has to be required that the instantiating free individual symbol is different from all the free individual symbols occurring earlier in the proof. This means that existential instantiation is not independent of the particular free singular terms occurring in the result of the process of existential instantiation. In deciding how many individuals are considered together in a step of a proof by natural deduction methods, we therefore have to count not only the free individual symbols which occur in the premisses of this particular step but also all the ones that occur at earlier stages of the proof. We may, for example, consider the conjunction of all the sentences reached up to a certain point and consider its degree instead of the degree of the individual lines of proof. (It may be called the degree of the set of sentences so far reached.) But if we do this, we find that natural deduction methods also conform to the pattern we have found. In them, too, we frequently have to add to the number of individuals we are considering together in order to be able to carry out the proofs we want to carry out; in other words, we have to add to the degree of the sets of sentences we are considering.

Natural deduction methods are interesting from our point of view because the synthetic element in them may be reduced to a single rule. In a suitable formulation of these methods there is only one rule that is synthetic, that is, that adds to the number of individuals one is considering in the sense just explained. This is just the rule of existential instantiation. If the other rules are formulated in a suitable way, the rule of existential instantiation thus takes all the blame for increasing the degree of the sets of sentences we have to consider in order to establish a logical truth of quantification theory. (Universal instantiation need not increase the degree, for it may be restricted to the cases where the instantiating free individual symbol is an old one, that is, occurs earlier in the argument.)

I conclude, then, that the logical truths of quantification theory cannot all be captured by (natural) rules of inference which would be analytic. In this sense, quantification theory is a synthetic theory.

We might also try to spell out more clearly which particular logical truths of quantification theory are synthetic in the most natural sense of the word based on criterion III (b). Such an attempt would bring us back, it seems to me, to the distinction between logical truths depending on the elimination of inconsistent constituents and those not depending on it. Almost all the logical truths as well as almost all the usual logical arguments that one finds in ordinary textbooks of logic will then turn out to be analytic in the relevant sense of the term, the main exception probably being offered by the laws for exchanging adjacent quantifiers. The details need not detain us here, however, since the main point is clear enough. The fact that many logical truths of quantification theory turn out to be analytic in one sense of the word but synthetic in another sense shows the importance of the distinction between the different senses. It also shows that it does make sense to ask whether the logical truths of quantification theory are analytic.

13. The traditions of analysis and synthesis

It remains to make good my promise to relate our findings to Kant's distinction between the analytic and the synthetic. I shall confine myself to a few general remarks only.

The basis of the connection may be expressed in terms of the history of the notions of the analytic and the synthetic. Like so many other important philosophical terms, they seem to have originated from the geometrical terminology of the Greeks.[22] Traditionally, there were two main variants of the concepts of the analytic and the synthetic.[23] In one of them, a synthetic argument was an ordinary step-by-step deductive argument, whereas in an analytic argument one started from what one wanted to prove and tried to reduce it to something known from which it could be proved. The other sense of the analytic and the synthetic was tied more closely to geometry, although these ties were by no means inseparable. Forgetting certain qualifications, we may say that a geometrical argument was called analytic in the second sense in so far as no constructions were carried out in it, that is, in so far as no new lines, points, circles, and the like were introduced during the argument. An argument was called synthetic if such new entities were introduced. Here we are interested in the second sense only.

Now it is well known that if the geometrical arguments of (say) Euclid's system are 'formalized' in the sense of being converted into the form of explicit logical arguments, most of them are instances of quantificational arguments. It is also fairly obvious that the distinction between the two kinds of geometrical arguments largely coincides with the distinction between the two kinds of quantificational arguments that I have been discussing. A geometrical argument in the course of which no new geometrical entities are 'constructed' – that is, introduced into the discussion – will normally be converted into a quantificational argument in the course of which no new free individual symbols are introduced and the degree of the sentences in question is not otherwise increased. The geometrical notion of analyticity definable in terms of the notion of a construction will thus virtually become a special case of the sense of analyticity that we characterized by means of the notion of degree. Elsewhere, I have argued that Kant's usage of the terms 'analytic' and 'synthetic' largely followed the mathematical paradigm.[24] He made it clear, furthermore, that he had in mind only the second of the two variant senses of the analytic and the synthetic which were listed above.[25] If I am right, Kant's usage therefore comes pretty close to the sense in which most logical truths of quantification theory were found above to be synthetic.

There is in the historical material also a half-implicit generalization of the geometrical notion of construction which may serve to establish an even closer connection between my suggested explication of the notion of analyticity and the meaning which the term 'analytic' has actually had. The part of the demonstration of a Euclidean theorem in which figures were introduced (drawn for the first time) was called the *ecthesis* or 'exposition'.[26] The same term was applied by Aristotle to a procedure, used in his syllogistic theory, that is very closely related to the rule of existential instantiation.[27] (Indeed, on one interpretation it virtually is this rule.) It has been suggested that Aristotle was here borrowing from Greek mathematical terminology;[28] but even if he was not, the two notions of *ecthesis* were frequently related to each other, as in fact may be done for perfectly good reasons. The result was a general but somewhat vague idea of something like the rule of existential generalization. I have suggested elsewhere that something like this idea was what Kant had in mind when he described the synthetic method of mathematics.[29] In fact, Kant indicates that mathematical truths are synthetic because they are based on the use of constructions. The general notion of a construction is explained by him as the introduction or 'exhibition' of an individual idea (individual term, as we may equally well say) to represent a general concept, an explanation strongly reminiscent of existential instantiation.[30] In the light of such explanations, we may safely say that for Kant something like the rule of existential instantiation was the paradigm of synthetic modes of reasoning in mathematics. Since we saw earlier that in a suitable system of quantification theory the rule of existential instantiation is the only one that increases the degree of the sets of sentences we are considering, this serves to relate Kant's notion of analyticity even more closely to the explication which can be given to this notion in terms of the degree of a sentence (or of a set of sentences). I think that in the light of this explication we can appreciate Kant's philosophy of mathematics and of logic much better than by means of any alternative explication of analyticity. In a sense, we may in this way even partially vindicate Kant's claim that most mathematical truths are synthetic. In certain other ways, too, we seem to have here a way of making certain parts of the traditional philosophy of mathematics more relevant to our own problems than modern philosophers sometimes think they are. What more can one ask of an explication of an old philosophical notion?[31]

NOTES

[1]   One of the main sources here is Frege, who defined analytic sentences as those that can be proved by using only general logical laws and definitions. See *Foundations of Arithmetic*, trans. by J. L. Austin (Basil Blackwell, Oxford, 1950), pp. 99ff.

[2]   As he was himself rather well aware of doing; he called his own distinction "klassisch" and "mächtig". See the *Prolegomena*, Secs. 3 and 5 (pp. 270 and 276 in Vol. V of the Academy Edition). Cf. also *Kant's Critique of Pure Reason*, trans. by N. Kemp Smith (Macmillan, London, 1933), p. 55 (B 19).

[3]   Cf. W. V. Quine, *From a Logical Point of View*, 2nd ed. (Harvard University Press, Cambridge, Mass., 1957), pp. 22ff.

[4]   Cf. Quine, *loc. cit.*; Morton G. White, *Toward Reunion in Philosophy* (Cambridge, Mass., 1955); and the evaluation of the subsequent discussion by Hilary Putnam in *Minnesota Studies in the Philosophy of Science*, Vol. 3, ed. by Herbert Feigl and Grover Maxwell (University of Minnesota Press, Minneapolis, 1962), 359–360. I do not want to imply that every characterization of analyticity along the lines of I is beyond salvation, although I do think that characterization I (a) is seriously mistaken.

[5]   Cf. Kant on his distinction between the analytic and the synthetic. In an analytic judgment "I have merely to analyse the concept; that is, to become conscious to myself of the manifold which I always think in that concept" (Kemp Smith, *op. cit.*, p. 49). In a synthetic judgment we sometimes "are required to join in thought a certain predicate to a given concept, and this necessity is inherent in the concepts themselves. But the question is not what we *ought* to join in thought to the given concept, but what we *actually* think in it, even if only obscurely" (*ibid.*, pp. 53–54; the italics are Kant's). The last sentence is remarkable in that Kant there explicitly countenances sentences which turn on 'necessities inherent in the concepts themselves', that is, which are analytic in sense I, but which for Kant are nevertheless synthetic. This suggests that Kant's intentions are not very well served by an explication of analyticity along the lines of sense I.

[6]   This view of Kant's is a generalization of his view on what he called 'Hume's problem'. For an early formulation of the problem, see the Academy Edition of Kant's works, II, 202–203. The general problem is there formulated as follows: "Wie soll ich es verstehen, dass weil Etwas ist, etwas Anderes sei?" Kant's answer is that this cannot happen 'durch den Satz des Widerspruchs', that is, analytically. Similar formulations occur in the first *Critique*, in the *Prolegomena*, and even in the *Critique of Practical Reason*; cf., e.g., *Prolego-*

mena, Academy Edition, Vol. 4, 257, 260, 277–278; the last passage shows the intimate connection between the justification of interindividual existential inferences and Kant's main problem of justifying synthetic judgments a priori.

[7] Suppose I know a sentence to be true. Then I can, e.g., leave out of consideration in making my plans and decisions all the alternatives excluded by the sentence. Clearly, the more possibilities I can thus rule out, the more I can say that I know. If I cannot rule out any possibilities, then I know nothing at all about the subject matter at hand. As Wittgenstein says, "I know nothing about the weather if I know that it is raining or not raining" (*Tractatus* 4.461).

This connection between the exclusion of possibilities and the amount of information a sentence conveys was first made explicit by Karl Popper and has subsequently been emphasized by him; see, e.g., *The Logic of Scientific Discovery* (Hutchinson, London, 1959), esp. Secs. 23, 31, and appendix *ix.

On the basis of this idea one can readily construct some very natural measures of the information which a sentence carries in propositional logic and in monadic quantification theory. Cf. Yehoshua Bar-Hillel and Rudolf Carnap, 'Semantic Information', *The British Journal of the Philosophy of Science* **4**, (1953–1954), 147–157. A tautology may then be defined simply as a sentence with zero information. In propositional logic it turns out that the tautologies so defined coincide with the logical truths of propositional logic.

[8] This question may be reformulated as a question whether one can extend in a natural and informative way the simple measures of semantic information which can be defined in propositional logic to other parts of logic in such a way that a sentence is logically true if and only if the information it carries is zero. This question has not been answered so far even in the case of the whole of quantification theory. The measures of semantic information proposed by Bar-Hillel and Carnap (*op. cit.*) yield unnatural results if one tries to extend them to the whole of quantification theory. According to these measures, every existentially quantified sentence carries zero information in an infinite domain of individuals, even if it is not logically true. If the domain of individuals is not allowed to become infinite, these measures assign zero information to every sentence that is not logically true but whose negation is satisfiable only in an infinite domain. (The denial of an axiom of infinity would be a case in point.)

[9] For if we could have such a finite list, we would have a decision method for many cases in which it is known to be unavailable.

[10] The depth $d(p)$ of an arbitrary quantificational sentence p may also be defined recursively as follows: $d(q)=0$ if q is an atomic sentence or an identity; $d(q_1 \ \& \ q_1)=d(q_1 \vee q_2)=\max(d(q_1), d(q_2))=$ the greater of the two numbers $d(q_1)$, $d(q_2)$; $d((Ex) q)=d((x) q)=d(q)+1$ (if q is here not a sentence and if $d(q)$ is therefore undefined, we may use instead the depth of any sentence obtained from q by substituting a free individual symbol for x). For instance, we have $d(P(a, b))=0$; $d((Ey) P(a, y))=d(P(a, b))+1=1=d((Ey) P(y, a))$; $d((Ey) P(a, y) \ \& \ (Ey) P(y, a))=max(d((Ey) P(a, y), \ d((Ey) P(y, a)))=max(1, 1)=1$; and hence $d((x) ((Ey) P(x, y) \ \& \ (Ey) P(y, x)))=2$. Similarly, the depth of $(x) ((Ey) P(x, y) \vee (Ey) (Ez) (P(y, z) \ \& \ P(z, x)))$ is 3.

[11] But are the individuals which nested quantifiers invite us to consider necessarily *different* individuals, as we seem to have assumed in counting them all? (This question was first raised to me by Professor Hector-Neri Castañeda.) The answer is simple, and instructive. The individuals which nested quantifiers introduce into our reasoning are necessarily different if and only if quantifiers are given what I have called an exclusive interpretation. (For this interpretation, see my article, 'Identity, Variables, and Impredicative Definitions', *Journal of Symbolic Logic* **21** (1956) 225–245.) Indeed, the difference between the usual

'inclusive' and the new 'exclusive' interpretation of quantifiers lies in this very requirement. Hence we must, strictly speaking, apply our notion of a degree only to quantificational sentences with exclusively interpreted quantifiers. It is not very difficult, however, to translate sentences with inclusively interpreted quantifiers into a language which makes use of exclusively interpreted quantifiers only (see *ibid.*). The degree of the translation may then serve as the degree proper of the original (inclusively interpreted) sentence. It turns out, moreover, that this translation very rarely makes any difference to the degree of our quantificational sentences. For this reason, the requirement of an exclusive interpretation of quantifiers makes little difference here. In fact, not very many points made in this paper turn on the peculiarities of an inclusive interpretation, and those that turn on it can easily be rewritten in terms of an exclusive interpretation. Cf. also my 'Distributive Normal Forms in Fist-Order Logic', reprinted as the last chapter of Hintikka, *Logic, Language-Games, and Information* (Clarendon Press, Oxford, 1973).

Similar remarks pertain of course also to the question whether the values of bound variables may coincide with the referents of free individual symbols occurring in the same sentence. Here, too, a change in the interpretation of quantifiers is called for in order to make my definition of degree applicable. Again, the change is so small as to make no difference to my present purposes, however.

[12] See Hintikka, *op. cit.*; *Distributive Normal Forms in the Calculus of Predicates* (*Acta Philosophica Fennica*, Vol. 6, 1953); 'Distributive Normal Forms and Deductive Interpolation', *Zeitschrift für mathematische Logik und Grundlagen der Mathematik* **10** (1964) 185–191.

[13] More accurately, this is what distinguishes constituents of degree two or more from those of degree one: the former may be inconsistent, but the latter never are. The interesting special case of monadic quantification theory reduces to the second of these two types of cases. Hence the situation in monadic quantification theory is exactly the same as in propositional logic; and hence the truths of the former are tautologies in exactly the same sense as those of the latter. This already shows that our notion of tautology has interesting applications outside propositional logic.

[14] These two reasons for the inconsistency of certain constituents are explained in a more systematic way in 'Distributive Normal Forms in First-Order Logic' (see note 11 above) as conditions (A) and (B). Strictly speaking, a third condition (C) is also needed. This condition is relatively trivial, however, as is shown, e.g., by the fact that it can be dispensed with if we use an exclusive interpretation of quantifiers. Hence I shall disregard it here. The conditions (A) and (B) have been discussed in an instructive special case by G. H. von Wright under the suggestive names 'fitting-in problem' and 'completion problem', respectively. See his *Logical Studies* (Routledge and Kegan Paul, London, 1957), p. 50.

[15] This follows from the completeness theorem of 'Distributive Normal Forms in First-Order Logic'. Every provable formula of quantification theory thus has in principle a proof of an especially simple structure. In each branch of the proof, only such relatively trivial rules are needed as enable us to convert formulae into distributive normal form and to add redundant parts to them so as to increase their depth, with but one essential exception in each branch. This exception is an application of one of the rules for changing the order of adjacent quantifiers.

[16] If so, all the truths of monadic quantification theory (monadic predicate logic) are analytic also in sense III. For (as mentioned in note 13) the truths of this part of logic do not depend on the elimination of inconsistent constituents.

This observation may be of some historical interest. In logic, the attention of most traditional philosophers, Kant included, was confined to traditional syllogistic, which is a part of monadic quantification theory. The fact that senses II and III of analyticity coincide with each other and with logical truth in this area may have been instrumental in leading traditional philosophers to think that they coincide everywhere.

[17] It is important to realize that the provability of this implication does not usually turn on the contradictoriness of its antecedents and that it therefore is not normally of the trivial kind. In fact, the antecedents of (5) are typically satisfiable. If one of them is not satisfiable then this merely means that there occurs as a part of (3) an inconsistent constituent of lesser depth which gives rise to the nontrivial provability of an implication of the same form (5).

[18] For instance, the following 'rule of proof' might be used (in combination with suitable propositional rules): From $(p \& p \& \dots \& p)$ (a conjunction with k members) infer q if and only if k is the Gödel number of a proof of q from p (in some standard formulation of quantification theory). This rule obviously suffices for all the proofs we want; and its applicability to a pair of formulae is obviously a recursive predicate of the Gödel numbers of these formulae. (A rule of this kind was first suggested to me by William Craig.)

[19] The rule mentioned above in note 18 does not satisfy this requirement because its applicability depends on the number of identical members of a conjunction which of course does not make any difference to it as a truth function.

[20] It is easy to see that the restrictions which I mentioned enable us to define a normal form of quantificational sentences which is somewhat cruder than the distributive normal form but which has the following properties. (a) If the free individual symbols and predicates of our sentences are limited to a finite set and if an upper bound is imposed on their depth (degree), then there is only a finite number of normal forms. (b) A sentence p can be inferred from q if and only if the normal form of the former can be inferred from the latter. Then it is easy to see that if we had a complete rule of inference which does not affect the degrees of our sentences, we should have a decision method for the whole of quantification theory, which is known to be impossible.

[21] Existential instantiation (specification, exemplification) is the transition from an existentially quantified sentence $(Ex)\, p$ to a sentence instantiating it, e.g., $p(a/x)$, where a is a free individual symbol and $p(a/x)$ the result of replacing x by a in p wherever it is bound to the initial quantifiers of $(Ex)\, p$. The rule which allows us to make this transition is not symmetrical with respect to the different free individual symbols, however. Those free individual symbols have to be barred from the role of a which occur at the earlier stages of the proof, even if they do not occur in the premise $(Ex)\, p$ itself. This restriction makes the natural deduction methods slightly unnatural from our point of view.

[22] See B. Einarson, 'On Certain Mathematical Terms in Aristotle's Logic', *American Journal of Philology* **57** (1936) 34–35 and 151–172, esp. 36ff.

[23] The history of the two versions is in many ways intertwined almost inextricably. It seems to me important to keep the two separate as much as possible, however. Some interesting remarks on the history and the interrelations of the two versions are made by Neal W. Gilbert in *The Renaissance Concepts of Method* (Columbia University Press, New York, 1960), pp. 31–35, 81–83, and 171–173.

[24] See Chap. 8 below and the further references given there.

[25] See the *Prolegomena* (Academy Edition), and Kant's inaugural dissertation of the year 1770, Sec. 1n.

[26] Thomas L. Heath, *The Thirteen Books of Euclid's Elements*, 2nd ed. (Cambridge University Press, Cambridge, 1926), pp. 129–131.

[27] See G. Patzig, *Die Aristotelische Syllogistik* (Vandenhoek und Ruprecht, Göttingen, 1959), pp. 166–180; J. Łukasiewicz, *Aristotle's Syllogistic* (Clarendon Press, Oxford, 1951), pp. 59–67.

[28] Einarson, *op. cit.*, pp. 161–162.

[29] Chapter 8 below and Chapter 8 of Jaakko Hintikka, *Logic, Language-Games, and Information* (Clarendon Press, Oxford, 1973).

[30] Kemp Smith (trans.), *op. cit.*, p. 577.

[31] An early version of this paper was a contribution to a symposium at the meeting of the American Philosophical Association, Western Division, in Columbus, Ohio, May 2–4, 1963. My thanks are due to my fellow symposiasts. Professor Hector-Neri Castañeda and Dr. Joseph S. Ullian, for their illuminating criticisms.

CHAPTER 8

KANT ON THE MATHEMATICAL METHOD

1. MATHEMATICAL METHOD TURNS ON CONSTRUCTIONS

According to Kant, "mathematical knowledge is the knowledge gained by reason from the construction of concepts." In this paper, I shall make a few suggestions as to how this characterization of the mathematical method is to be understood.

The characterization is given at the end of the *Critique of Pure Reason* in the first chapter of the Transcendental Doctrine of Method (A 713 = = B 741).[1] In this chapter Kant proffers a number of further observations on the subject of the mathematical method. These remarks have not been examined very intensively by most students of Kant's writings. Usually they have been dealt with as a sort of appendix to Kant's better known views on space and time, presented in the Transcendental Aesthetic. In this paper, I also want to call attention to the fact that the relation of the two parts of the first *Critique* is to a considerable extent quite different from the usual conception of it.

To come back to Kant's characterization: the first important term it contains is the word 'construction'. This term is explained by Kant by saying that to *construct* a concept is the same as to exhibit, a priori, an *intuition* which corresponds to the concept.[2] Construction, in other words, is tantamount to the transition from a general concept to an intuition which represents the concept, provided that this is done without recourse to experience.

2. A VULGAR INTERPRETATION OF KANTIAN CONSTRUCTIONS

How is this term 'construction' to be understood? It is not surprising to meet it in a theory of mathematics, for it had in Kant's time an established use in at least one part of mathematics, viz. in geometry. It is therefore natural to assume that what Kant primarily has in mind in the passage just quoted are the constructions of geometers. And it may also seem plausible to say that the reference to intuition in the definition of construction is calculated to prepare the ground for the justification of the use of such constructions which Kant gives in the Transcendental Aesthetic. What guarantee, if any, is there to make sure that the geometrical constructions are always possible? Newton had seen the only foundation of geometrical constructions in what he called 'mechanical practice' (see the preface to *Principia*). But if this is so, then the certainty of geometry is no greater than the certainty of more or less crude 'mechanical practice'. It may seem natural that Kant's appeal to intuition is designed to furnish a better foundation to the geometrical constructions. There is no need to construct a figure on a piece of paper or on the blackboard, Kant may seem to be saying. All we have to do is to represent the required figure by means of imagination. This procedure would be justified by the outcome of the Transcendental Aesthetic, if this can be accepted. For what is allegedly shown there is that all the geometrical relations are due to the structure of our sensibility (our perceptual apparatus, if you prefer the term); for this reason they can be represented completely in imagination without any help of sense-impressions.

This interpretation is the basis of a frequent criticism of Kant's theory of mathematics. It is said, or taken for granted, that constructions in the geometrical sense of the word can be dispensed with in mathematics. All we have to do there is to carry out certain logical arguments which may be completely formalized in terms of modern logic. The only reason why Kant thought that mathematics is based on the use of constructions was that constructions were necessary in the elementary geometry of his day, derived in most cases almost directly from Euclid's *Elementa*. But this was only an accidental peculiarity of that system of geometry. It was due to the fact that Euclid's set of axioms and postulates was incomplete. In order to prove all the theorems he wanted to prove, it was therefore not sufficient for Euclid to carry out a logical argument. He had to set out a diagram or figure so that he could tacitly appeal to our geometrical intuition which in this way could supply the missing assumptions which he had omitted. Kant's theory of mathematics, it is thus alleged, arose by taking as an essential feature of all mathematics something which only was a consequence of a defect in Euclid's particular axiomatization of geometry.[3]

This interpretation, and the criticism based on it, is not without relevance as an objection to Kant's full-fledged theory of space, time, and mathematics as it appears in the Transcendental Aesthetic. It seems to me, however, that it does less than justice to the way in which Kant actually arrived at this theory. It does not take a sufficient account of Kant's precritical views on mathematics, and it even seems to fail to make sense of the arguments by means of which Kant tried to prove his theory. Therefore it does not give us a chance of expounding fully Kant's real arguments for his views on space, time and mathematics, or of criticizing them fairly. It is not so much false, however, as too narrow.

3. KANT'S NOTION OF INTUITION

We begin to become aware of the insufficiency of the above interpretation when we examine the notion of construction somewhat more closely. The definition of this term makes use of the notion of *intuition*. We have to ask, therefore: What did Kant mean by the term 'intuition'? How did he define the term? What is the relation of his notion of intuition to what we are accustomed to associate with the term?

The interpretation which I briefly sketched above assimilates Kant's notion of an a priori intuition to what we may call mental pictures. Intuition is something you can put before your mind's eye, something you can visualize, something you can represent to your imagination. This is not at all the basic meaning Kant himself wanted to give to the word, however. According to his definition, presented in the first paragraph of his lectures on logic, every particular idea as distinguished from general concepts is an intuition. Everything, in other words, which in the human mind represents an individual is an intuition. There is, we may say, nothing 'intuitive' about intuitions so defined. Intuitivity means simply individuality.[4]

Of course, it remains true that later in his system Kant came to make intuitions intuitive again, viz. by arguing that all our human intuitions are bound up with our sensibility, i.e., with our faculty of sensible perception. But we have to keep in mind that this connection between intuitions and sensibility was never taken by Kant as a mere logical consequence of the definition of intuition. On the contrary, Kant insists all through the *Critique of Pure Reason* that it is not incomprehensible that other beings might have intuitions by means other than senses.[5]

The connection between sensibility and intuition was for Kant something to be proved, not something to be assumed.[6] The proofs he gave for assuming the connection (in the case of human beings) are presented in the Transcendental Aesthetic. Therefore, we are entitled to assume the connection between sensibility and intuitions only in those parts of Kant's system which are logically posterior to the Transcendental Aesthetic.

4. THE SYSTEMATIC PRIMACY OF KANT'S THEORY OF THE MATHEMATICAL METHOD

My main suggestion towards an interpretation of Kant's theory of the mathematical method, as presented at the end of the first *Critique*, is that this theory is not posterior but rather systematically prior to the Transcendental Aesthetic. If so, it follows that, within this theory, the term 'intuition' should be taken in the 'unintuitive' sense which Kant gave to it in his definition of the notion. In particular, Kant's characterization of mathematics as based on the use of constructions has to be taken to mean merely that, in mathematics, one is all the time introducing particular representatives of general concepts and carrying out arguments in terms of such particular representatives, arguments which cannot be carried out by the sole means of general concepts. For if Kant's methodology of mathematics is independent of his proofs for connecting intuitions and sensibility in the Aesthetic and even prior to it, then we have, within Kant's theory of the method of mathematics, no justification whatsoever for assuming such a connection, i.e., no justification for giving the notion of intuition any meaning other than the one given to it by Kant's own definitions.

There are, in fact, very good reasons for concluding that the discussion of the mathematical method in the Doctrine of Method is prior to, and presupposed by, Kant's typically critical discussion of space and time in the Transcendental Aesthetic. One of them should be enough: in the *Prolegomena*, in the work in which Kant wanted to make clear the structure of his argument, he explicitly appeals to his discussions of the methodology of mathematics at the end of the *Critique of Pure Reason* in the beginning and during the argument which corresponds to the Transcendental Aesthetic, thus making the dependence of the latter on the former explicit. This happens both when Kant discusses the syntheticity of mathematics (Academy edition of Kant's works, Vol. 4, p. 272) and when he discusses its intuitivity (*ibid.* p. 281; cf. p. 266).

Another persuasive reason is that at critical junctures Kant in the Transcendental Aesthetic means by intuitions precisely what his own definitions tell us. For instance, he argues about space as follows: "Space is not a... general concept of relations of things in general, but a pure intuition. For... we can represent to ourselves only one space. ... Space is essentially one; the manifold in it, and therefore the general concept of spaces, depends solely on the introduction of limitations. Hence it follows that an... intuition underlies all concepts of space" (A 24–25 = B 39). Here intuitivity is inferred directly from individuality, and clearly means nothing more than the latter.

5. The historical primacy of Kant's theory of the mathematical method

But I am afraid that, however excellent reasons there may be for reversing the order of Kant's exposition in the first *Critique* and for putting the discussion of mathematics in the *Methodenlehre* before the Transcendental Aesthetic, my readers are still likely to be incredulous. Could Kant really have meant nothing more than this by his characterization of the mathematical method? Could he have thought that it is an important peculiarity of the method of mathematicians as distinguished from the method of philosophers that the mathematicians make use of special cases of general concepts while philosophers do not? Isn't suggesting this to press Kant's definition of intuition too far?

The answer to this is, I think, that there was a time when Kant did believe that one of the main peculiarities of the mathematical method is to consider particular representatives of general concepts.[7] This view was presented in the precritical prize essay of the year 1764. Its interpretation is quite independent of the interpretation of Kant's critical writings. In particular, the formulation of this precritical theory of Kant's does not turn on the notion of intuition at all. It follows, therefore, that the idea of the mathematical method as being based on the use of general concepts *in concreto*, i.e., in the form of individual instances, was the starting-point of Kant's more elaborate views on mathematics. Whether or not my suggested reading of Kant's characterization of mathematics is exhaustive or not, that is, whether or not intuition there means something more than a particular idea, in any case this reading is the one which we have to start from in trying to understand Kant's views on mathematics.

It is useful to observe at this point that the reading of Kant which I am suggesting is not entirely incompatible with the other, more traditional, interpretation. On one hand, a fully concrete mental picture represents a particular, and therefore an intuition in the sense of the wider definition. On the other hand, particular instances of general concepts are usually much easier to deal with than general concepts themselves; they are much more intuitive in the ordinary sense of the word than general concepts. The two interpretations therefore don't disagree as widely as may first seem. What really makes the difference between the two is whether Kant sometimes had in mind, in addition to 'usual' intuitions in the sense of mental pictures or images, some other individuals that are actually used in mathematical arguments. This, I think, is something we must make an allowance for.

6. KANT ON ALGEBRA

In fact, if we have a closer look at Kant's actual theory of mathematics as presented at the end of the *Critique of Pure Reason*, we shall see that many things become natural if we keep in mind the notion of intuition as a particular idea in contra-distinction to general concepts. Usually, people read Kant's theory of the mathematical method in the light of what he says in the Transcendental Aesthetic. In other words, they read 'intuition' as if it meant 'mental picture' or 'an image before our mind's eye' or something of that sort. But then it becomes very difficult to understand why Kant refers to algebra and to arithmetic as being based on the use of intuitions. The point of using algebraic symbols is certainly not to furnish ourselves with intuitions in the ordinary sense of the word, that is, its purpose is not to furnish ourselves with more vivid images or mental pictures. Scholars have tried to reconcile Kant's remarks on algebra and arithmetic with his critical doctrines as they are presented in the Transcendental Aesthetic. The outcome of these attempts is aptly summed up, I think, by Professor C. D. Broad in a well-known essay on 'Kant's Theory of Mathematical and Philosophical Reasoning', where he says that "Kant has provided no theory whatsoever of algebraic reasoning."[8] This is in my opinion quite correct if we read Kant's description of the mathematical method in the light of what he says in the Transcendental Aesthetic. But then Broad's view becomes, it seems to me, almost a *reductio ad absurdum* of the assumption that the Transcendental Aesthetic is, in Kant's mind, logically prior to the discussion of mathematics at the end of the first *Critique*. For on this assumption the statements Kant makes on arithmetic and algebra are not only deprived of their truth but also of their meaning. If the Transcendental Aesthetic were logically prior to Kant's methodology of mathematics, it would become entirely incomprehensible what on earth Kant could have meant by his remarks on arithmetic and algebra which so obviously are at variance with his professed theories.

On the other hand, if we assume that by 'intuition' Kant only meant any representative of an individual when he commented on arithmetic and algebra, a number of things, although not necessarily everything, become natural. If we can assume that the symbols we use in algebra stand for individual numbers, then it becomes trivially true to say that algebra is based on the use of intuitions, i.e., on the use of representatives of individuals as distinguished from general concepts. After all, the variables of elementary algebra range over numbers and don't take predicates of numbers as their substitution values as the variables of a formalized syllogistic may do. Then we can also understand what Kant had in mind when he called algebraic operations, such as addition, multiplication, and division, constructions. For what happens when we combine in algebra two letters, say a and b, with a functional sign, be this f or g or $+$ or $\cdot$ or :, obtaining an expression like $f(a, b)$ or $g(a, b)$ or $a+b$ or $a \cdot b$ or $a:b$? These expressions, obviously, stand for individual numbers or, more generally, for individual magnitudes, usually for individuals different from those for which a and b stood for. What has happened, therefore, is that we have introduced a representative for a new individual. And such an introduction of representatives for new individuals, i.e., new intuitions, was just what according to Kant's definition happens when we construct something. The new individuals may be said to represent the concepts 'the sum of a and b', 'the product of a and b', etc.

Kant's remarks on algebra therefore receive a natural meaning under my interpretation, quite apart from the question whether this meaning is ultimately reconcilable with what Kant says in the Transcendental Aesthetic. We might say that the purpose of Kant's use of the term 'intuition' here is to say that algebra is *nominalistic* in Quine's sense: the only acceptable values of variables are *individuals*.

7. KANT ON ARITHMETICAL EQUATIONS

Kant's remarks on arithmetic present a somewhat more complicated problem. I shall not deal with them fully here, although they can be shown to square with the view I am suggesting. There is only one point that I want to make here.

In the case of the arithmetic of small numbers, such as 7, 5, and 12, the ordinary reading of Kant's remarks is not without plausibility. What Kant seems to be saying is that in order to establish that $7+5=12$ we have to visualize the numbers 7, 5, and 12 by means of points, fingers, or some other suitable illustrations so that we can immediately perceive the desired equation. He goes as far as to say that equations like $7+5=12$ are immediate and indemonstrable (A 164 = B 204). This is not easy to reconcile with the fact that Kant nevertheless described a procedure which serves, whether we call it a proof or not, to establish the truth of the equation in question and that he said that his view is more natural as applied to large numbers (B 16). I hope to be able to show later what Kant meant by saying that equations like $7+5=12$ are 'immediate' and 'indemonstrable'. He did not mean that the equation can be established without an argument which we are likely to call a proof. 'Immediate' and 'indemonstrable' did not serve to distinguish immediate perception from an articulated argument, but to distinguish a certain subclass of particularly straightforward arguments from other kinds of proofs. The ordinary interpretation of Kant's theory therefore fails here too. Of the correct view I shall try to give a glimpse later.

8. EUCLID AS A PARADIGM FOR KANT

One good way of coming to understand Kant's theory of mathematics is to ask: What were the paradigms on which this theory was modelled? The most obvious paradigm, and in fact a paradigm recognized by Kant himself, was Euclid's system of elementary geometry.[9] In the beginning of this paper, we saw that a usual criticism of Kant's theory of mathematics is based on a comparison between Kant's theory and Euclid's system. It seems to me, however, that it is not enough to make a vague general comparison. It is much more useful to ask exactly what features of Euclid's presentation Kant was thinking of in his theory. In view of the interpretation of Kant's notion of intuition that I have suggested, the question becomes: Is there anything particular in Euclid's procedure which encourages the idea that mathematics is based on the use of particular instances of general concepts?

It is easy to see that there is. For what is the structure of a proposition in Euclid? Usually, a proposition consists of five (or sometimes six) parts.[10] First, there is an *enunciation* of a general proposition. For instance, in proposition 20 of the *Elementa* he says: "In any triangle two sides taken together in any manner are greater than the remaining one." This part of the proposition was called the πρότασις.

But Euclid never does anything on the basis of the enunciation alone. In every proposition, he first applies the content of the enunciation to a particular figure which he assumes to be drawn. For instance, after having enunciated proposition 20, Euclid goes on to say: "For let *ABC* be a triangle. I say that in the triangle *ABC* two sides taken together in any manner are greater than the remaining one, namely, *BA*, *AC* greater than *BC*; *AB*, *BC* greater than *CA*; *BC*, *CA* greater than *AB*." This part of a Euclidean proposition was called the *setting-out* or *ecthesis* (ἔκθεσις, in Latin *expositio*). It is perhaps no accident that Kant used the German equivalent for setting-out (*darstellen*) in explaining his notion of construction, and that he used the term exposition for a process analogous to that of mathematical construction.

The setting-out or *ecthesis* is closely related to the following or third part of a Euclidean proposition, the *auxiliary construction*. This part was often called the *preparation* or *machinery* (κατασκευή). It consisted in stating that the figure constructed in the setting-out was to be completed by drawing certain additional lines, points, and circles. In our example, the preparation reads as follows: "For let *BA* be drawn through the point *D*, let *DA* be made equal to *CA*, and let *DC* be joined."

The construction was followed by the *apodeixis* or *proof* proper (ἀπόδειξις). In the proof, no further constructions were carried out.

What happened was that a series of inferences were drawn concerning the figure which had been introduced in the setting-out and completed in the auxiliary construction. These inferences made use (1) of the axioms, (2) of the earlier propositions, and (3) of the properties of the figure which follow from the way in which it was constructed.

After having reached the desired conclusion about the particular figure, Euclid returned to the general enunciation again, saying, e.g., 'Therefore, in *any* triangle, etc.'

9. 'ECTHESIS' AS A PARADIGM OF KANTIAN CONSTRUCTIONS

When this structure of a Euclidean proposition is compared with Kant's account of the mathematical method, the agreement is obvious. Kant's idea of geometry was, it may be said, Euclidean in more than one sense of the word. When Kant says that it is the method of mathematicians always to consider general concepts *in concreto*, in a particular application, he has in mind the setting-out or *ecthesis* of a Euclidean proposition where a general geometrical proposition is 'exhibited' or 'set out' by means of a particular figure. This is borne out by the examples by means of which Kant explains his theory of the mathematical method. He says that the superiority of the mathematical method over the philosophical one in geometry lies in the fact that the mathematician can draw actual figures and carry out proofs in terms of such figures. For instance, if a philosopher (*qua* philosopher) tries to prove that the sum of the internal angles of every triangle is equal to two right angles, he is reduced, Kant says, to analysing the concepts 'straight line', 'angle', and 'three', and is unable to get anywhere. A mathematician, in contrast, can draw a figure of a triangle, complete it by means of suitable additional constructions (i.e., introduce suitable new lines, circles, etc. into the argument) and thereby make the proposition to be proved obvious. (See A 716–717 = B 744–745.)[11]

This example shows that, in addition to the setting-out or *ecthesis* of a Euclidean proposition, Kant also had in mind the part of the proposition which follows the *ecthesis*, viz. the preparation or 'machinery'. Setting-out and preparation were the two parts of a Euclidean proposition where constructions in the usual sense of the word were made;

and we have seen that these two parts were also the ones in which constructions in Kant's abstract sense of the word were needed, i.e., where new individual points, lines, etc. were introduced. This, then, means that within geometry Kant's notion of construction coincides with the ordinary usage of the term 'construction'.

This outcome of our comparison between Kant and Euclid supports what was said earlier. It shows that Kant's notion of a construction accommodates as a special case the usual geometrical notion of construction. Now the constructions of the geometrical kind need not take place in the human mind. More often than not, they are carried out on a piece of paper or on the blackboard. What is common to all such constructions is that some new lines, points, or circles are introduced. If these geometrical entities are conceived of as individuals, they fit into Kant's general definition of an intuition. There is no need, therefore, to assume that the constructions of geometry mean for Kant something else than what we are prepared to call constructions.

But this is not all we can get out of the comparison. If we have a somewhat closer look at the relation between Kant's theory of the mathematical method and Euclid's practice, the relation serves to suggest several insights into Kant's theory. Here I shall only mention a few of them.

10. ANALYTIC AND SYNTHETIC METHODS

There is in geometry an ancient distinction between two kinds of methods. There is, on one hand, the method of assuming a desired result to be achieved, for instance, of assuming that we have succeeded in making a desired construction, in the ordinary sense of 'construction'. From these assumptions one then argues 'backwards', so to speak, to the conditions on which this construction is possible and to the ways in which it can be effected. This is called the analytic method. It was sometimes ascribed to Plato, but it was not to be employed explicitly and systematically in a large scale until the analytic geometry of Descartes, the very name of which is derived from the 'analytic' method in question. The other method was the synthetic one. In applying it one tries to effect the desired result, for instance, to make a desired construction, by actually carrying out constructions. What distinguishes the two methods, therefore, is broadly speaking the fact that in the analytic method no constructions are made while the synthetic method is based on the use of actual constructions.[12]

Kant indicates that what makes mathematics in general and geometry in particular *synthetic* is the use of intuitions, i.e., the use of constructions. We have seen that his notion of construction coincides, in geometry, with the ordinary mathematical usage of the term 'construction'. What this means, then, is that Kant's distinction between analytic and synthetic is modelled, within mathematics at least, on a usage of mathematicians which was current at his time. (Mathematicians to-day still speak of synthetic geometry, meaning geometry which turns on the use and study of geometrical constructions.) This suggestion is supported by Kant's own comments on the subject, which serve to narrow down his sense of synthetic so as to connect it explicitly with constructions in an almost geometrical sense. The distinction between analytic and synthetic in geometry was earlier often used to separate two methods of *finding a desired proof or construction*, or, in some cases, to separate two methods of exposition. What Kant needed was a distinction between two different means of *carrying out a proof*. For him, the paradigm of synthesis was precisely synthesis in the geometrical sense of the word, i.e., the completion of a figure by means of the introduction of new geometrical entities. This he distinguished from the other usage which was based on the paradigm of proceeding 'inversely' from a ground to a consequence. This difference is stated by Kant, if not in so many words, in a footnote to the first paragraph of his *Dissertation* of the year 1770.[13]

11. KANT AND ANALYTIC GEOMETRY. 'INDEMONSTRABLE' EQUATIONS

There is another way in which an awareness of the respective geometries of Euclid and Descartes helps us to understand Kant. We can make a particularly interesting observation if we compare Euclid's geometry with Descartes'. According to Descartes, the main idea of the analytic geometry was a correlation or analogy between algebraic and geometrical operations. Just as all we need in arithmetic are the four or five basic operations of addition, subtraction, multiplication, division, and the extraction of roots, exactly in the same way we need in geometry only a few basic constructions, Descartes says.[14] What we are interested in here is the analogy between algebraic and geometrical operations, in particular the fact that algebraic operations correspond to certain geometrical constructions. This gives, I think, the key to what Kant means by saying that simple arithmetical equations, such as $7+5=12$ are 'immediate' and 'indemonstrable'. We see this if we try to cast the argument by means of which $7+5=12$ is verified into the form of a Euclidean proposition. Because of the analogy between algebraic operations and geometrical constructions, the actual addition of 7 and 5 corresponds to the third stage, i.e., the preparation or 'machinery', of a Euclidean proposition. Kant's explanations also show that, according to him, the numbers 7 and 5 must somehow be 'set out' or 'exhibited' before the actual operation of addition, in analogy to the 'ecthesis' of a Euclidean proposition. (This is what his remarks on "points or fingers" illustrate.) But what, then, corresponds to the proof proper, to the *apodeixis*? Obviously, all that we have to do in order to show that $7+5=$ $=12$ is to carry out the operation of addition; the proof proper is reduced to a mere minimum, to the mere observation that the result of the addition equals the desired result 12. In a perfectly good sense, therefore, one can say that no proof (proper), no *apodeixis* is needed to establish that $7+5=12$. This equation is 'immediate' and 'indemonstrable' in the precise sense that it can be established by the mere auxiliary construction or *kataskeue* of a Euclidean proof. This is all that Kant's statement amounts to. And the fact that this really was Kant's idea is shown by a letter of his to Schultz, dated November 25, 1788. The main difference is that, instead of using the terminology which pertains to the *theorems* of the Euclidean geometry, Kant in this letter makes use of the parallel terminology pertaining to geometrical *problems*.

This is important, I think, over and above the interpretation of particular passages, for it shows how Kant intended the intuitivity of arithmetic to be understood. The immediacy of arithmetical truths is not due to the fact that simple equations like $7+5=12$ are perceived to be true and not argued for, but to the fact that the only thing we have to do in order to establish such equations is to carry out the computation. This serves to explain why Kant said his account of the equations is more readily understood in the connection of large numbers (B 16; cf. A 78 = B 104).

12. APODEICTIC INFERENCES ANALYTIC

I suspect that a particularly perplexing passage in the first *Critique* receives a natural explanation pretty much in the same way as the remarks on arithmetic. I mean the statement Kant makes in B 14 to the effect that all the inferences (*Schlüsse*) of mathematicians are based on the principle of contradiction "which the nature of all apodeictic certainty requires." This passage becomes very natural if we take Kant for his word and understand him as referring solely to the apodeictic or 'proof proper' part of a Euclidean proposition. Taken literally, the proof proper or apodeixis is after all the only part of a Euclidean proposition where inferences are drawn. Taken in this way Kant's statement expresses precisely what he would be expected to hold on my interpretation, viz. that the distinction between on one hand *apodeixis* and on the other hand *ecthesis* and the auxiliary construction separates the analytic and the synthetic parts of a mathematical argument.

13. INTUITIONS MADE INTUITIVE

What have we accomplished so far? We have seen that in Kant's theory of the mathematical method, presented towards the end of the first *Critique*, one has to keep in mind the possibility that by intuitions Kant means particular representatives of general concepts. We have seen that a number of things about Kant's theory of algebra, arithmetic, and geometry become natural from this point of view. But, it may be said, the possibility of intuitions which are not sensible is ruled out in the Transcendental Aesthetic. Kant argues there that all the use of intuitions in mathematics is based on the intuitions of space and time, and that these intuitions are due to the structure of our sensibility. There is, therefore, no room left in mathematics for intuitions that are not connected with sensibility.

I have no desire to deny that this is what Kant says. But I want to point out that the disagreement between the above interpretation of Kant's methodology of mathematics and his theory of space and time in the Transcendental Aesthetic does not disprove my interpretation. The discrepancy between the two parts of Kant's system belies my reading of Kant only if the account of mathematics given in the Transcendental

Aesthetic is correct. Kant claims there that the use of intuitions in mathematics can only be understood if we assume that all these intuitions are due to our sensibility. If there now are intuitions, say the individual variables or 'intuitions' of algebra, which have no relation to our sensibility, then the only possible conclusion is not that these alleged intuitions are not intuitions at all in Kant's sense. The other possibility is to say that they are genuine intuitions but that Kant just was wrong in saying that all the intuitions used in mathematics are *sinnlich*, i.e., due to our sensibility.

But then it remains to be explained how Kant came to entertain the mistaken doctrine. I have implied that the notion of the mathematical method as being based on the use of individual instances was the starting-point of Kant's better-known theory that all the intuitions we use in mathematics are due to our sensibility. What is there in the notion of an intuition as an individual instance which made Kant think that this conclusion is inevitable? We have discussed the role of intuitions, in the sense of representatives for individuals, in algebra, in arithmetic, and in geometry. What is the common feature of these uses which can only be explained, according to Kant, by assuming that the mathematical intuitions are sensible? What is the common denominator of all the mathematical 'constructions' we have discussed?

14. 'ECTHESIS' IN LOGIC

It seems to me that a natural generalization is virtually contained in the above analysis of Euclid's propositions. The most important part of a Euclidean proposition which is intuitive in Kant's sense is the setting-out, the *ecthesis*. Now this notion of *ecthesis* occurs not only in Greek geometry. It also occurs in the Aristotelian logic. Aristotle never explains explicitly what the procedure called *ecthesis* is, but we can perhaps say that it was a step in which Aristotle moved from considerations pertaining to a general term over to considerations pertaining to a particular representative of this general term. For instance, in *Analytica Priora* I, 2, 25a15, Aristotle seems to argue as follows: If no A is a B, then no B is an A. For if not, then some B's are A's. Take a particular b of this kind. This particular b has both the property B and the property A and shows, therefore, that it is impossible that none of the A's is a B as we assumed. This contradiction proves the conclusion. A later passage (*Analytica Priora* I, 41, 49b33ff.) seems to indicate that Aristotle took the logical *ecthesis* to be essentially the same as the geometrical one.[15]

I suggest that this notion of *ecthesis* offers a very good reconstruction of Kant's notion of construction, i.e., of the notion of the exhibition of a general concept by means of particular representatives. It agrees, as we see, very well with the way in which Kant defines the notion of construction. Its use in the Aristotelian logic may perhaps explain why Kant criticized (in the essay on the 'false subtlety of the four syllogistic figures') certain parts of this logic. He went as far as to reject, in effect, all the syllogistic modes except the first two modes of the first figure. The explanation may perhaps lie in the fact that the particular application of *ecthesis* I just outlined was calculated to prove one of the rules of conversion which Aristotle needed in order to reduce all the syllogistic modes to the first two modes. Since the use of *ecthesis* was for Kant a typically mathematical method of reasoning, he could not use it in logic in the way Aristotle did. For this reason, Kant could not reduce all the syllogistic modes to the two modes of *Barbara* and *Celarent* which he recognized as the basic ones, and was bound to reject all the others as being 'impure' and 'confusing'.

The notion of *ecthesis* can be made precise in terms of modern logic.[16] It becomes, in effect, identical with one of the most important rules of inference of quantification theory (existential instantiation). And, in terms of the notion of *ecthesis* so reconstrued, we can see in what sense the equation $7+5=12$ can be said to be based on the use of particular representatives of general concepts, i.e., on the use of *ecthesis*. It would take us too far, however, to go into this question here.[17]

15. PARTICULARS PARTICULARLY INTUITIVE?

I shall conclude this paper by sketching very briefly and in un-Kantian terms how the reconstruction of Kant's notion of construction in terms of *ecthesis* or in some similar way makes sense of his attempt to connect the mathematical method with sensibility. It was already suggested that the notion of construction may perhaps be identified with certain methods of proof in modern logic. If this is so, then Kant's problem of the justification of constructions in mathematics is *not* made obsolete by the formalization of geometry and other branches of mathematics. The distinction between intuitive and nonintuitive methods of argument then reappears in the formalization of mathematical reasoning as a distinction between two different means of logical proof. But does there remain any sense in which the use of such 'intuitive' methods is problematic? Would Kant have accepted such a reconstruction of the notion of intuition as a premise of his argument that all intuitions are due to our sensibility?

The answer to the questions is, I think, yes. We can see why it was natural for Kant to make the transition from the use of individual instances of any kind to their connection with sensibility. I shall briefly outline two explanations.

Historically, it may be said, nothing was more natural for Kant than to connect individuals with the use of our senses. Aristotle already held that "it is sense-perception alone which is adequate for grasping the particulars" (*Analytica Posteriora* I, 18, 81b6). All knowledge, therefore, which is obtained by means of particulars, must be perceptual. How natural the application of this general Aristotelian idea to the case of constructions in Kant's sense was, is perhaps shown by the fact that Alexander the Commentator already applied Aristotle's idea to the process of *ecthesis*. Alexander held that the singular term introduced in the *ecthesis* is given by perception, and that the proof by *ecthesis* therefore consists in a sort of perceptual evidence.[18] And the general Aristotelian assumption about individuals and senses was echoed by Kant's German predecessors.

16. CONSTRUCTIONS AS ANTICIPATIONS OF EXISTENCE

Another, and perhaps a more important way of making Kant's ideas plausible may be derived from the division of the Euclidean propositions into parts. We have seen that for him, the use of constructions took place in the second and the third part of a Euclidean proposition, while in the fourth part the argumentation was purely nonconstructive or, which amounts to the same, purely analytic. Now the distinction between these parts of a Euclidean proposition corresponds, according to a widespread view of which Kant seems to have accepted, to a distinction between two kinds of principles of Euclid's system. The principles of construction are the so-called postulates, while the principles of proof proper are called axioms (common notions). It is significant that the examples Kant gives of analytic principles used in geometry (B 17) obviously fall into the second category. (This shows, incidentally, that Kant's notion of construction in geometry was not, as sometimes has been suggested, something alien to the axiomatic treatment of geometry. The very examples Kant gives of geometrical constructions are based either directly on Euclid's postulates, or else on explicit propositions Euclid has proved earlier; a fact of which Kant scarcely could have been unaware. In point of fact, the main construction needed in Kant's favourite example, the theorem about the internal angles of a triangle, is based on the postulate of parallels which Kant himself had tried to prove.)

Hence, the distinction between intuitive and logical ways of reasoning was for Kant, within geometry at least, equivalent with the distinction between the use of postulates, i.e., principles of construction, and the use of axioms, i.e., principles of proof. What, then, constitutes the latter distinction? According to a wide-spread view which may be traced back to Aristotle and certainly back to the Greeks, postulates are assumptions of *existence*. Kant's problem of the justification of constructions, therefore, amounts to the problem of justifying the use of existential assumptions in mathematics.

17. HOW CAN CONSTRUCTIONS YIELD A PRIORI KNOWLEDGE?

Stated in this form the whole problem may seem spurious. There is certainly nothing that could prevent a mathematician from studying axiom systems which incorporate general existential assumptions.

The problem only makes sense if we are concerned with the applicability of mathematical reasoning to reality. But this certainly is something Kant was concerned with in the Transcendental Exposition, in spite of the fact that he insists that he is speaking of pure mathematics only. (This appears particularly clearly from paragraphs 8–9 of the *Prolegomena*; cf. Vaihinger's discussion of these paragraphs.) We may ask: what happens when we apply to reality a particular mathematical argument in the course of which a postulate, i.e., a general existential assumption, has been used? In applying it, we have to introduce a representative for a new individual, as Kant puts it "without any object being present, either previously or now, to which it could refer." The introduction of the new representative for an individual is carried out a priori. The existence of the individual object in question, in other words, is not given by experience. Kant describes the situation by saying that the intuition or, in our terms, the representative for an individual object precedes its object. The only thing to make sure that there is any object at all corresponding to the representative is the general existential assumption. But it may seem as if there is no general justification for the application of existential assumptions at all unless we are in fact acquainted with the objects that are assumed to exist, which simply is not the case with applications of our a priori knowledge. It seems, as Kant puts it, impossible to intuit anything a priori. For in the absence of actual acquaintance there is in reality nothing to make sure that we can always find objects which the representatives we have introduced really stand for or that they have the properties we expect them to have.[19]

Kant's solution of this (real or apparent) problem consists in saying that there is one and only one case in which we can be sure that the individuals we have assumed to exist really do so and have the desired properties. This is the case in which we have ourselves created the objects in question or ourselves put the desired properties and relations into them.[20] And he seems to think that there is only one stage of our coming to be aware of objects in which this kind of 'putting properties into objects' can take place. Or, rather, there is only one stage in which we can 'put properties' into all (individual) objects. This stage is sensible perception. For sensible perception is the only way in which an individual object can 'make its way' into our consciousness. Outer sense is the only way in which we can become aware of external objects. For this reason, it is the only stage of our coming to know objects at which we can ourselves give spatial relations to all external objects. Therefore, the spatial relations postulated in geometry must be due to the structure of our outer sense.

I am putting forth this partial reconstruction only as a first approximation to what Kant had in mind in the Transcendental Exposition. This reconstruction is related fairly closely to Kant's 'transcendental argument' for his theory of space and time especially as it is presented in the *Prolegomena*. I have merely tried to fill in those steps which Kant does not himself emphasize in the light of his general assumptions. The relation of my partial reconstruction to Kant's other arguments for his views is more complicated, and requires a longer discussion than I can undertake here.

I want to emphasize that I am not at all claiming that Kant's argument is correct. The main purpose which the reconstruction serves here is to suggest that Kant's problem of the possibility of constructions in mathematics, and his attempted solution to the problem, makes perfectly good sense even when by 'construction' one only means 'the introduction of a new individual representative for a general concept'.

18. THE STRUCTURE OF KANT'S ARGUMENT

The structure of Kant's argument in the form presented here is nevertheless worth a closer look. Its several stages may be represented in the light of what has been said somewhat as follows:

(1) Mathematical reasoning is principally concerned with the existence of individuals.

(2) The results of mathematical reasoning are applicable to all experience a priori.

In virtue of Kant's general 'Copernican' assumptions ("we can know a priori of things only what we ourselves put into them") (1) and (2) force us to conclude:

(3) The existence of the individuals with which mathematical reasoning is concerned is due to the process by means of which we come to know the existence of individuals in general.

Of course, what really matters is not the existence of the individuals as such (there are plenty of individuals existing in the world) but the existence of individuals having the appropriate relations to each other. Hence we may perhaps paraphrase (3) as follows:

(4) The mutual relations of the individuals with which mathematical reasoning is concerned is due to the process by means of which we come to know the existence of individuals.

These systems of mutual relations may be expected to be reflected by the structure of mathematical reasoning.

Now Kant has been seen to assume that

(5) the process by means of which we come to know the existence of individuals in general is perception (sensation).

From (4) and (5) it follows that

(6) the structure of mathematical reasoning is due to the structure of our apparatus of perception.

Now (6) is in effect a basic feature of Kant's full and final doctrine of the mathematical method, as complemented by the results he thought he had achieved in the Transcendental Aesthetic.

19. ARE INDIVIDUALS 'GIVEN TO US'?

This line of thought (1)–(6) is not without interest and even without certain plausibility. Since we have seen that Kant's point can be translated so as to apply to modern logic, we are therefore led to ask what the corresponding argument will look like as applied to symbolic logic. Steps (1)–(2) and (4) do not seem to me completely implausible as applied to logic instead of mathematics. It is in (5) that Kant really goes wrong. It is simply not true that we usually or always come to know the existence of individuals in the world by means of perception in the sense that perception is the whole of the process involved. It may even be asked whether any perception at all need be involved. When we come to establish the existence of a number of a certain kind, it is mistaken to assume that perception is always involved. (But is a number really an individual? Maybe not; but certainly a number was an individual for Kant when he called the symbols of algebra intuitions, i.e., representatives of individuals. Kant's account of algebra stands or falls with the assumption that 'individuals' of the sort represented by the variables of algebra are also known by the sole means of perception.) The concept of an inner sense to which Kant resorts here is one of the weakest points of his system. To think of all knowledge of individual objects as being due to perception is to succumb to a temptation which for Kant may have been very real but which it is important to get rid of. This is the temptation to think that the basic materials of human knowledge are *given* to us passive receivers who do not have to actively search for these materials. On this fallacious idea the human mind, often conceived of as a disembodied spirit inhabiting an alien machine, has to wait until the signals from the outside strike its receptors. (It is interesting in this connection to observe the way in which Kant stressed the passive nature of perception, speaking, e.g., of how objects are *given to us* in perception.) The fact that the mind can indirectly spur the machine into a movement is not thought to alter the situation materially. Nor is the situation essentially changed by the fact that according to Kant the human mind can in many ways actively organize the raw-materials thus obtained, add to them and perhaps even modify them.

I hope that I do not have to argue here that this picture is *grundfalsch*, thoroughly false. It is more interesting to ask for a better account. If perception is not the general concept which covers all that we want, what is? It seems to me that insofar as we can give a general name to all the processes by means of which we come to know the existence of individuals, they may rather be called processes of searching for and finding than acts of perception, albeit we have to accommodate the accidental perception of an object as well as the deliberate construction of an object as special cases of 'searching' and 'finding' in this broad (broadest possible) sense. Hence we have instead of (5):

(5)* The process by means of which we come to know the existence of individuals is that of searching for them.

Instead of (6) we thus have to conclude:

(6)* The structure of a logical argument is due to the structure of the processes of searching for and finding.

My attempted partial reconstruction of the main point of Kant's philosophy of mathematics as applied to modern symbolic logic instead of mathematics thus gives rise to an interesting suggestion for our present-day philosophy of logic. The suggestion is to consider the logic of quantification as being essentially the logic of the notions of searching for and finding (suitably generalized). It seems to me that this suggestion is likely to give rise to interesting and important considerations, if carried out systematically.

NOTES

[1] In referring to the *Critique of Pure Reason*, I shall use the standard conventions A = first edition (1781), B = second edition (1787). All decent editions and translations give the pagination of one or both of these editions. In rendering passages of the first *Critique* in English, I shall normally follow Norman Kemp Smith's translation (Macmillan, London and New York, 1933).

[2] *Loc. cit.*

[3] A paradigmatic statement of this view occurs in Bertrand Russell's *Introduction to Mathematical Philosophy* (George Allen and Unwin, London, 1919), p. 145: "Kant, having observed that the geometers of his day could not prove their theorems by unaided arguments, but required an appeal to the figure, invented a theory of mathematical reasoning

according to which the inference is never strictly logical, but always requires the support of what is called 'intuition'." Needless to say, there does not seem to be a scrap of evidence for attributing to Kant the 'observation' Russell mentions.

[4] See, e.g., Kant's *Dissertation* of 1770, section 2, §10; *Critique of Pure Reason* A 320 = B 376–377; *Prolegomena* §8. Further references are given by H. Vaihinger in his *Commentar zu Kants Kritik der reinen Vernunft* (W. Spemann, Stuttgart, 1881–1892), Vol. 2, pp. 3, 24. Cf. also C. C. E. Schmid, *Wörterbuch zum leichteren Gebrauch der Kantischen Schriften* (4th ed., Cröker, Jena, 1798) on *Anschauung*.

[5] "We cannot assert of sensibility that it is the sole possible kind of intuition" (A 254 = B 310). Cf. e.g. A 27 = B 43, A 34–35 = B 51, A 42 = B 59, A 51 = B 75 and the characteristic phrase 'uns Menschen wenigstens' at B 33.

[6] The opening remarks of the Transcendental Aesthetic seem to envisage a hard-and-fast connection between all intuitions and sensibility. As Paton points out, however, they have to be taken partly as a statement of what Kant wants to prove. See H. J. Paton, *Kant's Metaphysic of Experience* (George Allen and Unwin, London, 1936), Vol. I, pp. 93–94.

[7] This has been brought out clearly and forcefully by E. W. Beth, to whose writings on Kant I am greatly indebted, although I do not fully share Beth's philosophical evaluation of Kant's theories. See 'Kants Einteilung der Urteile in analytische und synthetische', *Algemeen Nederlands Tijdschrift voor Wijsbegeerte en Psychologie* **46** (1953–54) 253–264; *La crise de la raison et la logique* (Gauthier-Villars, Paris, 1957); *The Foundations of Mathematics* (North-Holland Publishing Company, Amsterdam, 1959), pp. 41–47.

[8] *Proceedings of the Aristotelian Society* **42** (1941–42) 1–24.

[9] See the Academy Edition of Kant's works, Vol. 2, p. 307. Concerning the *Elementa*, see Sir Thomas Heath's translation and commentary *The Thirteen Books of Euclid's Elements* (Cambridge University Press, Cambridge, 1926).

[10] Heath, *op. cit.*, Vol. 1, pp. 129–131.

[11] We can see here that according to Kant the peculiarity of mathematics does not lie in the *axioms* and *postulates* of the different branches of mathematics, but in the mathematical mode of argumentation and demonstration.

[12] We have to realize, however, that the mere difference of the directions in which one is proceeding in an analysis and in a synthesis, respectively, was sometimes emphasized at the expense of the questions whether constructions are used or not. One could thus distinguish between a 'directional' and a 'constructional' (or 'problematic') sense of analysis and synthesis. Cf. my paper, 'Kant and the Tradition of Analysis', in *Deskription, Existenz und Analytizität*, ed. by P. Weingartner (Pustet, Munich, 1966), reprinted as Chapter 9 of Jaakko Hintikka, *Logic, Language-Games, and Information* (Clarendon Press, Oxford, 1973).

[13] Cf. also, *Prolegomena*, §5 (Academy Edition, Vol. 4, p. 276, note). We can also say that Kant's remarks in effect serve to distinguish between the directional and the constructional (problematic) sense of analysis and synthesis, and to indicate that Kant opts for the latter. (See the preceding note and the article mentioned there.)

[14] See *La Géométrie*, the first few statements (pp. 297–298 of the first edition).

[15] Concerning the notion of *ecthesis* in Aristotle, see W. D. Ross, *Aristotle's Prior and Posterior Analytics: A Revised Text with Introduction and Commentary* (Clarendon Press, Oxford, 1949) pp. 32–33, 412–414; Jan Łukasiewicz, *Aristotle's Syllogistic from the Standpoint of Modern Formal Logic* (Clarendon Press, Oxford, 1951), pp. 59–67; Günther Patzig, *Die Aristotelische Syllogistik* (Vandenhoeck und Ruprecht, Göttingen, 1959), pp. 166–178; B. Einarson, 'On Certain Mathematical Terms in Aristotle's Logic', *American Journal of Philology*, **57** (1936) 34–54, 151–172, esp. p. 161. As will be seen from these discussions, the

precise interpretation of the Aristotelian notion of *ecthesis* (as used in his logic) is a controversial problem to which no unambiguous solution may be available. The interpretation which I prefer (and which I shall rely on here) assimilates logical *ecthesis* to the 'existential instantiation' of modern logic. I cannot argue for this interpretation as fully here as it deserves. For Aristotle's use of the term *ecthesis* in geometry, which seems to me to be closely related to the logical *ecthesis*, cf., e.g., *Analytica Priora* I, 41 49b30–50a4 and *Analytica Posteriora* I, 10, 76b39–77a2.

[16] I am here presupposing the interpretation mentioned in the preceding note. For further remarks on this interpretation, cf. my paper, 'Are Logical Truths Analytic?.' *Philosophical Review* 74 (1965) 178–203, reprinted as Chapter 7 of this volume, and E. W. Beth's discussion of the relation of *ecthesis* and modern logic in 'Semantic Entailment and Formal Derivability', *Mededelingen van de Koninklijke Nederlandse Akademie van Wetenschappen, Afd. Letterkunde*, N. R., 18, no. 13 (Amsterdam, 1955), pp. 309–342.

[17] Some remarks on these points are contained in my paper, 'Kant Vindicated', in *Deskription, Existenz und Analytizität*, ed. by P. Weingartner (Pustet, Munich, 1966), reprinted as Chapter 8 of *Logic, Language-Games, and Information* (note 12 above).

[18] Alexander of Aphrodisias, *In Aristotelis Analyticorum Priorum Librum I Commentarium*, ed. by M. Wallies, in *Commentaria in Aristotelem Graeca*, Vol. 2 (a) (Berlin 1883), p. 32, cf. pp. 32–33, 99–100, 104; Łukasiewicz, *op. cit.*, pp. 60–67. An attempt to explain and to justify the mathematical *ecthesis* from an Aristotelian point of view also easily gives rise to striking anticipations of Kantian doctrines. Thus we find, for instance, that according to Theophrastus mathematical objects "seem to have been, as it were, devised by us in the act of investing things with figures and shapes and ratios, and to have no nature in and of themselves..." (Theophrastus, *Metaphysica* 4a18ff., pp. 308–309 Brandisii). Cf. also Anders Wedberg, *Plato's Philosophy of Mathematics* (Almqvist and Wiksell, Stockholm, 1955), p. 89, who emphasizes that Aristotle likewise seems to anticipate some of the most salient features of Kant's theory of mathematics.

[19] This difficulty was emphasized by Kant's early critics. For instance, J. G. E. Maas writes in his long paper, 'Ueber die transcendentale Aesthetik', *Philosophisches Magazin* 1 (1788) 117–149, as follows, apropos Kant's notion of an a priori intuition: "Hierbey kann ich (I) die Bemerkung nicht vorbeilassen, dass eine Anschauung *a priori*... nach Kants eigenen Erklärungen nicht denkbar sey. Eine Anschauung ist eine Vorstellung. Sollte sie *a priori* seyn, so müsste sie schlechterdings nicht vom Objecte hergenommen werden, und eine Anschauung ist doch nur möglich, sofern uns der Gegenstand gegeben wird, dieses aber ist wiederum nur dadurch möglich, dass er das Gemüth auf gewisse Weise afficiere. Eine Anschauung *a priori* ist demnach unmöglich, und kann mithin auch in Ansehung des Raumes nicht zum Grunde liegen" (pp. 134–135). Maas does not realize, however, that the possibility of a successful use of a priori intuitions is precisely the problem Kant was trying to solve in the Transcendental Aesthetic.

[20] In B xviii Kant says that he is "adopting as our new method of thought... the principle that we can know *a priori* of things only what we ourselves put into them." Cf. also B xii–xiv. I have commented briefly on the historical background of this Kantian assumption in 'Kant's "New Method of Thought" and his Theory of Mathematics', *Ajatus* 27 (1965) 37–47, reprinted above as Chapter 6 of this volume, and in 'Tieto on valtaa', *Valvoja* 84 (1964) 185–196.

CHAPTER 9

A PRIORI TRUTHS AND THINGS-IN-THEMSELVES

1. KANT'S DOCTRINE OF SYNTHETIC A PRIORI TRUTHS CAN BE VINDICATED

This chapter was first presented as a response to the question, 'Are mathematical and logical truths synthetic a priori?' The outlines of the partial answer that I can offer to this question have been argued for on other occasions.[1] In the present chapter, I shall first summarize the relevant aspects of the answer. The question was initially posed by Kant, and most existing discussions of it refer in so many words to Kant. On pain of gross historical distortion, one therefore cannot help discussing the question in Kantian terms. Now the examples of mathematical reasoning Kant mentions and discusses are typically reproducible in first-order logic. Hence any historically accurate reading of the question turns it into a problem concerning the status of logical rather than mathematical truths. Again, by 'synthetic truths' Kant did not mean truths that do not turn solely on the meanings of the terms they contain, as a contemporary philosopher is likely to mean. I have argued that the best explication we can offer of Kant's notion of an analytic truth (in first-order logic) is what I have called *surface tautology*. Interpreted in this way, Kant's doctrine of the existence of synthetic a priori truths in what he took to be mathematics turns out to be correct in an almost trivial fashion, for there are easily any number of valid (and provable) sentences of first-order logic that are not surface tautologies.

Instead of offering yet another exposition of these points, I shall in this paper comment on one particular aspect of the situation which I have not elaborated elsewhere and which seems to possess a great potential interest from a general philosophical point of view. This aspect is the nature of the kind of information (surface information) that goes together with the notion of surface tautology. An examination of this concept seems to open wide philosophical perspectives which are highly relevant to the traditional discussion of the possibility of synthetic a priori truths and to its background in idealistic philosophy.

2. A SURVEY OF FIRST-ORDER LOGIC

For the purpose, let me first recapitulate how the concept of surface information can be defined and how it behaves.[2] Let us assume that we are dealing with a given fixed first-order language with a finite number of predicates but (for simplicity) without individual constants. Define the *depth* of a sentence s as the length of the longest chain of nested and connected quantifiers in s. (Two quantifiers which contain the bindable variables x and y and of which the latter occurs within the scope of the former, are *connected* if there are quantifiers which occur within the scope of the former and which contain the variables $z_1, z_2, ..., z_k$ such that x and z_1, z_i and z_{i+1} $(i = 1, 2, ..., k-1)$, z_k and y occur in the same atomic formula in s.) Each closed sentence of depth d can be effectively transformed into a disjunction of pairwise exclusive sentences of an especially simple structure, called (closed) *constituents* of the same depth. Likewise, each open sentence of depth d (with certain individual variables $z_1, ..., z_k$) can be transformed into a similar distributive normal form (i.e., into a disjunction of constituents with the same depth and with the same variables). Some of these are effectively recognized as being, in a specifiable sense, *trivially inconsistent*. Roughly speaking, this means that two parts (not necessarily consecutive) of such a constituent contradict each other propositionally. Since there is no decision procedure for the whole of first-order logic, there must exist nontrivially inconsistent constituents, too, which cannot be effectively recognized.

There exists, however, a systematic procedure for weeding out more and more inconsistent but not trivially inconsistent constituents. All we have to do is to keep on adding to the depth of our constituents (while preserving of course the same predicates and the same individual variables). At each addition to the depth of a constituent, it is usually split into a disjunction of a number of deeper constituents, which are said to be *subordinate* to the given one. These can be tested for trivial inconsistency, and it may happen that they are all trivially inconsistent although the original, shallower constituent was not. Moreover, it can be shown that at a sufficiently great depth the inconsistency of each inconsistent constituent and, hence, the inconsistency of each inconsistent sentence, is eventually betrayed in this way. This result, which I have proved in detail elsewhere, constitutes a completeness theorem for our method of enumerating inconsistencies.

If a probability-like measure (system of weights) is defined on the set of all consistent sentences, the weight of each consistent constituent is split up between all its consistent subordinate constituents (of a fixed depth). Such weights will be called *measures of inductive probability*, and by their means one can define in the usual way measures of information, called *depth information*.[3] One especially simple way is to put $\text{cont}_{\text{depth}}(s) = = 1 - p_{\text{ind}}(s) = p_{\text{ind}}(\sim s)$, where 'cont' means 'informative content' and 'p_{ind}' 'inductive probability'.

3. DEPTH INFORMATION NONRECURSIVE

It is remarkable that all natural-looking principles of assigning measures of inductive probability and depth information are nonrecursive. For instance, if the weight w of each constituent of depth d is always divided evenly between all the consistent subordinate constituents of depth $d+1$, one can tell the weight of one of the latter constituents (as a function of w) if and only if one knows the number of these consistent subordinate constituents. However, being able to tell this number is easily seen to be tantamount to being able to tell which of the constituents in question are inconsistent and, hence, tantamount to having a decision procedure for first-order logic.[4] And this, of course, we cannot accomplish recursively. For this reason, measures of depth information cannot in general be effectively calculated. Hence they cannot in any realistic sense be operated with directly. They do not reflect faithfully the realities one has to deal with in logic and in mathematics.

This becomes especially striking if one recalls the close relationship between the concept of information and the idea of the elimination of uncertainty. Part of the uncertainty we inevitably have to face is the uncertainty as to which constituents (and other sentences) are inconsistent and which of them are consistent. In order to take into account the elimination of this kind of uncertainty in our measures of information, we have to use other systems of weights than those given to us by measures of inductive probability.

4. SURFACE INFORMATION

A much better candidate for a genuinely realistic measure of informative content is obtained by assigning a nonzero weight to each constituent that is not trivially inconsistent. It may be stipulated that, whenever a constituent of depth d is split up into a disjunction of a number of constituents (none of which is trivially inconsistent) of depth $d+1$, its weight is divided between these (each of them receiving a nonzero weight) by some definite principle. When the sum of weights is normalized to 1, we again obtain a probability-like measure p_{surf}, which will be called *surface probability* or *prelogical probability*. This may be thought of as the degree of belief it is rational to associate with a sentence before one has done to it any of the many things that logic enables us to do in order to spell out its implications more and more fully. (Hence the half-serious term 'prelogical probability'.) In terms of such probability-like measures, we can in the usual way define measures of *surface information*. One such measure is $\text{cont}_{surf}(s) = 1 - p_{surf}(s)$.

What has been said does not yet suffice to explain fully how these measures are obtained, for so far we have not said anything about what happens to the weight of a constituent $C_0^{(d)}$ of depth d which is not trivially inconsistent but whose subordinate constituents of depth $d+1$ are all trivially inconsistent. It turns out unnatural to let the weight of $C_0^{(d)}$ simply get lost. The natural procedure seems to be to reassign the weight of $C_0^{(d)}$ to its several 'next of kin'. By this I mean the following: Constituents that are not trivially inconsistent form a tree. When we have a situation of the kind just discussed, a branch comes to an end with the constituent $C_0^{(d)}$ in question. When this happens, we trace the branch in question back till we come to the most recent branching point – say, to the constituent $C_0^{(c)}$ ($c < d$) – from which at least one such branch emerges as reaches down to depth $d+1$. The weight of $C_0^{(d)}$ is then divided among all the constituents $C_i^{(d+1)}$ subordinate to $C_0^{(c)}$ which are not trivially inconsistent. This division proceeds stepwise, and follows some specified principles. For instance, if we otherwise follow even distribution of weights to subordinate constituents of the next greater depth, we can follow even distribution here, too.

This suffices to define measures of surface probability and surface information. By a *surface tautology of depth d* we can now mean the disjunction of all the constituents of depth d (with the given predicates and variables, of course) which are not trivially inconsistent, and, more generally, any sentence of depth d that has this disjunction as its distributive normal form. So defined, surface tautologies are precisely those sentences whose surface information is zero. This preserves the important systematic connection between the notion of informativeness and the notions of tautology and analyticity which was already relied on by Kant when he called analytic judgments merely 'explicative' (*Erläuterungsurteile*).

An arbitrary surface tautology of depth d will be called in the sequel $t^{(d)}$.

Among sentences s of depth d or less, the conditional probability $p_{surf}(s \mid t^{(d)})$ (defined in the usual way) satisfies the customary Kolmogorov axioms of probability calculus (with the exception of countably infinite additivity). In view of the familiar betting-theoretical motivation of these axioms,[5] our observations imply that these conditional probabilities can be thought of as possible betting ratios for a rational agent who thinks of all those events as possible which are described by such constituents of depth d as are not trivially inconsistent. (Rationality may here be taken to mean simply ability to avoid Dutch Books made against oneself.) This throws some light on the nature of our notions of surface probability and surface information. Notice, incidentally, that p_{surf} $(s \mid t^{(d+e)})$ is simply the surface probability of the distributive normal form of s at depth $d+e$.

5. DEPTH INFORMATION AS A LIMIT OF SURFACE INFORMATION

Further light is thrown on our notions by an examination of what happens to $\text{cont}_{surf}(s \mid t^{(d+e)}) = 1 - p_{surf}(s \mid t^{(d+e)})$ when e grows. The direction of change depends on the particular sentence in question. We do not always have $\text{cont}_{surf}(s \mid t^{(d+e)}) \le \text{cont}_{surf}(s \mid t^{(d+e+1)})$. This inequality nevertheless holds, even as a strict inequality, whenever one of the constituents in the distributive normal form of s (at the original depth d) becomes trivially inconsistent for the first time at depth $d+e+1$ while the same happens to no constituent of the same depth that does not occur in the normal form of s. (This is very much in keeping with the idea of information as elimination of uncertainty. The information s conveys to us – relative to $t^{(d+e)}$ – grows whenever we can omit one of the possibilities s seemed to allow to begin with and among which we had to be uncertain, while no competing possibility is likewise omitted.) Moreover, from the completeness theorem mentioned earlier it follows that the limit $\lim_{e \to \infty} \text{cont}_{\text{surf}}(s \mid t^{(d+e)})$ is a measure of depth content. What is more, the distribution principle that gives us this depth information is related in a simple way to the distribution principles used in assigning the surface information in question. For instance, if $p_{\text{surf}}(s)$ is based on the principle of even distribution of weights where we move from a given depth to the next greater depth, then so is the $p_{\text{ind}}(s)$ which we obtain as $\lim_{e \to \infty} p_{\text{surf}}(s \mid t^{(d+e)})$. More generally, one can easily see that ratios between weights are in a certain natural sense preserved when one thus moves from $p_{\text{surf}}(s)$ to the corresponding $p_{\text{ind}}(s)$. In the sense that appears from these remarks, we can say that the depth content of a sentence s is the limit to which surface content converges when we gradually draw out from s all its more or less hidden implications. In short, depth information is the limit of surface information.

6. SURFACE INFORMATION AS DEDUCTIVE INFORMATION

These observations perhaps help to illustrate the naturalness of our measures of surface information as a measure of the kind of information we actually (and not just 'implicitly') have. In view of the obvious need of realistic measures of this kind, it is not surprising that some of the theoreticians of subjective probability have recently expressed interest in (not explicitly specified) probability-like measures which are supposed to resemble ours in not being invariant with respect to logical equivalence.[6] Perhaps our measures of 'prelogical' probability are answers to their prayers.

There is nothing subjective about our measures, however. Rather, they give us perfectly objective – and, I have suggested, fairly realistic – measures of information which show that there are senses of information in which logical and mathematical reasoning yields new information in a perfectly objective sense of 'information'. This provides a definitive counterexample to the often-repeated neopositivistic thesis that the only sense in which logical or mathematical reasoning gives us new information is purely psychological or subjective, and thus also provides a partial answer to the Kantian question from which we started in this chapter. Elsewhere, I have explored the relation of my answer to the traditional philosophy of mathematics, especially to Kant.

All this leaves open a group of absolutely crucial questions, however, which have to be raised before we can hope to understand fully the notion of surface information. Speaking of information prompts the question: Information about what? How do the operations that increase our surface information enhance our grasp of some subject matter or other? In the last analysis, one would like to see how an increase in surface information enables us to deal more efficiently with the reality – the 'external' non-conceptual world that we presumably are primarily interested in.

7. Surface information is about reality

In order to answer these questions, let us assume that I receive an item of information from a source that I know to be absolutely reliable, and let us assume that this news item is expressed in the form of a first-order sentence s of depth d. What does that sentence 'really' tell me about the aspect of reality of which it ostensibly speaks? This can in principle be spelled out by seeing which possibilities concerning the world s admits and which possibilities it excludes, i.e., by transforming s into its distributive normal form of depth d. (This point can be greatly strengthened. One might say, for instance, that to specify what a sentence s 'really' tells me about reality is to specify what kinds of individuals I can expect to find in the world when s is true and, after I have found one of them, how the further kinds of individuals are related to it which I may come across, etc. But what the distributive normal form of s does is just to answer all such questions as fully as one can do without going beyond the depth of s, i.e., going beyond the resources of expression already used in s.) However, this normal form does not yet give me everything I can extract from s without the benefit of further factual discoveries and without the benefit of further messages with a factual content. The reason for this is that some of the possibilities that s seems to admit at depth d may turn out be only apparent.

I have tried to illustrate this state of affairs by comparing constituents not to pictures of reality, but to recipes for constructing such pictures.[7] This analogy can in fact be profitably developed further in several directions. The main point relevant here is that some of these recipes may misfire in the sense that no picture can be constructed by their means. From the recipe alone one cannot see whether this is the case or not. Barring further information (surface information!), I therefore have to be prepared for the truth of any constituent in the normal form of s that is not trivially inconsistent. The reality and even urgency of this need merits some emphasis. For instance, in the normal form of s there may be some constituents asserting the existence of certain kinds of individuals (or n-tuples of individuals). Even though all these constituents are in the last analysis inconsistent, I cannot discount them as long as I have not actually ascertained their inconsistency. Before I have done that, I may even find myself making practical preparations for actually running into the kinds of individuals my (inconsistent) constituents assert to exist. A rich stock of detailed illustrations of the phenomenon involved here, drawn from a slightly different department of first-order logic, are offered by the domino problems of Hao Wang and his collaborators.[8] In the same way as one cannot see from a constituent whether it yields a consistent 'picture' of the world or not, in the same way one cannot see from one of these domino problems whether it admits of a positive solution or not. For my purposes, the domino problems are illustrative in two different respects. First, a completed domino problem – i.e., an Euclidean plane filled with domino chips of specifiable kinds – is closely reminiscent of a 'picture of the world', especially of a completed jigsaw-puzzle picture. Second, domino problems show how very far one sometimes has to carry out an attempted 'picture construction' before one can see its impossibility, thus strikingly illustrating the kind of combinatorial information needed to rule out some merely apparent alternatives.

The unavoidability of this predicament follows from the undecidability of first-order logic, which is thus seen to contain important morals for our concept of information.

Our description of the actual situation one faces when one receives a piece of information expressed in first-order language also shows what the practical (pragmatic) advantages are that accrue from an increase in surface information. It was pointed out above that, as far as s and its successively deeper and deeper normal forms are concerned, we obtain more surface information essentially insofar as we can eliminate some of the constituents in its normal form at the initial depth d as being inconsistent. The more such inconsistent constituents we can eliminate, the more narrowly we can restrict the range of eventualities we have to be prepared for when we know that s is the case. It is true that no new empirical observations and no further messages with a factual import are needed for the elimination. The fact nevertheless remains that this elimination is not automatic and that it is not a merely subjective process of getting rid of mental blocks that cloud our vision of what there already is in front of us. The elimination involves further work whose extent can be objectively measured.

8. SURFACE INFORMATION AS CONCEPTUAL INFORMATION

Thus we can see a good reason for saying that the uncertainty we get rid of when our surface information grows is uncertainty concerning the reality our sentences speak of. The same is presumably true of the concept of information involved here. (This could also be construed as a reason for saying that nontrivial logical and mathematical knowledge is 'synthetic' in a rather striking sense of the word.) At the same time, it is clear that the insights we obtain when we gain new surface information are in some important sense conceptual, almost linguistic. They pertain to the ways in which our language can or cannot represent reality. They are not comparable to having a look at a picture so as to see what that part of the world is like which the picture represents; they are, rather, like realizing that certain structures that might at first seem to be pictures do not really stand for anything. The information gained thus seems to be purely conceptual.

9. THE DUAL CHARACTER OF SURFACE INFORMATION

This double nature of surface information might seem very puzzling, almost paradoxical. Rightly viewed, it nevertheless points to a feature of the conceptual situation we are studying which seems to me highly interesting. The paradoxical double nature of surface information illustrates the important fact that whatever we try to say about reality is inextricably interwoven with the contributions of our own conceptual system. What we can directly and immediately express or grasp is a complex outcome which embodies both elements due to nonconceptual reality and elements due to the conceptual system we are relying on. The better we know the conceptual system, the more fully we know what is contributed to this complex outcome by our conceptual system. By discounting this we can therefore ipso facto know to the same extent what is contributed to it by the reality we in the first place want to describe (or want to have described to us). For this reason, the deeper understanding of our own conceptual system – in the case at hand, the wider mastery of first-order logic – which an increase in surface information amounts to can at the same time mean an elimination of uncertainty concerning the objective state of affairs 'out there' in reality.

The metaphor that inevitably suggests itself here is the following: We do not and cannot 'touch' the reality directly, but only by means of a conceptual system. This system works like a highly complex instrument that connects our knowledge with the reality this knowledge is about. This instrument is so intricate that we do not know which of its registrations are due to the influence of the reality we are interested in and which of them merely reflect the mode of functioning of the instrument itself. The better we know the instrument, the more of the merely apparent registrations we can disregard. This also means that we can use the instrument more efficiently than before for the purpose of coming to know the reality its feelers touch.

Thus we can see how surface information may legitimately be thought of both as conceptual information and at the same time as information concerning objective reality. Strictly speaking, this is of course true only of that increase in surface information which takes place when a sentence is expanded into a disjunction of increasingly deeper constituents.

10. THE INEXTRICABILITY OF CONCEPTUAL AND 'REAL' INFORMATION

The most interesting feature of the situation is the inextricability of conceptual elements from those contributed by mind-independent reality. One reason why this is interesting is that it is closely related to a well-known thesis of certain traditional philosophers who are sometimes inaccurately referred to as *idealists*. These philosophers have claimed that all our knowledge – or at least all our 'better' knowledge, which for Kant meant synthetic knowledge a priori – presupposes, and depends on, concepts that are of the nature of the mind's own creations. (Cf. Chapters 4 and 6 above.) As a corollary to this dependence of all our knowledge on our own concepts, it is maintained that 'things in themselves', as they would be independent of all our concepts and therefore of our own activity, are unknowable and indescribable. At best, one school of thought avers, the concept of a *Ding an sich* is useful as an idealized limit that our knowledge can approximate but never fully reach. In brief, reality is for these philosophers inseparable from our concepts – and vice versa.

The simple but representative case of first-order languages offers us a handy testing ground of these 'idealistic' theses. In view of what has been said, these theses can in fact be understood so as to be in certain respects essentially correct. In terms of the metaphor, it *is* the case that (in general) we cannot effectively decide which registrations of the apparatus to which we are comparing our conceptual system are informative about 'objective' reality and which registrations are, in contrast, merely due to the mode of operation of our registering apparatus. In a sense, whatever we may try to say of *Dinge an sich* in first-order terms is normally shot through with elements (apparent possibilities) which are entirely due to the specific way in which first-order sentences are related to the reality they strive to mirror. In this sense, reality and our concepts *are* inextricably interwoven with each other in all nontrivial use of first-order discourse. Furthermore, the central role of this discourse strongly suggests that my point can be generalized.

The inextricability of conceptual from objective factors in first-order languages is due to the undecidability of first-order logic. Looked upon from the point of view of the present paper, Church's undecidability result thus turns out to have decidedly idealistic implications. Our modern version of a time-honoured idealistic thesis undoubtedly appears undramatic as compared with the imagery that is usually associated with the original version or versions. For instance, the 'things in themselves' that our version may perhaps be claimed to involve do not constitute a special class of unknowable but nevertheless in some strange way causally active entities. Speaking of one's knowledge of 'things in themselves' means for us merely a *façon de parler* – a counterfactual way of speaking – of one's knowledge such as it would be if all elements contributed to it by our conceptual apparatus were eliminated. In short, it means for us speaking of depth information instead of surface information. There is nothing illegitimate about doing so, as long as we realize that there is no way of actually (i.e., effectively) dealing with the nonrecursive concept of depth information.

In spite of this undramatic appearance of our quasi-idealistic conclusions, it seems to me that they are in a deep sense connected with what is true and important in the original thesis. (Cf. Chapter 10 below.) Among other things, I believe that thinking of *Dinge an sich* as a separate, unknowable class of entities has always been a case of fallacious hypostatization. If this connection really exists, it is not surprising that as a by-product we can also partially vindicate the old Kantian doctrine of the synthetic a priori character of nontrivial mathematical (and, for us, logical) truths.

NOTES

[1] See Chapters 6–8 of the present volume, Chapters 5–10 of my *Logic, Language-Games, and Information* (Clarendon Press, Oxford, 1973), and 'On Kant's Notion of Intuition (*Anschauung*)', in *The First Critique: Reflections on Kant's 'Critique of Pure Reason'*, ed. by Terence Penelhum and J. H. MacIntosh, in the series Wadsworth Studies in Philosophical Criticism (Wadsworth Publishing Co., Belmont, Calif., 1969), pp. 38–53.

[2] A background for the following discussion is given by the following papers (in addition to those mentioned in the preceding note): 'Distributive Normal Forms in First-order Logic', in *Formal Systems and Recursive Functions: Proceedings of the Eighth Logic Colloquium, Oxford, July 1963*, ed. by J. N. Crossley and M. A. E. Dummett (North-Holland Publishing Co., Amsterdam, 1965), pp. 47–90; and 'Distributive Normal Forms and Deductive Interpolation', *Zeitschrift für mathematische Logik und Grundlagen der Mathematik* **10** (1964) 185–191.

[3] For the different kinds of information, cf. my paper 'The Varieties of Information and Scientific Explanation', in *Logic, Methodology, and Philosophy of Science, Proceedings of the Third International Congress, Amsterdam, 1967*, ed. by B. van Rootselaar and J. F. Staal (North-Holland, Amsterdam, 1968), pp. 151–171.

[4] Assuming that we know the number of consistent constituents (and therefore also the number of inconsistent ones) of a given depth, a simple method of deciding which constituents of this depth are consistent is to list all valid sentences in order until the right number of constituents are among their negations. Since we know this number, we know that the remaining constituents are all consistent. In the same way, one can see more generally that the decision problem of the axiom system whose only nonlogical axiom is a constituent $C_0^{(d)}$ (of depth d, say) is of the same degree of unsolvability as the function (of e) that indicates how many of the constituents subordinate to $C_0^{(d)}$ and of depth $d + e$ are inconsistent.

[5] For the original works by Ramsey and de Finetti, see the handy anthology, *Studies in Subjective Probability*, ed. by H. E. Kyburg and H. E. Smokler (John Wiley, New York, 1964). For a more recent treatment, see the papers by John G. Kemeny, Abner Shimony, and R. Sherman Lehman in *Journal of Symbolic Logic* **20** (1955) 263–273; 1–28; and 251–262, respectively.

[6] See Leonard J. Savage, 'Difficulties in the Theory of Personal Probability', *Philosophy of Science* **34** (1967) 305–310, and Ian Hacking, 'Slightly More Realistic Personal Probability', *ibid* 311–325.

[7] See my 'Are Logical Truths Analytic?' (Chapter 7 above).

[8] See Hao Wang's paper, 'Remarks on Machines, Sets, and the Decision Problem', in *Formal Systems and Recursive Functions*, ed. by J. N. Crossley and M. A. E. Dummett (North-Holland, Amsterdam, 1965) pp. 304–320.

CHAPTER 10

'DINGE AN SICH' REVISITED

1. THE IMPORTANCE OF BEINGS 'AN SICH'

One of the most important questions both in interpreting and in evaluating Kant's philosophy concerns the status of his 'things in themselves'. Are they to be understood ontologically, as a genuine class of entities, or is all the talk of *Dinge an sich* merely an epistemological *façon de parler*, an oblique illustration of the necessity of considering the objects of our knowledge qua objects of the operations which we use in gaining information of them and which inevitably also colour our knowledge of them?

This contrast implies, or at least suggests, other major problems. It reflects immediately on the other half of the dichotomy of phenomena vs. things in themselves. Are phenomena also to be thought of realistically as *things* capable of, e.g., causal relationships, their phenomenal character amounting simply to the epistemological footnote that they are not being considered *an sich*? Or are they to be thought of phenomenalistically as being mere appearances, mere affections of the hidden reality behind our sense-perceptions? It is not hard to find traces of either view in Kant's writings, and not much harder to be tempted to elevate this interpretational contrast into an explicit doctrine of a 'double affection' à la Adickes.[1] Even though Adickes was able to assemble material from the *Opus postumum* which seems to indicate that Kant himself yielded to this temptation in his extreme old age, it remains a most unsatisfactory way out, a multiplication of interactions between entities without necessity. Barring such desperate solutions, we have here a contrast in emphasis and interpretation which is not unrelated to the recent cleavage between ontological and neo-Kantian commentators.[2] This cleavage effectively shows how one's reading of Kant's concept of things-in-themselves is apt to have *folgenschwere* repercussions both for the interpretation and for the evaluation of Kant's whole thought.

2. An epistemological perspective on things in themselves

An interesting perspective on this problem seems to be opened by the interpretation of Kant's philosophy of logic and mathematics which I have outlined in the last few years (partly as a further development of the suggestions of the late E. W. Beth).[3] One of the main stumbling-blocks in interpreting Kant is on any view the question as to how the alleged role of *Dinge an sich* as transcendent causes of our sensations is to be reconciled with their epistemological task of marking the impossibility of separating mind's own contributions to our knowledge of things from the contributions of these things themselves. It seems to me that we can appreciate better this double role of things-in-themselves when we realize what Kant's basic reasons were for adopting his theory of space, time, and mathematics. In a nutshell, the conceptual situation is this: Kant had a theory of the mathematical method according to which it turns on considering particular representations ('intuitions') of general concepts. In brief, mathematics traffics in individuals in contradistinction to general concepts. (A modern logician would express this by saying that the gist of the mathematical method lies in the use of instantiation rules.) Now according to Kant's general transcendental method, the only way of explaining why such modes of reasoning can yield synthetic knowledge a priori is to assume that the mind has itself somehow put the relevant properties and relations into the objects of our knowledge in the act of coming to know them. But what is this act? How is it that we come to know individuals (particulars)? Here Kant unhesitatingly answers: through sense-perception.[4] Hence the synthetic knowledge a priori that we can obtain through the mathematical method must be due to the form (mode of operation) of our faculty of sense-perception. This form Kant identifies with space and time.

If I am right, this is the objective basis of the role Kant assigns to sense-perception or, to use another jargon, to receptivity in his philosophy. It may very well be that Heimsoeth is right in the sense that historically and psychologically Kant's views were conditioned by the metaphysical contrast between finite beings who are restricted to receptivity (sense-perception) in their dealings with the world of particulars as contrasted to the possibility of divine spontaneity which itself creates the objects of its knowledge in an act of 'intellectual intuition'.[5] Whatever one can say of the historical background and the psychological motivation of Kant's views, however, his crucial systematical reason for assigning sense-perception the place it occupies in his philosophy and for thereby making things in themselves into transcendent pseudo-causes of our sensations is an *epistemological* one. It is basically just an acceptance of the traditional idea, which goes back all the way to Aristotle, that "it is sense-perception alone which is adequate for grasping particulars" (*Analytica Posteriora* I, 18, 81b6). Without this assumption, Kant could not connect the use of those particular representations which he designated by the loaded term 'intuitions' with sense-perception.[6] Heimsoeth and his ilk have never taken seriously the fact that the processes through which we come to know particulars could be different both from the receptive registration of sensations by us humans and from the creative operations of the Divine understanding.

3. THE MISSING 'TERTIA VIA'

In fact, the arguments I have proffered in my interpretation of Kant's theory of logic and mathematics suggest a third possibility, mistakenly overlooked by Kant himself no less than by his commentators. The processes through which we humans come to know individuals are not passive sensations literally given to us, but the active operations of searching und looking for the individuals in question. Hence the correct Kantian view would be that the synthetic a priori truths of mathematics[7] reflect, not the structure of our faculty of sense-perception, but the rules of our 'language-games' of seeking and finding.[8] This view I have argued for on independent grounds, and I believe that a closer examination of the behaviour of our logical expressions in natural languages will vindicate it further.[9]

Even though these observations are evaluative and critical rather than exegetical, they provide useful interpretational clues. They help us to appreciate the reasons for the unmistakable tension there is in Kant's system between the epistemological and the ontological elements. After having reached his view of things in themselves as unknowable causes of appearances, Kant was subsequently driven time and again to ascribing to these appearances all sorts of realistic attributes, and vice versa to making things in themselves subject to the same conditions as appearances. (How close to a *contradictio in adjecto* both Kant and his interpreters have been forced may perhaps be illustrated by means of a claim which one of the best recent commentators puts forward with special emphasis: "... it is impossible to explain how a synthesis of perceptions can yield *knowledge, unless the objects themselves are also products of a mental synthesis.* This is in fact the line Kant's argument takes." Quoted from R. P. Wolff, *Kant's Theory of Mental Activity*, Harvard University Press, Cambridge, Mass., p. 169, italics as in the original.) Intellectual tensions of this kind become understandable as consequences of Kant's false step in assimilating the epistemological contrast between things in themselves and empirical objects to the altogether different ontological dichotomy of noumena vs. phenomena.

Before following these clues a little deeper into the interpretation of Kant's doctrines, we must see what the constructive implications of my tentative reconstruction of the concept of 'things in themselves' are. If the process which gives us our knowledge of particulars is not sense-perception, but active seeking and finding, what becomes of the a priori knowledge which is based on the anticipation of the course of such processes? The applicability of such knowledge is now seen to depend on considering its objects as (potential) objects of the activities of seeking and finding, and will reflect the structure of these activities. This is analogous to Kant's view that mathematical knowledge applies to objects only in so far as they are objects of sense-perception, and reflects the form of our faculty of sense-perception. It seems to me that there is a large grain of truth in our modern analogue to Kant's theory of space, time, and mathematics. There is for instance a perfectly good sense in which the so-called laws of first-order logic (quantification theory) merely reflect the structure of our 'language-games' of seeking and finding. Hence this approach to first-order languages provides us with a fully worked-out, detailed example of how Kantian ideas are applicable to contemporary problems, albeit in a form different from Kant's own. The possibility of such detailed examples separates my theories sharply from the vague and woolly general suggestions of the neo-Kantians.

In particular, we can now see in what way the things in themselves can be said to be unknowable. They are unknowable merely in the sense that in so far as we are registering, recording, or transmitting information about objects in first-order terms, we are inevitably considering these objects qua objects of seeking and finding. And if it were the case, as some philosophers think,[10] that first-order languages can serve as the 'canonical notation' of *all* objective knowledge, then the same would hold of all empirically determinate knowledge. We simply could not express intelligible knowledge of objects except in so far as they are objects of seeking and finding. An attempt to step outside the language-games of seeking and finding in order to obtain knowledge of objects in themselves, that is, considered independently of these language-games, would be impossible.

I do not think that quantificational (first-order) language-games are universal.[11] Hence the remarks just made should be relativized. However, even so they will give us an interesting perspective on what a reconstructed notion of things in themselves might look like. It is especially striking that no duplication of entities is involved at all. We do not have a special class of transcendent entities casting their shadows on the phenomenal world, but a special way of obtaining, registering, and codifying information of perfectly ordinary objects.

4. THE INEXTRICABILITY OF THINGS IN THEMSELVES FROM EMPIRICAL OBJECTS

My reconstructed Kantian theory may be illustrated further by pushing it deeper in one particular direction which is left implicit by Kant but which is important enough to deserve some independent systematic attention. The whole notion of things in themselves would lose much of its interest and persuasiveness if we could separate the contributions of our own epistemic activities to their end-product from the contributions of things in themselves. Kant never faced this question squarely, as far as I can tell, but implicit in his philosophy is the presupposition that such a separation is impossible. Otherwise, many of the things he says would be simply nonsensical or at best utterly uninteresting.[12]

On my partial analogue of the Kantian theory the partial inseparability can be demonstrated.[13] Any non-trivial quantificational sentence S – we may think of it as expressing my knowledge – inevitably admits of apparent possibilities for which I must be prepared but each of which can be eliminated by purely conceptual considerations. They constitute the inevitable back side of our own contributions to the kind of knowledge that S can express. However, there is no rule (effective procedure) for locating all of them in the case of many sentences S. In this sense, the effects of the inevitable presence of our own knowledge-seeking activities simply cannot be eliminated. The reasons for this, which are connected with the unsolvability of the decision problem for first-order logic, are spelled out elsewhere. We can in any case explain the situation by means of an analogy. The activities of seeking and finding operate in the same way as a complex recording instrument whose mode of operation influences its registrations. Moreover, these influences cannot even be completely separated from the effects of the very process which they serve to record.

Thus we obtain an interesting perspective on – and perhaps even a partial vindication of – the notion of *Ding an sich*. However, many of the things Kant says or intimates about things in themselves are seen to be mistaken, if my reconstruction is correct. These apparent mistakes include the idea of sense-perception as the way in which things in themselves affect us, the duplication of entities into things in themselves and phenomena, and the non-spatial and non-temporal mode of existence of *Dinge an sich*.

5. INDIVIDUALS CONSTITUTED THROUGH CROSS-IDENTIFICATION

Can these views be also vindicated by pushing the interpretation further? There are in fact other interesting systematic perspectives which help us to appreciate the interest of Kant's ideas, if not their correctness.

Among other things, the Kantian connection between the empirical, the sensible, and the spatio-temporal appears to admit of a powerful second line of defense. The leading ideas of this defense are in fact connected with a highly interesting possibility of relating Kantian ideas to certain recent developments in philosophy and of using these to appreciate Kant's philosophy.[14]

The basic idea of this line of thought is that the notion of an individual (particular) is itself problematic as soon as we begin to consider such 'intentional' concepts as knowledge – the consideration of which is of course very much characteristic of Kant's transcendental method. In using such concepts, we have to consider, however tacitly, our individuals as members of more than one possible state of affairs or course of events, in brief, as members of more than one 'possible world'. In such contexts, we do not have well-defined individuals capable, e.g., of serving as values of the variables of quantification until we possess a method of recognizing (re-identifying) these individuals in different possible worlds.[15] The point of view which I have argued for is that the methods of re-identification (better, cross-identification, that is, of drawing 'trans world heir lines' connecting the manifestations of one and the same individual in several possible worlds) are not given by God or by Logic alone, but are (in principle) constituted by ourselves. Our structuring and conceptualizing activity is in other words involved in the constitution of the very objects of our knowledge. (Cf. Section 3 above.)

6. CROSS-IDENTIFICATION TURNS ON A SPATIOTEMPORAL FRAMEWORK

This idea is already strongly reminiscent of Kant, and it can be pushed still further.[16] What is especially interesting for the purposes at hand is the intimate connection there obtains between cross-identification (we might also call it individuation) on the one hand and space (and time) on the other. Spatiotemporal continuity (the possibility of tracking individuals back and forth in time) seems to me to constitute one of the main vehicles of cross-identification.[17]

This is already suggestive of Kant's idea of space and time as the framework in which particulars appear to us (because we have imposed this framework on them). It also suggests a highly interesting (although not necessarily a Kantian) answer to the question as to the sense in which spatial and temporal relations are objective and in what sense they are imposed on objects by ourselves. They are imposed by us on the objects of our knowledge in the sense that these objects are constituted by means of these relations. To the extent they are being relied on in individuation, to that extent it does not even make sense to speak of the objects of such propositional attitudes as knowledge and belief otherwise than as spatial and temporal.

7. CROSS-IDENTIFICATION AND VISUAL SPACE

There are even closer connections between cross-identification problems and Kant's doctrines. The main systematic insight we have recently gained in this area is, it seems to me, that there are in our actual conceptual repertoire two entirely different types of cross-identification methods, descriptive methods and demonstrative methods (or, rather, methods turning on acquaintance).[18] The contrast is sharpest in the case of a perceptual situation. There the different 'possible worlds' considered are all the different states of affairs compatible with what someone, say a, perceives. Now if he sees (seems to see) certain objects in certain (subjective) locations, there *are* such objects at these locations in all these possible states of affairs. They can thus be cross-identified by means of their location in a's visual geometry.

This kind of cross-identification (demonstrative or perceptual cross-identification) can be extended to certain other propositional attitudes. It is strikingly reflected in our language in the direct-object construction with such verbs as 'sees', 'perceives', 'remembers', and 'knows', for (I have argued) the semantics of these constructions turns on individuation by acquaintance.[19] It also has very close affinities with Kant's theory of space, time, geometry, and the mathematical method, and might prima facie seem to vindicate these almost completely. It seems to re-establish the connection between the idea of an individual object, geometry, and perception which I disparaged earlier. And if this connection obtains, then all our knowledge of particular objects is obtained through processes which involve, or presuppose, individuation of these objects by means of their location in perceptual space-time. If so, we must at least give a new hearing to the Kantian idea that the properties and relations which we somehow must have put into objects in order to be able to apply the synthetic, a priori truths of mathematics to them are imposed on them in sense-perception. We seem to be pushed all the way back to Kant.

8. KANT OVERLOOKS DESCRIPTIVE CROSS-IDENTIFICATION

This second line of defense of the orthodox Kantian position is a mistaken one, however. The mistake in question is nevertheless a highly instructive one.[20] Once again the best antidote to Kant's mistakes is his own idea of emphasizing the mind's own contributions to the total structure of our knowledge. If our individuals are *au fond* constituted by ourselves, we must in principle be able to carry out the constitution in different ways. As was already indicated, it is my thesis that we do it all the time in practice, too. In fact, if one does not visually recognize the persons and objects one sees, this clearly means that in different possible states of affairs compatible with what one sees they can be different individuals. But of course in saying this we are presupposing a method of cross-identification different from the perceptual or demonstrative one. It is what I have called the descriptive method.[21] Without trying to spell it out in detail, I can say that it relies heavily on the same principles in cross-identifying individuals between different worlds as we constantly use in re-identifying them between different moments of time. These are of course completely independent of the viewpoint of any particular perceiver, knower, or believer. If there is a major conceptual element here which goes beyond objective spatio-temporal continuity, it is undoubtedly similarity. For instance, when in a perceptual situation I don't see who the man in front of me is, this means that my visual perceptions of him leave so much room for the variation of his other (unseen) attributes that when they are used as a basis of cross-identification the perceived man is objectively speaking a different person in the different situations compatible with what I see.

Kant's mistake, from this perspective, lies in not distinguishing the two modes of individuation, or perhaps rather neglecting descriptive methods in favour of individuation by acquaintance (especially by perception).[22] The mistake of course spoils the Kantian theory. In particular, it spoils the alleged connection between our idea of individual and perception. Descriptive individuation is in no way dependent on perceptual perspectives, and hence no reference to perception is involved in our idea of individual in so far as descriptively individuated individuals are concerned. Moreover, obviously it is just descriptively cross-identified individuals that are alone important in scientific contexts.

Kant's mistake can nevertheless be seen to be very natural, hence illustrating the subtlety of the philosophical problems involved. Earlier we saw that one major true element in Kant's philosophy is appreciated when the dependence of descriptive cross-identification on space and time (continuity, etc.) is realized. This dependence lends after all a spatiotemporal character to our individuals. If Kant could have identified the space (and time) involved here with the perceptual space (and time) relied on in perspectival individuation, he would have been almost completely right. Thus the basic flaw of Kant's theory is connected with his frequently registered failure to distinguish between physical and perceptual space and time, although it is more general than this particular failure.

9. PERCEPTUAL CROSS-IDENTIFICATION AND LANGUAGE-GAMES OF SEEKING AND FINDING

Even here there are ways of making Kant's theory more understandable, albeit not more correct. One of the fundamental questions in applying the insights of possible-worlds semantics here is what the relevant 'possible worlds' (possible courses of events or possible states of affairs) are. Without excluding other ways of bringing possible-worlds semantics to bear on Kant, it is fairly clear that one major application is to identify the 'possible worlds' with different contexts of language use in so far as they involve our relations of particulars – roughly, different perceptual contexts. One partial systematic reason why this application is important is that cross-identification between such contexts is important for the language-games of seeking and finding.

In language-games in which we search for particular individuals we must be able to recognize them in a variety of different circumstances, viz. those that constitute end-points of search.[23] It is perhaps not unnatural to connect this problem with Kant's notion of synthesis.

The relevant occasions or contexts of use will then be perceptually quite different, although we are not excluding the possibility that each of them may involve perception. The crucial point is that cross-identification between these 'possible contexts of use' cannot be perceptual. We just cannot survey at one glance all the different contexts of use needed, say, in a language-game of seeking and finding so as to be able to cross-identify between them perceptually.

However, it is precisely here that Kant's passive, un-Kantian ideas of how we come to know individual objects betray him. He thinks that we humans have our intuitions literally *given to us* in perception. We do not look for them, only look at them. This view would destroy one of the major reasons why we cannot perceptually bridge the gap between the different relevant contexts of use, and would on the contrary suggest that all the particulars given to us can be located in the one perceptual space and time in which we behold all particulars. This encourages the idea that the relevant possible worlds or possible contexts of language use are essentially perceptual worlds, that is, perceptual alternatives to a given state of affairs. Thus Kant's basic mistake in his theory of space, time, and mathematics has important repercussions to the views he in effect holds about individuation and related matters. It leads him to consider perceptual cross-identification as the basic form of individuation by running together the different occasions on which we rely on perceptual individuation. According to Kant, I am tempted to say, we as it were look at the world always from the same perspective.

This is connected with several central Kantian doctrines, among them the idea of the unity of experience. All our different experiences can be pooled together in one and the same framework, if Kant is right. Another factor here may be Kant's thesis of the ideality of time which makes it easier for him to join temporally different occasions together. These doctrines do not offer much real support to the primacy of perceptual individuation, however.[24]

10. The contrast 'Dinge an sich' vs. empirical objects reconstructed

All this has important consequences for our understanding of Kant's notion of things-in-themselves. The fundamental connection is obvious enough: Members of the actual world are *Dinge an sich*, individuals in perceptual alternatives (or in something like perceptual alternatives) are appearances, if perceptually individuated.

It is quite striking that if Kant had been right in restricting (in effect) his attention to individuation by acquaintance, especially perceptual individuation, he would likewise have been right in thinking of the relationship of *Dinge an sich* to empirical objects (objects of perception, memory, etc.) as a (pseudo-)*causal* one. I have in fact argued elsewhere[25] on completely independent grounds that perceptual world lines (more generally, world lines of individuals individuated by acquaintance) are extended from alternative worlds to the actual one by means of causal principles. For instance, a visual object x of mine in fact is the real-world object a just in case a has in some appropriate sense caused me to have x. (Certain restraints have to be put on the way it causes this, however.)

In fact, in the present-day semantics of perceptual concepts we have a small-scale example of the Kantian problem of the unknowability of things-in-themselves. For on the basis of (say) my visual impressions alone I cannot trace any world line to the actual world. The visual impressions give me a set of possible worlds (more precisely, short segments of possible worlds). I can cross-identify between these, but that alone does not enable me to follow any world line back to the actual world. Hence in a sense my perceptual objects must be said to be caused by actual objects, but I cannot tell perceptually which ones. More generally, on the basis of perceptual information alone I can only speak of perceptual objects qua perceptual objects, not unlike Kant's 'appearances'.

Notice that this is no longer true of third-person perceptual statements. Kant is therefore here prey (to some extent) to the first-person fallacy which has plagued philosophy since Descartes.

Notice also that the Kantian problem of the duplication of entities also has a partial analogue in the present-day semantics of epistemic (including perceptual) concepts. In a sense, a perceptual object (perceptually individuated individual) is one and the same entity in all its manifestations in the different possible worlds we are considering, and the problem of locating it in the actual world is from this perspective a further question concerning this unique individual. This corresponds to thinking of a *Ding an sich* and the corresponding empirical object as being basically identical, that is, one and the same entity. However, in a sense each world has its own supply of individuals (members of its domain) which are correlated by ourselves so as to form trans world heir lines. (This task is relatively easy as long as different perceptual alternatives are being compared with each other. The difficult case is going from them to the actual world.) Hence this way of looking at the semantical situation is analogous to thinking *Dinge an sich* and empirical objects as two different classes of entities altogether.

Of course there is not really any conflict between the two viewpoints. The problem is nevertheless a subtle one, as shown by the repeated demands of some logicians and philosophers to be told which ones are 'really' the individuals of our semantics, individual members of the several possible worlds or the world lines connecting the manifestations of one and the same individual in these worlds.

Other Kantian problems can likewise be partly reconstrued in the framework of possible-worlds semantics. A case in point is the notorious problem as to whether our own acts of knowing belong to the noumenal or the phenomenal world. (If the former, we have direct access to it, contrary to what Kant seems to say. If the latter, we only *appear* to know what we think we know, which is completely contrary to the spirit of Kant's enterprise.) Another, related example is the question of the status of the human ego.

These questions are connected with the problem of the status of one's self-knowledge.[26] Are we to think of one's self as being perceptually or descriptively individuated? More specifically, if we are aware of our own knowings, which way do we then identify ourselves? What, in general, does the semantics of self-knowledge look like? Without discussing these controversial questions here, I want to emphasize their close connections with some of the most basic problems connected with Kant's philosophy.

11. 'DINGE AN SICH' RECOGNIZED

Our visit to *Dinge an sich* has thus shown them to be somewhat different from what Kant told us. In particular, they have turned out to be much less outlandish than people earlier thought. We can nevertheless recognize them without difficulty from Kant's descriptions. The central problems concerning them in Kant's time and now are in fact similar to a truly remarkable degree, it seems to me.

NOTES

[1] Erich Adickes, *Kant und das Ding an sich* (Berlin, 1924); *Kants Lehre von der doppelten Affektion unseres Ich* (Mohr, Tübingen, 1929).

[2] Cf. the useful surveys by Martin J. Scott-Taggart, 'Recent Work on the Philosophy of Kant', in *Kant Studies To-Day*, ed. by Lewis White Beck (Open Court, La Salle, Illinois, 1969), pp. 1–71, and George Schrader, 'The Thing In Itself in Kantian Philosophy', *Review of Metaphysics* 2 (1949) 30–44.

[3] Much of this work has been collected in *Logic, Language-Games and Information: Kantian Themes in the Philosophy of Logic* (Clarendon Press, Oxford, 1973). See also Chapters 6–9 above as well as my papers 'On Kant's Notion of Intuition *(Anschauung)*', in *The First Critique: Reflections on Kant's 'Critique of Pure Reason'*, ed. by Terence Penelhum and J. J. MacIntosh (Wadsworth Publ. Co., Belmont, Calif., 1969), pp. 38–52,

and 'Kantian Intuitions', *Inquiry* **15** (1972) 341–345. For E. W. Beth, see the bibliography of his writings in *Synthese* **16** (1966) 70–106.

[4] Cf. A 19 = B 33: "Objects are *given* to us by means of sensibility, and it alone yields us intuitions...".

[5] Cf. Heinz Heimsoeth, *Studien zur Philosophie Immanuel Kants*, Kantstudien, Ergänzungshefte, Vol. 71 (1956).

[6] See here especially Chapter 8 above.

[7] Since most of the actual examples of mathematical reasoning Kant considered belong to first-order logic, Kant's theory of mathematical reasoning and mathematical truth is really a theory of what is nowadays considered mathematical logic rather than mathematics proper.

[8] Cf. *Logic, Language-Games, and Information* (note 3 above), Chapters 3 and 5.

[9] In this way, we obtain a powerful and natural theory of the semantics of quantifiers in natural language. Notice also that in view of the more active nature of these operations as compared with the essentially passive sense-perception, we might even offer the paradoxical suggestion that our theory represents a more truly Kantian doctrine than Kant's own, for Kant's characteristic and important tendency is to emphasize what "reason ... produces after a plan of its own" (B xiii).

[10] Cases in point (not without qualifications) are W. V. Quine and Donald Davidson.

[11] It turns out that not even all relatively simple quantificational sentences of natural language can be translated into first-order notation.

[12] The unknowability of things-in-themselves depends heavily on this inseparability.

[13] See here *Logic, Language-Games, and Information*, Chapter 10, and Chapter 9 above.

[14] This possibility was foreshadowed in the last section of Chapter 6 'Semantic for Propositional Attitudes', of my *Models for Modalities* (D. Reidel, Dordrecht, 1969). It has since been developed further by Robert Howell; cf. his paper 'Intuition, Synthesis, and Individuation in the Critique of Pure Reason', *Nous* **7** (1973) 207–232.

[15] Cf. my *Models for Modalities* (note 14), especially Chapter 7. The pragmatic limits of such recognition have been the gist in W. V. Quine's criticism of quantified modal logic.

[16] This is essentially Howell's strategy (see note 14 above, and also his forthcoming work along the same lines).

[17] Cf., e.g., my 'Semantics of Modal Notions and the Indeterminacy of Ontology', in *Semantics of Natural Language*, ed. by Donald Davidson and Gilbert Harman (D. Reidel, Dordrecht, 1972), pp. 398–414.

[18] Cf. my 'On the Logic of Perception', Chapter 9 of *Models for Modalities* (note 14 above).

[19] See my 'On the logic of Perception' (note 14), 'Objects of Knowledge and Belief: Acquaintances and Public Figures', *Journal of Philosophy* **67** (1970) 869–883.

[20] If I am right, it also underlies Bertrand Russell's onetime thesis of the 'reducibility to acquaintance'. See my paper, 'Knowledge by Acquaintance – Individuation by Acquaintance', in *Jenseits von Sein und Nichtsein*, ed. by Rudolf Haller (Akademische Druck- und Verlagsanstalt, Graz, 1972); also in *Bertrand Russell* (Modern Studies in Philosophy), ed. by David Pears (Doubleday, Garden City, N.J., 1972), pp. 52–79, reprinted as Chapter 11 below.

[21] See note 19 above.

[22] It seems to me that several other philosophers have likewise been led astray by their use of perception as a paradigm of a propositional attitude. A systematic study of this fallacy might be in order. To what extent was, say, Husserl prey to this fallacy?

[23] See Chapter 3 of my *Logic, Language-Games, and Information* (note 3 above). The difference between looking for particular individuals and looking for individuals of a certain kind is relevant here, but does not invalidate my point.

²⁴ Notice that Kant is nevertheless *verbally* very nearly right in some of his formulations. These are the ones where he says that we come to individuals through sensation. Here a direct-object construction (knowing *objects*) is being employed. Whatever the precise truth-conditions of such direct-object statements are, they are in terms of first-hand epistemic relations with individuals. The paradigm case of such relations is the relation of perceiving an object. (Direct-object construction.) Hence Kant would be very nearly correct if his statements were only calculated to cover our knowledge of objects by acquaintance. – Yet this verbal correctness is beside the point, for the kind of knowledge Kant was concerned with certainly included knowing what, who, where, when, etc., and most importantly, included knowing about physically (descriptively) individuated objects. (Such knowledge cannot be construed as direct-object knowledge, but turns on presuppositions which can only be expressed in terms of interrogative constructions.) Otherwise, Kant's epistemology simply would not be applicable to such impersonal knowledge as is found in science.

²⁵ 'Information, Causality, and the Logic of Perception', forthcoming.

²⁶ This shows how very central the (apparently quite small) problems in reality are which have come up in my exchanges with Hector-Neri Castañeda. See my paper, 'On Attributions of "Self-Knowledge"', *Journal of Philosophy* 67 (1970) 73–77, and the further references given there.

CHAPTER 11

KNOWLEDGE BY ACQUAINTANCE –
INDIVIDUATION BY ACQUAINTANCE

1. ACQUAINTANCE AND PROPOSITIONAL ATTITUDES

The purpose of this paper is to try to see what the logical gist of Bertrand Russell's doctrine of knowledge by acquaintance is. I take the outlines of what Russell says on this topic as being familiar enough.[1] What is not equally clear is how Russell's doctrine is to be understood and evaluated. At least this was not clear to myself before I came upon some ideas in the semantics of propositional attitudes which suddenly made the logic of Russell's views – if not their correctness – perspicuously clear. Hoping that this clarity is not an illusion, I shall try to capture and preserve it by conveying it to others.[2]

By propositional attitudes I mean here the same sorts of things as Russell – knowledge, belief, wish, hope, etc.[3] The boundaries of this class of concepts are prima facie somewhat unclear. For instance, memory and especially perception seem to be concerned with an entirely different sort of relation of a man to his past or present environment than typical propositional attitudes – a relation much less propositional and at least partly causal and genetic.[4] Yet for the purposes of my semantical analysis they are on a par with knowledge and belief.

Sometimes propositional attitudes are characterized by saying that the verbs expressing them can be used with a that-construction and a personal subject.[5] Yet this is not the only construction in which they – or at least some of them – occur. Interrogative constructions (knowing who, remembering when, perceiving where, etc.) do not appear too far removed from the that-construction, and I have argued elsewhere at some length that they can be reduced (apart from minor qualifications) to the that-construction plus quantification over suitable entities.[6] For instance,

(1)   *a* knows (remembers, perceives) who did B

KNOWLEDGE BY ACQUAINTANCE

may be paraphrased as

(1)* $(Ex)\ a$ knows (remembers, perceives) that x did B

with the bound variable x assumed to range over persons.

2. ACQUAINTANCE AND THE DIRECT OBJECT CONSTRUCTION

However, many verbs for propositional attitudes also have a direct object construction. This might even seem to be *sui generis*, apart from such harmless uses of the direct object construction to do odd jobs for other constructions as 'knowing the answer' for 'knowing what the answer is', etc. Especially in the case of perception, the direct object construction might also seem to express the primary use of the concept involved. This easily makes perception appear rather unpropositional. Perhaps this does not make much difference between different propositional attitudes, however, for the ubiquity and importance of the direct object construction with other verbs easily encourages us to think that what they express is also typically a relation between a person and an object or a set of objects, rather than a relation involving a person and a proposition (or something else equally propositional). These objects are then so called in a double sense, for they will be the objects of the attitude in question. One of the most important questions in this area is precisely whether this is the right view of the objects of knowledge, belief, memory, and perception. It is not surprising to see profound thinkers like Husserl turning the question about the nature of this 'intentional' relationship of our acts of perception, belief, desire, etc., to their objects into one of the main problems of their philosophy.

At the stage of his philosophical biography with which we are here concerned, Russell subscribes to a closely related view as applied to judgment. "A judgment, as an occurrence, I take to be a relation of a mind to several entities, namely, the entities which compose what it judged," Russell writes.[7] This theory of judgment was, according to Russell's own account, one of the main bases of his views concerning the nature of knowledge by acquaintance, and in particular concerning its primacy over knowledge by description. In any case, it is not much of an exaggeration to say that Russell's thinking around 1910 was dominated by something of a contrast between the kind of knowledge expressible by a propositional construction and the kind expressible by the direct object construction. For instance, in *Our Knowledge of the External World* he contrasts 'acquaintance' and 'knowledge about'. The latter is "knowledge of propositions, which is not necessarily involved in acquaintance with the constituents of the propositions." (*Op. cit.*, George Allen and Unwin, London, 1914, p. 145.)

The direct object construction with 'knows' is especially interesting for our purposes here because what it expresses can both idiomatically and fairly accurately be said to be just acquaintance. In other words,

(2)   *a* knows *b*

(where *b* is an individual) and

(3)   *a* is acquainted with *b*

may be taken to be near-synonyms, if we disregard the social overtones of 'is acquainted with'. Russell makes liberal use of the direct object construction with 'knows' in expounding his views on 'knowledge by acquaintance'. (He also calls acquaintance [a special kind of] knowledge of things; see *The Problems of Philosophy*, p. 46.) To a considerable extent, studying the nature of acquaintance will therefore mean studying the logic of such expressions as (2) and (3).

3. Possible-worlds semantics for knowledge

Recent logical and philosophical work on propositional attitudes – which is largely an upshot of the development of a satisfactory semantics (model theory) for modal logics – overwhelmingly suggests, however, that the key to their nature does not lie with the direct object construction but with the overtly propositional aspects of their logical behavior. Although the theories that have been developed here are not without their subtleties, the basic ideas are almost ridiculously simple.[8]

They can be uncovered by asking: What is it to specify what somebody knows (believes, remembers, perceives, etc.)? The obvious, and correct, answer is to say: We have to specify what is compatible with what he knows (and by implication what is incompatible with it). Now the force of the first 'what' here is not restricted to the sundry aspects of what there actually is and what actually happens. We have to specify also what unrealized states of affairs and courses of events would still have been compatible with his knowledge in contradistinction to those which his knowledge is powerful enough to exclude. For simplicity of terminology and for vividness of imagery, I propose to dub all these realized and unrealized states of affairs and courses of events *possible worlds*.[9] Technically, specifying what *a* knows (in a world *W*) means specifying which possible worlds are alternatives (more fully, epistemic *a*-alternatives) to *W*, i.e., compatible with what *a* knows in *W*.

The same account applies at once to other propositional attitudes. One main qualification to keep in mind here is that in the context of some notions (e.g., perception), a 'possible world' is a possible momentary *state of affairs*, while in the case of others (e.g., knowledge) it often, and maybe typically, has to be interpreted as a possible *course of events* (a possible 'world history').

The crucial point is that in discussing people's propositional attitudes, we have to consider several possible worlds within the same 'logical specious present'. This immediately shows, among other things, that there is nothing surprising or disconcerting in the breakdown of the usual laws of identity and quantification whenever propositional attitudes are at issue. For instance, if we are discussing what *a* knows (and fails to know), the truth of '$b = c$' does not guarantee substitutivity *salva veritate*. For its truth means that the terms '*b*' and '*c*' pick out the same individual in the actual world, which does not preclude their referring to different objects in some relevant alien worlds, i.e., in some of the epistemic *a*-alternatives to the actual world.

4. EXISTENTIAL GENERALIZATION AND UNIQUE REFERENCE

Likewise, we cannot 'existentially generalize' with respect to (say) the term '*b*' in '$F(b)$' so as to obtain '$(Ex) F(x)$', for '*b*' may refer to different individuals in different possible worlds under consideration, therefore giving us no foothold for maintaining that, for some particular individual *x*, it is true that $F(x)$ as '$(Ex) F(x)$' says. For instance, I can believe certain things about (say) the next Governor of California without there being any particular person of whom I believe them, viz., if the phrase 'the next Governor of California' picks out different politicians under the different courses of events I believe to be possible. Similar examples can be given in terms of proper names instead of definite descriptions.

Existential generalization with respect to '*b*' in (say) '*F(b)*' is legitimate if and only if '*b*' picks out one and the same individual in all the relevant possible worlds. These worlds are the ones as a member of which we are considering *b* in '*F(b)*'. They are indicated by the way '*b*' occurs in '*F(b)*' (by the *modal profile* of '*F(b)*' with respect to '*b*'). If '*b*' occurs only outside the scope of all epistemic, doxastic, etc., operators, we are considering *b* as the member of the actual world only. If '*b*' occurs within the scope of '*a* knows that', we are considering *b* as a member of the 'epistemic alternatives' to the actual world (with respect to *a*). If '*b*' occurs within the scope of two operators, *b* is considered as a member of certain alternatives to alternatives, and so on.

The simplest – and yet fully representative – situation is one in which '*b*' occurs only within the scope of '*a* knows that'. Then the relevant possible worlds are the epistemic *a*-alternatives to the actual world. Since something is true in all these worlds if and only if it is known by *a* to be true, the uniqueness of reference of '*b*' in these several worlds is naturally expressed by

(4) (Ex) *a* knows that $(x = b)$

whose colloquial counterpart was already found to be

(5)   *a* knows who *b* is.

This is the extra premiss needed to guarantee uniqueness of reference here, and hence amenability to existential generalization.

All this is conditional on the assumption that the relevant possible worlds are those compatible with what *a* actually knows. For other situations and other concepts, we have similar or parallel premisses. In the parallel cases for belief, memory, and perception, they are of the form

(6) (Ex) *a* believes (remembers, perceives) that $(x = b)$

whose vernacular counterparts are

(7)   *a* has an opinion as to (remembers, perceives) who *b* is.

Philosophers have occasionally played with the tempting idea that there are some singular terms which *for conceptual reasons* cannot but refer to one individual, i.e., which pick out this individual in *all* possible worlds (insofar as they pick out anything at all). Such terms would presumably satisfy *all* 'uniqueness premisses' of form (6) as well as all other, more general uniqueness requirements. They are called by Russell *logically proper names*.[10] It seems to me, however, that this idea is a chimera and that the realistic procedure is usually to relativize one's discussion to some fixed set of alternatives to some given possible world.[11] Conditions (4)–(7) illustrate what the uniqueness of reference amounts to in such restricted circumstances. In some situations, we may have to consider other sets of possible worlds, perhaps alternatives to alternatives to the actual world. In each case, only a relatively small subset of the set of all possible worlds is considered, however. What the uniqueness premisses for all the different cases look like can almost be gathered from what we have already said, and is discussed in some detail in my essay, 'Existential Presuppositions and Uniqueness Presuppositions', in *Models for Modalities* (note 2 above), pp. 112–47. These uniqueness premisses express the conditions on which the usual quantificational modes of inference, in particular existential generalization, apply to free singular terms in different contexts.

5. THE PROBLEM OF CROSS-IDENTIFICATION

So far, so good. There is a pervasive assumption at work here, however, which has to be brought to the open. We have been speaking freely of a singular term's picking out *different individuals* (or *the same individual*) in different possible worlds. This clearly presupposes that we can *cross-identify*, i.e., tell (in principle) whether an inhabitant of one possible world is or is not the same as a given inhabitant of another. We cannot make sense of quantification (in a context in which we are overtly or tacitly considering several possible worlds) unless and until we can cross-identify between these possible worlds. Such considerations, however tacit, are from a logician's point of view unavoidable as soon as we quantify into a propositional-attitude context, i.e., bind a variable to a quantifier across a verb expressing a propositional attitude.

Since we can make sense of such expressions as (4)–(7) which blatantly involve quantification into a propositional attitude, we obviously can do this (up to a point at least) in our conceptual repertoire. But precisely how do we manage this neat trick? The depths of this profound question cannot be fathomed here. The best I can do is to register two claims for which I have argued at length elsewhere:

(A) Cross-identification relies on the properties and interrelations of individuals in the two worlds we are considering. In other words, it amounts to a comparison between these worlds.[12]

(B) in the context of perception, memory, and knowledge, cross-identification can take place in two different ways.[13]

Here (A) prepares the ground for (B), by showing that the notion of identity (for individuals in different possible worlds) cannot be taken as an unproblematic, given notion.

6. DEMONSTRATIVE VS. DESCRIPTIVE CROSS-IDENTIFICATION

As to (B), I have proposed to call the two kinds of methods of cross-identification *descriptive* methods and methods relying on *acquaintance*.[14] (Occasionally the latter may also be called *demonstrative*, *perspectival*, or *contextual* methods.) The former can be described briefly by saying that they are just the kinds of methods we use in trying to cross-identify between real life and a *roman à clef*. (This example illustrates not only the general nature of these methods but also the difficulty of spelling them out.) To describe these methods a little bit more fully, one can say that they often rely on the continuity of individuals in space and time. This frequently enables one to trace them back (or forth) all the way to the 'inner story' consisting of those facts about our individuals which are common to all the possible worlds considered. In our example, these worlds are the actual world and the world as described by the hypothetical *roman*. In more realistic cases, the common parts of these worlds typically consist of all the facts whose negations are incompatible with the propositional attitude in question. Once we come to this 'common ground' in following the world lines of two individuals in their respective worlds, it suffices to see whether they coincide or not.

If continuity conventions of this sort fail, we have to fall back on similarities and dissimilarities between the members of the different possible worlds to decide whether or not they are identical.

In contrast to these impersonal comparisons, cross-identification by acquaintance relies on the role of the person whose attitudes we are discussing. Let us suppose that that individual is myself and that the propositional attitude in question is memory. Then my own firsthand memories of persons, times, places, and objects create a framework which serves to cross-identify people, places, objects, etc. As long as they play the same role in my personally remembered past, I can treat them as identical (say in two autobiographical novels, both compatible with everything I remember) even though I do not remember enough of them to say (truly) that I remember who, where, or what they are, and although they therefore are not well-defined individuals by the descriptive criteria.

Even more strikingly, my visual space (at some given time) creates a similar framework. Even if I do not see who *that* man over *there* is, in all states of affairs compatible with what I see (seem to see), there is a man there, whom I can treat as one and the same man.

7. DEMONSTRATIVE CROSS-IDENTIFICATION AND THE DIRECT OBJECT CONSTRUCTION

A moment's thought also shows that b's having such a location in my visual space is just what my seeing b means. (Direct object construction!) We are tempted to say that a has a place in my visual space if and only if a is one of my *visual objects*, and that being one of my visual objects is precisely what 'my seeing a' means. There is no harm in yielding to this temptation as long as we remember that the distinctions between 'visual objects' and 'physical' or 'public' or 'descriptive objects' is entirely a matter of interworld comparisons and that no possible world therefore contains a special class of individuals called 'visual objects'. Likewise, I remember b (direct object construction again!) if and only if I can place him in the context of my personally remembered past.

This establishes an interesting connection between cross-identification by acquaintance and the direct object construction. This connection can be made even more striking by recalling the dependence of quantification (quantification *into* a context governed by a propositional-attitude verb) on cross-identification. Without cross-identification, we have not defined the entities our variables range over. No entity without cross-identity, we might say. By way of an alternative slogan, we might also say that in speaking of propositional attitudes the 'real' ('unique', 'well-defined') individuals are in the last analysis the 'world lines' that connect the manifestations or embodiments of the same individual in different possible worlds. Now that we have uncovered two different sets of such world lines, there must likewise be two different kinds of quantifiers in the offing.

Let us use '(Ex)', '(y)', etc., as quantifiers relying on descriptive cross-identification and '$(\exists x)$', '$(\forall y)$', etc., as quantifiers relying on acquaintance. Then

(8) $(\exists x)$ a remembers that $(b=x)$

will say that as far as cross-identification by acquaintance is concerned, the term 'b' picks out a unique individual. This individual b is accordingly one whom a can place in the frame of reference of personal reminiscenses, i.e., he is an individual of whom it is true to say

(9) a remembers b.

The same goes for other attitudes. For instance, a sees b if and only if a can find a room for b among those individuals whose place in his visual geometry is definite, i.e., if and only if the following is true:

(10) $(\exists x)$ a sees that $(b=x)$.

By the same token, (2) and (3) can (omitting minor qualifications) be said to be expressible as

(11) $(\exists x)$ a knows that $(b=x)$.

8. IDENTIFICATION AS INDIVIDUATION. ITS IMPLICATIONS

A terminological point may be in order here. The values of quantified variables are intended to be individuals in the fullest sense possible. Since it is seen that quantification is nevertheless relative to the principles of cross-identification, these principles could equally well be called principles of *individuation*. The notion of a (well-defined) individual is in a perfectly good sense relative to a cross-world comparison method as soon as one starts quantifying into propositional attitudes.

This may seem misleading, for a distinction is often made between individuation (roughly, the splitting up of one world or one state of affairs into individuals) and identification (roughly, tracing the 'world-line' of an individual from one temporary state to another or from one possible world to another). This terminology seems to me highly unfortunate, for it hides the fact that in many important circumstances (e.g., in all contexts involving quantification into a propositional-attitude context) we simply do not have well-defined individuals before cross-identification. Cross-identification is thus almost as much part and parcel of an individual as so-called 'individuation'. From now on, I shall accordingly use 'cross-identification' and 'individuation' more or less interchangeably.

Here we perhaps begin to see in what sense 'the understanding of meanings comes through acquaintance', as it, according to David Pears, comes on Russell's theory. (See Pears, *Bertrand Russell and the British Tradition in Philosophy*, Collins, London, 1967, p. 182; Random House, New York.) Acquaintance gives us a method of individuation (cross-identification). Without such a method, no singular term could be said (or denied) to specify a unique individual in different 'possible worlds'. In other words, without such a method, there would not be any telling what the individuals are that are picked out by our singular terms.

We also begin to see the great interest of individuation by acquaintance for philosophy. We have already reached a logical analysis of the direct object construction in terms of the that-construction for several propositional-attitude verbs. The prima facie reasons mentioned above for thinking of propositional attitudes as possibly involving a relation of a person to an object are thus eliminated – or at least considerably weakened.[15] Propositional attitudes *are* indeed inextricably propositional. The fact that the reduction of the direct object construction to the that-construction involves a special sense of quantification does not weaken this point at all.

More specifically, in (11) we have discovered the logical form of the relation we express by 'acquaintance'. This gives us a useful starting point for further observations.

For one thing, if what I have said is right, then we have here a disproof of Russell's claim that "our knowledge of *things*, which we may call acquaintance" is "logically independent of knowledge of truths" (*The Problems of Philosophy*, p. 46). For an inspection of (11) shows that the only context in which the concept of knowledge is used there is in the that-construction, which presumably must be thought of as expressing 'knowledge of truths'. Yet (11) was found to express a paradigmatic instance of our 'knowledge of things' (including of course here also persons).

It is important to realize, however, that in a sense different from the one I just presupposed Russell may be quite right. In the kind of logical semantics envisaged here, the truth-value of statements of the form (8), (10), or (11) is not determined by the truth-values of simpler statements involving no quantifiers. Our friend a's knowledge of any number de facto identities of the form '$b = d$' does not by itself determine whether he knows b or not, and the same goes for a's knowledge of de facto truths about b. In this important sense, our knowledge of things is indeed logically independent of our knowledge of any particular facts about them.

This is not a peculiarity of the direct object construction, however, for the same things can in principle be said about the who-construction (4) as about the direct object construction (11) in this respect.

9. SENSE-DATA RECONSTRUCTED

One class of objects of acquaintance that we find in Russell and in a number of other philosophers are the so-called sense-data. Their status is an intricate problem in its own right. However, I have argued on an earlier occasion that the job which sense-data were essentially intended to do by the most careful and perceptive sense-datum theorists is done by quantifiers relying on perceptual individuation (individuation by acquaintance for perceptual contexts).[16] If the 'values' of variables bound to such quantifiers could be hypostatized into separate entities, they would be indistinguishable from sense-data (apart from certain psychological and phenomenological assumptions), I have ventured to suggest. However, this hypostatization is illicit, for perceptual quantifiers are not distinguished from the descriptive ones by the individuals they range over in any particular world, but rather by a special method of cross-world comparisons.

In order to see the connection between sense-data and quantifiers relying on perceptual cross-identification, one may recall what sense-data were supposed to be in the first place: objects of immediate perception, i.e., the individuals which our judgments of immediate perception are about. The role of the immediacy requirement here is to rule out all consideration of the actual physical situation. Thus sense-data are supposed to be those individuals we judge about perceptually when we do not perceive (or otherwise know) what descriptive (physical) individuals they are. This is precisely the service which individuation by acquaintance (perceptual individuation) renders us here: it provides us with individuals which we can speak of (judge about) even when we abstract completely from the actual physical objects involved. What quantifiers 'ranging over' such individuals take as values are precisely 'objects of immediate perception' or 'perceptual objects', one is tempted to say. Sense-data are thus part and parcel of the same group of ideas as acquaintance for us no less than for Russell.[17] They are the objects of 'perceptual acquaintance'.

The main reason why traditional sense-data do not look like the values of my acquaintance-quantifiers is an assumption or, rather, a prejudice as to what we can immediately (spontaneously, noninferentially) perceive. For Russell or Moore, sense-data are typically like patches of colour and shade and not three-dimensional occupants of one's perceptual space because they did not think that our sense-perceptions – especially visual ones – are spontaneously articulated into (apparent) three-dimensional objects, such as tables, bridges, and people. For this reason, sense-data are traditionally made much more ephemeral than my perceptually cross-identified individuals. However, the main reason for this immaterialization of sense-data seems to be a mistake about the phenomenology of perception, a mistake which could be disproved by a closer phenomenological and psychological analysis of the situation. All the careful analysts of our spontaneous, unedited sense-impressions seem to agree that they are to be described in terms of perceiving, e.g., persons and material objects, not in terms of perceiving, e.g., colours and shades. (Michotte and others have even studied the perception of causality.)

10. THE CONTEXTUAL NATURE OF DEMONSTRATIVE INDIVIDUATION

We can also see why some propositional attitudes are more prone to the direct object construction than others. It was seen that this construction involves individuation by acquaintance. This in turn presupposes a certain point of view of perspective, i.e., it presupposes that the person whose propositional attitudes are being discussed is interacting or has interacted with the objects of his attitude in such a way as to create a conceptual 'perspective' on them. For otherwise there is not the kind of framework present in the different possible worlds involved here which would enable us to cross-identify perspectivally.

Now we always perceive from a certain vantage point, and remember people and events because we were personally there. Furthermore, our first-hand knowledge of persons and places is based on our actual cognitive interaction with them. In contrast, we can believe what we choose of sundry entities without having had much to do with them. No wonder, therefore, that we do not have a direct object construction with 'believes' parallel to the direct object constructions we have studied.

Not too much deep significance should be read into this fact, however, for it may very well be merely a matter of degree.

Likewise we can now see that (other things being equal) the direct-object construction with propositional-attitude verbs is the more important for a philosopher the likelier he is to think of these attitudes in terms of a personal, first-hand situation, for instance of knowing on the model of perceiving. For the cross-identification relied on in the direct-object construction makes essential use of such situations. Since we found above in Chapter 3 (see especially Sections 6 and 13) that such Greek philosophers as Plato and Aristotle exhibited this situational inclination in their conceptual practice, it is not surprising that the important conceptual paradigm for them (especially for Plato) was one expressible in terms of the direct object construction. (Witness Chapter 1 above, especially Sections 10–11.) In Plato we even find a direct object construction with the verb *doxazein* (in a sense analogous to 'knowing John') which corresponds to the English 'believing'. (See *Theaetetus* 209B.) The absence of an English construction like 'opining John' or 'believing John' with a meaning parallel to 'knowing John' thus indeed looks like a matter of historical accident.

11. THE PARALLELISM OF KNOWING WHO AND KNOWING + DIRECT OBJECT

Notice, finally, the neat parallelism of the respective logical structures of the constructions (4) (i.e., (5)) and (11) (i.e., (2)). The only thing that distinguishes them is the kind of quantifier involved. This logical observation suggests a commonplace moral. It would be surprising if things so similar were always sharply distinguished in ordinary usage. In fact, the sharp distinction I have made above between the interrogative constructions and the direct object construction in terms of 'knows' has to be taken with a grain of salt. It is easily seen that in ordinary language one construction is frequently used to denote what would be expressed perhaps slightly more appropriately by the other.[18] Language is at best a partial and incomplete guide to logic here. Acquaintance *may* be what 'knowing who' naturally expresses in suitable circumstances.

An important example of this will be found in the opening lines of Russell's essay on 'Knowledge by Acquaintance and Knowledge by Description'.[19]

12. RUSSELLIAN ACQUAINTANCE

Our distinction between the two kinds of individuation methods appears to be new in the literature. However, it seems to me that individuation by acquaintance has in effect been discussed by philosophers more or less openly in several interesting contexts, of which Russell's theory of knowledge by acquaintance is the best known example.

As was already indicated, Russell opens his paper, 'Knowledge by Acquaintance and Knowledge by Description', by saying that its object "is to consider what it is that we know in cases where we know propositions about 'the so-and-so' *without knowing who or what the so-and-so is*" (my italics). Taken literally, this is simply false, for Russell's favourite examples concern our knowledge of Bismarck and of Julius Caesar. (Surely we know, in the most straightforward sense of the expression, who these gentlemen are.) Hence some slightly unusual sense of knowing who (or what) must be presupposed. Russell's explanations show amply that what is involved is just a switch to individuation by acquaintance, at least insofar as particulars are concerned. (I shall here in this essay leave alone Russell's remarks on universals.) One can scarcely come closer than Russell to our symbolic treatment of individuation by acquaintance, as exemplified by

$$(\exists a) \text{ we know that } (a = \text{the so-and-so}),$$

when he says that "... we have '*merely* descriptive knowledge' of the so-and-so when ... we do not know any proposition 'a is the so-and-so,' where a is something with which we are acquainted."[20]

Many of the details of Russell's discussion are also reminiscent of what has already been said in this paper. For instance, my remarks on the perspectival nature of contextual individuation (one's own personal role in the situation creates a frame of reference) are matched by Russell's emphasis on the relational character of acquaintance, i.e., on "the need of a subject which is acquainted".[21] Russell's prime example of the objects of acquaintance is the same as the first example given above of contextual individuation, viz., sense-data (except for my disclaimer that they do not exist as a separate class of entities in any particular world).[22] Russell's sometime claim that "there are only two words which are strictly proper names of particulars, namely, 'I' and 'this'" is neither true nor even plausible unless individuation by acquaintance is presupposed.[23] (In saying this, I am of course presupposing the connection between the notion of a logically proper name and uniqueness of reference mentioned earlier.)

More than one aspect of Russell's theory of knowledge by acquaintance can be discussed from the vantage point we have reached. For instance, we can now see why it was possible for Russell to maintain – as David Pears has argued that he did[24] – without any logical difficulties that one can have acquaintance with individuals which are not actually present, provided that one has come across them in the past. As was pointed out, personal memories normally give one enough reference-points to individuate persons and things by their means. In a sense, there is but a difference in degree between individuation by perceptual criteria and individuation by means of personal memory. Both can be classified as cases of individuation by acquaintance.[25]

13. REDUCIBILITY TO ACQUAINTANCE

More important is the possibility of partly reconstruing within our approach and evaluating Russell's famous thesis of the reducibility to acquaintance: "Every proposition which we can understand must be composed wholly of constituents with which we are acquainted."[26]

The first main point to be noted here is that Russell's thesis is primarily semantical and ontological and not only epistemological. That is, he is not only discussing the interrelation of different types of knowledge, but also the different types of entities involved in our propositions. As far as singulars are concerned, such questions of ontology lead us immediately to questions of individuation and cross-identification. It is in fact clear that at least a large part of what Russell is claiming can be expressed within our framework as a thesis to the effect that the only irreducible individuals are those created by contextual methods of cross-identification. In contrast to some secondhand expositions, Russell's own formulation of the reducibility thesis is in terms of understanding a proposition rather than coming to know it.

It seems clear to me that the gist of Russell's reducibility thesis can be recaptured in this way as a thesis to the effect that only demonstrative methods of cross-identification (individuation by acquaintance), not physical (descriptive) ones, are indispensable. Even apart from Russell, this thesis is important enough to be discussed in some detail.

Is it true? I believe it is not. However, I do not have any single knock-down argument to this effect. What can be done is to indicate some of the great difficulties that face any serious attempt to dispense with individuals descriptively individuated, and also to give partial and conditional arguments for the indispensability of individuals descriptively individuated. It seems to me that the cumulative force of all these arguments is strong enough to justify our considering Russell's thesis as false.

For this purpose, it may be noted that merely interpreting singular terms as definite descriptions fails to accomplish the elimination of 'public' individuals, contrary to what Russell in effect assumed earlier in the penultimate paragraph of 'On Denoting' (1905). One reason for this is almost acknowledged by Russell.[27] It is based on the fact that, given a singular term, say 'Bismarck', we can make two different kinds of statements in terms of it. We can make a statement about whoever may be picked out by that term, i.e., whoever may meet the correlated description. One may also make a statement about that individual who in fact is (or was) Bismarck.[28] For instance, someone (say a) may believe that whoever Bismarck was, he was an astute diplomat. This can be formulated as

(12) a believes that Bismarck was an astute diplomat.

If he had instead had the same belief concerning Bismarck the man, we would have to say something different. Recalling that it is bound variables that range over individuals ('individuals themselves', not individuals characterized in a certain way), we can see that this can be expressed as follows:

(13) $(Ex) ((x = \text{Bismarck})$ & $(a$ believes that x is an astute diplomat$))$.

Suppose someone proposes to replace the proper name 'Bismarck' in (13) by a definite description which in the last analysis is in terms of what can be experienced. This does not bring us any closer to a reduction to acquaintance, for in (13) the quantifier may very well rely on public (descriptive) methods of cross-identification. If so, it is the bound variable and not the name 'Bismarck' that forces us to consider public individuals and not merely acquaintances. Then no juggling with the free singular term 'Bismarck' will help the reduction.

· It seems to me that Russell betrays awareness of the distinction (12)–(13) when he discusses propositions which outsiders can only 'describe' but cannot 'affirm'. These, it appears from Russell's discussion, are intended to be precisely propositions about the man (the individual) himself, not as described in this or that way.

Russell describes the situation in terms of judging rather than believing, but this is an insignificant discrepancy. He writes: "It would seem that, when we make a statement about something only known by description, we often intend to make our statement, not in the form of involving the description, but about the *actual thing described*. That is to say, when we say anything about Bismarck, we should like, if we could, to make the judgment ... of which he himself is a constituent. In this we are necessarily defeated, since the actual Bismarck is unknown to us. But we know that there is an object B called Bismarck, and that B was an astute diplomatist. We can thus describe the proposition we should like to affirm, namely, 'B was an astute diplomatist' where B is the object which was Bismarck" (*Mysticism and Logic*, p. 218, my italics).

Notice how close Russell comes to my formulation (13). In fact, the judgment he is describing might almost be expressed as follows:

(Eb) $(b = \text{Bismarck}$ & we judge that b was an astute diplomatist)

with a 'b' taking actual objects as its values.

A minor discrepancy is nevertheless created by the fact that Russell is, in the quoted passage, apparently thinking of knowledge (individuation) by acquaintance in saying that Bismarck is 'unknown to us'. Hence '∃' rather than 'E' may best catch his intentions here. However, the logical point he is making is independent of the style of quantifiers (mode of individuation) employed.

14. RUSSELL'S MISTAKES

The mistake Russell makes here is that he assumes that the reason why someone cannot assert a describable but unassertable proposition about Bismarck must be that he is not acquainted with Bismarck or with whomever we are talking about.[29] This is of course circular. It is true only if our quantifier in (13) presupposes individuation by acquaintance. If it relies on individuation by descriptive methods, the impossibility of using the name 'Bismarck' to express one's beliefs about the person in question will be due to one's failure to *know who* Bismarck was, not to a failure to *know* (to be acquainted with) him. It is difficult to suppress the suspicion that Russell is tacitly assimilating the notion of 'knowing who' (or 'knowing what') to the notion expressed by the (irreducible) direct object construction with 'knows', i.e., to the notion of acquaintance. On a number of occasions (see, e.g., *The Problems of Philosophy*, pp. 44–45) Russell contrasts being acquainted with someone (knowledge by acquaintance) with merely knowing (truly judging) that he exists (knowledge by description). This is a false dichotomy, however, because there also is a third type of a proposition here, viz., knowing who that someone is.

In any case, the main official reason Russell himself gives for the reducibility thesis is circular in that it in effect assimilates the two methods of individuation to each other. "The chief reason for supposing the principle true is that it seems scarcely possible to believe that we can make a judgment or entertain a supposition without knowing what it is that we are judging or supposing about."[30] From this it does not follow that we must be acquainted with what we are judging about, but rather that we must know what it is in the straightforward sense which does not seem to reduce to acquaintance.

Behind Russell's explicit arguments there nevertheless seems to lurk a deeper reason for concentrating on individuation by acquaintance. As was already mentioned, Russell tried to interpret judgment as some sort of relation between a mind and the objects proper to the judgment.[31] Anything like a normal concrete relation can be found between them only in the case of judgments (statements) about individuals cross-identified by acquaintance, as I have indicated, not in the case of descriptively individuated particulars, for only in the case of acquaintance does the position of the knower, perceiver, or rememberer make any difference. Hence Russell's theory of judgment predisposes him to concentrate on individuation by acquaintance.

A full-dress criticism of Russell's theory of judgment is impossible here. The best criticism is in the long range likely to be a superior alternative theory, which I cannot attempt to sketch here. It may nevertheless be pointed out that the principle Russell is appealing to is much less plausible than it might first seem. What is needed for us to understand a judgment, it seems to me, is not that we are acquainted with the objects of this judgment, or that we know who or what they are, but rather that we know what possibilities (one may think of them as possible experiences) it excludes. For this purpose, it is not required that we know in advance what objects give rise to these experiences. Suppose I form a judgment as to what I might find in an unknown environment, e.g., on Mars. Surely in some obvious sense I can do that without having any inkling as to what the individual objects are that I might encounter there.[32] Thus Russell's theory of judgment is not obviously superior to its alternatives. In my view, it overlooks an important aspect of the essentially propositional character of judgment.

I am thus criticizing Russell at two essentially different levels. First, I am suggesting that there is no need for us to know the individuals which we are judging about – or, rather, no need that our judgments always be *about* any particular individuals at all. Secondly, I have pointed out that even when a judgment is about a definite individual, this definiteness may be of the nature of our *knowing who* (or what) we are judging about, not of the nature of our *knowing him* (or it).

Moreover, one of the main reasons – at least plausible reasons – for thinking of any propositional attitudes as involving (logically speaking) relations between a person or a mind and the objects of these attitudes has already been disposed of. This reason was the prevalence of the (non-elliptical) direct object construction with many of the verbs expressing propositional attitudes, which suggests that the proper analysis of these attitudes involves some kind of a direct relation. This construction was seen to be reducible to the that-construction, however.

What about topical reasons for or against the reducibility? One thing is in any case clear. Although our discussion has mostly been in informal terms, it goes together with an explicit semantical theory of propositional attitudes. Although I cannot discuss any details here, this semantics makes it clear that, in the simple languages consisting of quantification theory plus verbs for propositional attitudes, there is no hope whatsoever of reducing one kind of quantification to the other. If our semantics is correct on the whole, any reduction would thus have to turn on some concepts not represented in these languages. What these further concepts could be seems impossible to gather from the literature or to excogitate on theoretical grounds. Hence there appear to be good grounds for thinking that Russell's acquaintance thesis is wrong. In any case, the onus of proof is very much on the upholders (if any) of Russell's thesis.

NOTES

[1] The main sources are Russell's essay 'Knowledge by Acquaintance and Knowledge by Description', *Mysticism and Logic* (Longmans, Green and Co., London, 1918), pp. 209–32; Barnes and Noble, Inc., New York, parts of which had appeared previously in the *Proceedings of the Aristotelian Society* 11 (1910–11) 108–28, and Chapter 5 of *The Problems of Philosophy*, which follows the Aristotelian Society paper and to which I shall refer in the Galaxy Book (Oxford Paperback) edition (1959). Much of Russell's other early work is also relevant here, particularly some of the other essays in *Mysticism and Logic* and the essays reprinted in *Logic and Knowledge*, ed. by R. C. Marsh (George Allen and Unwin, London; 1956; Macmillan, New York).

[2] The main thesis of the early parts of the present paper, viz., the existence of a duality between two kinds of individuation methods, was put forward and explained in my paper 'Objects of Knowledge and Belief: Acquaintances and Public Figures', *Journal of Philosophy* 67 (1970) 869–83. For background and for special cases, cf. also the following papers of mine: 'The Semantics of Modal Notions and the Indeterminacy of Ontology', *Synthese* 21 (1970) 159–75; 'On the Logic of Perception', in *Perception and Personal Identity*, ed. by N. S. Care and R. H. Grimm (The Press of Case Western Reserve University, Cleveland, 1969), pp. 140–73 (reprinted in Jaakko Hintikka, *Models for Modalities* (D. Reidel Publishing Co., Dordrecht, 1969), pp. 151–83); 'On the Different Constructions in Terms of the Basic Epistemological Concepts", in *Contemporary Philosophy in Scandinavia*, ed. by R. E. Olson and A. M. Paul (Johns Hopkins Press, Baltimore, 1971), pp. 105–122; 'On Attributions of "Self-Knowledge"', *Journal of Philosophy* 67 (1970) 73–87. Cf. further my *Models for Modalities* (mentioned above) and *Knowledge and Belief* (Cornell University Press, Ithaca, N.Y., 1962).

[3] The term 'propositional attitude' nevertheless belongs to a much later period of Russell's

philosophical activity. See *An Inquiry into Meaning and Truth* (George Allen and Unwin, London, 1940; Macmillan, New York).

[4] Thus Russell writes in *An Inquiry into Meaning and Truth:* "Memory, when veridical, is causally dependent upon previous perception."

[5] This seems to be Russell's position in *An Inquiry into Meaning and Truth*, for he says there of words involving what he calls "propositional attitudes" that all of them, "when they occur in a sentence, must be followed by a subordinate sentence telling what it is that is believed or desired or doubted."

[6] See the works mentioned in note 2 above. It seems to me that the point is also fairly clear without much elaborate argument. It is to be admitted, however, that in the colloquial interrogative constructions there may be sundry presuppositions of uniqueness present which are not necessarily captured by our paraphrases. This is not a very important point, however.

[7] *Mysticism and Logic*, p. 219.

[8] For my own work in this area, see note 2 above. The papers mentioned there contain references to the work of others.

[9] The fact that we do not always know (believe, remember, etc.) the logical consequences of what we know (believe, remember, etc.) shows that often we have to consider here 'worlds' that only appear possible to our logically unperspicacious mind's eye, over and above worlds that are 'really' possible. This complication does not matter to our present purposes, however.

[10] See the further explanations of the meaning of this term in Russell and of its role in Russell's thinking given by David Pears, *Bertrand Russell and the British Tradition in Philosophy* (Collins, London, 1967; Random House, New York).

[11] This is one of the main theses of my paper 'The Semantics of Modal Notions and the Indeterminacy of Ontology' (note 2 above).

[12] See my paper 'The Semantics of Modal Notions and the Indeterminacy of Ontology' (note 2 above).

[13] See my paper 'Objects of Knowledge and Belief: Acquaintances and Public Figures' (note 2 above).

[14] See 'Objects of Knowledge and Belief' and 'On the Logic of Perception' (note 2 above).

[15] They are not completely eliminated because I have not yet dealt with two further questions which may seem to encourage the simple-minded relational analysis of perception. These questions are the possibility of a *de re* interpretation of perceptual statements and the causal element in our perceptual concepts. Both problems can be dealt with without weakening my point, although I cannot do so here for reasons of space.

[16] See 'On the Logic of Perception' (note 2 above).

[17] "When we ask what are the kinds of objects with which we are acquainted, the first and most obvious example are *sense-data*" (Russell, *Mysticism and Logic*, p. 210).

[18] For examples, see my paper 'Objects of Knowledge and Belief' (note 2 above).

[19] *Mysticism and Logic*, p. 209 (note 1 above).

[20] *Op. cit.*, p. 215.

[21] *Op. cit.*, p. 210.

[22] *Loc. cit.*

[23] *Mysticism and Logic*, p. 224.

[24] *Op. cit.*, pp. 71, 181–82.

[25] On p. 133 of *Logic and Knowledge*, Russell seems to restrict the range of things experienced in the past much more narrowly than this. It may appear from his formulation that an acquaintance with a past object is possible only "in immediate memory of some-

thing which has just happened." This has also provoked some criticism against Pears. (See J. O. Urmson's discussion of Pears's book in the *Philosophical Review* **78** (1969) 510–15.) However, all we have in the case of acquaintance by memory is strictly parallel with acquaintance by perception *apud* Russell. There, too, the range of entities that we can be acquainted with is narrowed very much by Russell for largely psychological reasons, in fact narrowed to rather ephemeral sense-data and to ourselves, these allegedly being the only entities we can 'immediately' (noninferentially) perceive. Likewise, Russell seems to have thought that the things we can immediately remember are few and fleeting. In fact, Russell refers here to the 'psychology of memory' as a source of his opinions. I do not see anything here to belie the logical point made in the text.

26 *Mysticism and Logic*, p. 219; *The Problems of Philosophy*, p. 58.

27 With the following, compare pp. 216–18 of *Mysticism and Logic*.

28 This is to all intents and purposes the old *de dicto-de re* distinction. For a brief discussion of it, see my paper 'Semantics for Propositional Attitudes' in *Models for Modalities* (note 2 above).

29 The reason why Russell says that "the actual Bismarck is unknown to us" obviously cannot be that we do not know who Bismarck is, but rather the earlier (p. 217) announced fact that we do not know Bismarck, i.e., are "not ... acquainted with the entity in question."

30 *Mysticism and Logic*, p. 219.

31 See, e.g., *Mysticism and Logic*, pp. 219–21.

32 Of course Russell does not claim that we must *know*, sight unseen, what these objects are. However, in order to reconcile such situations with his reducibility to acquaintance, he was forced to resort to such more or less desperate remedies as acquaintance with universals, propositions that can be described but not asserted, and the replacement of virtually all names (and other singular terms) by definite descriptions. I cannot here criticize these attempted ways adequately. However, the very need to resort to them is perhaps enough to suggest the difficulties with Russell's theory judgment.

INDEX OF NAMES

Adickes, E. 197, 209n.
Adkins, A. W. H. 33
Ackrill, J. L. 73, 74, 76n., 79n.
Aeschylus 73
Alexander, H. G. 133n.
Alexander the Commentator 176, 183n.
Anscombe, G. E. M. 84–88, 97n., 120, 125n.
Aquinas, St. Thomas 84, 99, 109, 115–116
Arendt, H. 45
Aristophanes 71
Aristotle VIII, 1, 8, 11–12, 16, 35, 38, 41, 44–45, 47–49, 50–79, 81, 84, 89–95, 97n., 132, 174–177, 182n., 183n., 199, 224
Arnauld, A. 125n.
Augustine, St. 98–99, 114–115, 118, 124n.
Austin, J. L. 155n.
Ayer, A. J. 76n.

Bacon, F. VIII, 81–82, 86, 110
Balz, A. G. A. 124n.
Bar-Hillel, Y. 78n., 156n.
Barr, J. 76n.
Beck, L. J. 123n.
Berlin, I. 126
Beth, E. W. 182n., 183n., 198, 210n.
Black, M. 76n.
Blanchet, L. 122
Bluck, R. S. 59, 77n.
Boole, G. 138, 141
Borowski, L. E. 132n.
Broad, C. D. 134n., 165

Campanella, T. 98
Carnap, R. 156n.
Cassirer, E. 103, 132n., 134n.
Castañeda, H.-N. 156n., 159n., 211n.
Church, A. 194
Cicero 77n.
Collingwood, R. G. 42–44, 75, 79n.
Copernicus, N. 127
Cornford, F. M. 25, 64, 74, 78n.
Craig, W. 158n.
Cratylus 62
Crombie, I. M. 15, 19, 22

Davidson, D. 210n.
Descartes, R. IX, 83–86, 90, 94, 98–125, 170–172, 208
Diodorus Cronus 57–58
Diogenes Laertius 57, 77n.

Einarson, B. 158n., 159n., 182n.
Eleatics 3, 5
Empedocles 60
Euclid 130–131, 134n., 153–154, 161, 167–174

Filmer, R. 85
Finetti, B. de 195n.
Frede, M. 24
Frege, G. L. VIII, 70
Friedländer, P. 79n.
Fränkel, H. 67, 71, 78n., 79n.
Föllesdal, D. 97n.

Galilei, G. 90
Gassendi, P. 101, 109, 114, 121
Geach, P. T. 77n., 120, 125n.
Gilbert, N. W. 158n.
Gilson, É. 122
Goodman, N. 76n.
Gouhier, H. 124
Gould, J. 29, 32–34, 39
Greenberg, J. 76n.
Grene, M. X
Gueroult, M. 100, 103, 123n., 124n.
Gulley, N. 21, 77n.
Gundisalinus, D. 97n.

Hacking, I. 196n.
Hailperin, T. 123n.
Hare, R. 19, 21–22
Havelock, E. 71–73, 77n.
Heath, T. L. 134n., 158n., 182
Hegel, G. W. F. 50
Heimsoeth, H. 198–199, 210n.
Heraclitus 62
Hobbes, T. 82, 114, 125n., 127–128, 133n.

Homer 59, 63, 73, 77n.
Howell, R. 210n.
Hume, D. 126, 155n.
Husserl, E. 210n.
Höffding, H. 133n.

Isocrates 6

Jaeger, W. 44
John of Spain 97n.

Kahn, C. 23
Kant, I. VII, IX, 1, 88, 126–134, 135, 137, 153–158, 160–211
Kemeny, J. G. 195n.
Kemp Smith, N. 124n., 125n.
Kluckholm, E. R. 76n.
Kneale, M. 57, 74, 77n., 79n.
Kneale, W. 57, 77n., 79n.
Kolmogorov, A. N. 188
Koyré, A. 119

Leblanc, H. 123n.
Lehman, R. S. 195n.
Leibniz, G. W. 68, 123n.
Lenz, J. W. 77n.
Locke, J. 85–86, 126
Long, A. A. 77n.
Łukasiewicz, J. 158n., 182n.
Lyons, J. 19

Maas, J. G. E. 183n.
Maimonides, M. 80–82, 96n.
Malcolm, N. 125n.
Mates, B. 57–58, 77n.
Megarians 57
Michotte, A. 223
Moore, G. E. 76n., 223n.
Moravcsik, J. E. M. 24
Morin, J. B. 124n.

Newton, I. 90, 126, 128–129, 133n.

Olsen, C. 84
Owen, G. E. L. 67–68

Parmenides 3, 16–17, 22–23, 27–28, 66–67, 77n., 78n.
Paton, H. J. 182n.
Patzig, G. 158n., 182n.

Pears, D. 221, 226, 232n., 233n.
Peirce, C. S. 111, 141
Philo the Megarian 58
Plato VIII, 1–49, 59–60, 62–64, 66–68, 72–75, 77n., 78n., 79n., 110, 170, 224
Popkin, R. 110, 124n.
Popper, K. R. 156n.
pre-Socratics 12
Prior, A. N. 76n.
Putnam, H. 155n.

Quine, W. V. IX, 51, 76n., 155n., 167, 210n.

Ramsey, F. P. 195n.
Remes, V. 97n.
Ross, W. D. IX, 35, 90
Rousseau, J.-J. 126, 133n.
Runciman, W. G. 18, 59, 62, 64, 77n., 78n.
Russell, B. A. W. 76n., 78n., 133n., 134n., 181n., 210n., 212–233

Sanchez, F. 81
Sartre, J.-P. 84–85
Savage, L. J. 196n.
Schmid, C. C. E. 134n., 182n.
Scholz, H. 98, 122n.
Schoolmen 98
Schrader, G. 209n.
Schrecker, P. 124n.
Schultz, J. 172
Scott-Taggart, M. J. 209n.
Sextus Empiricus 57, 77n.
Shimony, A. 195n.
Snell, B. 6–7, 12–13, 17, 24, 28, 31–33, 58–59, 77n.
Socrates 4, 29–34, 36–37, 39–43, 45, 48, 63
Solmsen, F. 78n.
Sophists 3
Souilhé, J. 6–7
Spengler, O. 78n.
Sprague, R. 5, 15, 24
Stenius, E. 24
Stenzel, J. 17
Stoics 57, 77n.
Strodtbeck, F. L. 76n.

Taran, L. 78n.
Taylor, A. E. 30, 60

Theophrastus 183n.
Toulmin, S. 133n.

Ullian, J. S. 159n.
Urmson, J. O. 233n.

Vaihinger, H. 133n., 177, 182n.
Vico, G. 82–86, 91, 96n.
Vlastos, G. 33, 39

Walsh, W. H. 133n.
Wang, Hao 191, 196n.

Wedberg, A. 183
White, M. G. 155n.
Whitehead, A. N. 83–84
Whorf, B. L. 43
Williams, D. C. 76n.
Wittgenstein, L. J. J. VIII, 1, 14, 138–139, 156n.
Wolff, R. P. 200
Wright, G. H. von 125n., 157n.

Xenophanes 12–13, 28, 36

INDEX OF SUBJECTS

Acquaintance VIII, 204, 212, 214, 229–230
  objects of 222, 226
  and knowing who 225
  by memory 233
  by perception 233
acts of knowing, noumenal or phenomenal (Kant) 209
aidion 67
aionion 67
akrasia 92
algebra 130
  Kant on 134, 165, 166, 180
  algebraic operations, analogous to geometrical constructions 172
ambiguity 14
  pros hen 38
analogy 1
analytic, analyticity IX, 97, 138, 149, 151, 154–156, 171, 176
  and the truths of logic 135
  analytic truth as a conceptual truth 135
  analytic truth as tautological truth 135
  analytic methods 135–136
  analytic sentence 136
  analytic argument-step 136
  analyticity and the number of individuals considered together 137
  analytic argument 137
  analytic argument never carries us from the existence of an object to a different object 137
  analytic proof 137, 150
  the history of the notion 153
analysis, the method of 89–91
analysis, geometrical 89–90, 92–94, 96–97, 153, 170
Anschauung 129, 134, 182–183
apodeixis 168, 172
  analytic in Kant's sense 173
arete 29, 39
  as knowledge 30, 32–33
  as skill 32
  as knowledge of definitions 40

argument against contradiction (Plato) 24
arithmetical equations 167, 172
artists, Plato's criticism of 40
atemporal being 66, 68
auxiliary constructions 94–95, 168–169, 173
axioma 57, 74–75
axioms 177

belief 203, 212, 216
  must have an object for Plato 8
  as a *dynamis* 9, 44
  objects of 9, 11, 24, 26–27
  as propositional 21
  as separated from faith 28
bound variable 100

calendar 71
cause 84
changing truth-value 53–55, 57, 69
chronology, Greek neglect of 71, 75
clear and distinct ideas (Descartes) 116
cogitare 118–122
cogito-argument IX, 1, 14, 43–44, 49–51, 58
  as an inference 99–102, 109, 116
  the indubitability of 108, 116–117
  as a performance 108–110, 112–118
  and doubt 109–110, 113
  role of thinking in 109–110, 113
  and introspection 110
  as a factual statement 110
  singularity of 111–112
  not generalizable 112
  momentariness of 113–114
conceptual assumptions VIII, 1, 14, 43–44, 49–51, 58
conceptual and real information inseparable 193–195
consciousness 116, 119–120
constituents 193
  of propositional logic 138–139, 142
  in quantification theory 142–144
  inductive definition of 145
  inconsistent 145, 146–148, 149, 185, 192

like jigsaw puzzles 146–148, 191
why sometimes inconsistent 147
inconsistent, yield synthetic truths 149
inconsistent, yield interindividual inferences 149
the elimination of the inconsistent ones
149–150
trivially inconsistent 185–187, 191
subordinate 185
constructions 154, 160, 170, 175, 177, 179
context-dependency 20
craftsman, as a paradigm of knower 32,
37, 41–43, 45, 47–48
creation 44
cross-identification, descriptive 204–205,
218, 228
perceptual 205, 207, 222
demonstrative 205, 218, 227
contextual 218
demonstrative, and direct object construction 219
by acquaintance, and direct object construction 219

decision problem 224
definite descriptions 227–228
definition 39, 41, 61–62
degree, notion of 139, 142, 150, 152, 155
as the number of individuals considered
140–142
deliberation 89–91, 93–96
demiurge 44
demonstration 82, 127
depth, notion of 139–141, 185, 187–188
defined recursively 156
depth information nonrecursive 186,
189, 195
depth information as a limit of surface
information 188
Dinge an sich, see also things in themselves
IX, 194, 197–211
context-dependent 224
diorismos 93
direct object construction VII, 19–20, 22,
211, 213–214, 219, 222, 224, 229, 230
distributive normal forms 142, 144, 190
doing vs. making 13, 45, 80
domino problems 191
double affection (Adickes) 197
doubt 118, 122

doxa 6, 8, 10, 27–28, 53–54, 62–63
doxazein 224
dynamis 5–6, 15
as having only one product 7–8
individuated by its objects 9
must have an object 16

ecthesis 173, 175
as existential instantiation 154, 168
as a paradigm of construction 169
in logic 174–175
and perception 176
elenchus 34
seeks definitions 39
empeiria 35
ends-and-means 91–93, 95
entailment 105
enunciation 168
episteme 6, 11, 13, 27–28, 31–35, 39, 41–
42, 78
as skill 29
presupposes awareness 35–36, 45
episteme of episteme 38
teachability of 44
ergon 7–8, 15
Erläuterungsurteile 188
essential nature 84
existential inconsistency 104–108, 111
116, 122
existentially inconsistent sentences vs.
existentially inconsistent statements 107
existential presuppositions 102, 105, 112
in Descartes 103
existential self-verifiability 108, 116
expositio; see ecthesis

fact-stating discourse 106
faith 28
fallacies IX, 5, 14
Plato's alleged answer to 4
falsity as misidentification 26
first-order logic, see quantification theory
first-person fallacy 208
first-person pronoun 107, 111, 226
Forms, Platonic 10, 41, 63–64
Aristotelian 41

generalization, existential 215–216

geometry 82, 89, 128, 153, 160, 177, 204
  certainty of 161
  analytic 83, 94, 171
  synthetic 83, 171
  geometrical imagination not appealed
    to by Kant 128
good 97

history 82
  historical relativity 64

imagination, mathematical 130
imitation of nature 45
implication, Stoic controversies about 57
  material 58
individuation 203, 220–221, 227
  by acquaintance 205, 207, 221–223,
    225–227, 229–230
  by perception 205, 207, 222–223
  descriptive 205, 223, 229
inductive probability 186
infinity 81
information as elimination of uncertainty
  186
instantiation 130
  existential 151–152, 154, 158, 175
  existential, as a paradigm of synthetic
    modes of reasoning 154
  universal 152
  instantiation rules 198
intentio 97
intentional action 87
interrogative construction 211–212, 225,
  232
introspection 110–111
intuition 182
  as a mental picture 162, 165
  as a representation of an individual 162
  and sense-perception 163, 173
  intellectual 99, 199
  in Kant 128–131, 133–134, 160–166,
    170, 198–199, 206, 210
  intuitions a priori 178, 183

judgment, Russell's theory of 213, 222,
  228, 230, 233
  propositional character of judgments
    230

kataskeue 168, 178

knowhow 41
knowing, different kinds of 49
  how 32, 34–35, 37, 43, 46, 48
  that 32–33, 35, 37, 43
  what 37, 39, 46–48
  who 212, 216, 224, 229–230
  who and acquaintance 225
  the material factor 48
knowledge 203, 212, 218
  by acquaintance VIII, 58, 212–214,
    225–226, 229, 231
  by description 213, 225, 229, 231
  vs. true belief 2, 10, 13, 16, 21, 63–64, 67
  as a dynamis 9, 44
  objects of 9, 11–13, 15, 24, 26–27, 43,
    59, 77–78, 197, 203, 231
  maker's knowledge VIII, 47, 49, 80–85,
    87, 89, 91, 96, 127
  user's knowledge 47–48
  implies truth 11, 17, 28, 61
  and skill 13, 28, 31–33, 37–38
  as realizing itself in its objects 13, 43
  alleged identity of the knowledge and
    the known 16, 18, 41
  as mental seeing or touching 21, 59, 64
  as propositional 21, 32
  and saying, analogous 22
  and belief, same objects, same or
    different? 27
  as unerring skill 29, 46–47
  knowledge of knowledge 38
  based on observation 58–60
  without observation 84–86
  as 'having seen' its object 58–59
  only of what is eternal 58, 60–61, 64, 75
  of an eyewitness 59–60, 64
  as perception 60, 62–64, 224
  genuine knowledge only of what is un-
    changeable 60–61, 63
  of universals only in Aristotle 61
  and time 65
  and change 66
  as power 81
  human 81–82
  demonstrative 82, 127
  historical 82–83, 86
  intentional 84–85, 87–88, 202
  intentional knowledge: objects of 85
  practical 84–87
  of causal connections 85–86

a priori 88, 128, 177–178, 193, 198
  synthetic a priori 127
  mathematical 160, 200
  of particulars 200
  of facts 222
  of things 221–222
  of truths 221

language, extensional 88
  intensional 88
  language games of seeking and finding
    181, 199–202, 206
lekton 57, 75
  compared with proposition 57, 74
logical truth 135
  logically proper names 217, 226

maker's knowledge, the scope of 83
  making vs. doing 13, 45, 80
mathematical methods, Kant on 160
mathematical truth VII
mathematics, Kant's theory of 128–129,
  131, 161, 163–165
  mathematical truths synthetic 155
meaning, representative theory of 24
  name theory of 24
meaningful falsity, the problem of 2, 14,
  22–25
megista gene 25
memory 35, 212, 216, 218–219, 226, 232
modal profile 216
monolithic concepts IX
most general kinds in Plato 25–26

natural deduction 151–152
Nature 45
not-being 23, 26
now 52, 68–69, 71–72
  always the same for Aristotle 70

objects of knowledge 213
  of belief 213
  of memory 213
  of perception 213
omniscience, implies omnipotence in
  Plato 39
  alleged omniscience of sophists 40
omnitemporality vs. eternity 67–68
opinion: see *doxa* and belief
oral tradition 73

paideia 44
past 78, 226, 232
perception 20, 61, 131, 163, 197–200, 202,
  204–205, 212, 216, 218, 222
  and particulars 132, 176, 179, 199
  allegedly passive 132, 177
  as a paradigm of propositional attitude
    210
perceptual acquaintance 223
perceptual cross-identification VIII
perceptual objects 208, 223
perceptual space 204
performatory utterance 105, 116
phenomena 197, 200
  vs. things in themselves 197, 200
picture theory of language 147
pistis 28
poiesis 80
political science 82–83
possible worlds 68, 138, 203–204, 206–
  209, 215–217, 219
  possible world semantics 206, 209, 214
  alternative ones 215–216
postulates 176–177
  as assumptions of existence 177
power: see *dynamis*
practical syllogism 89–90, 93, 95
  major premiss of 91–92, 97
  minor premiss of 91–92, 95, 97
praxis 80
prelogical probability 187, 189
present 78
present-tense statement, conjunctive sense
  65–66
  expressing knowledge 65
probability, subjective 189
proposition 53, 57, 69
  concept missing in Plato and Aristotle
    74
  Russell's analysis of 226
propositional attitudes 203, 212–215, 217,
  219, 221, 230–232
  propositional construction 19

quantification theory 100–102, 137–139,
  142, 145–146, 151, 175, 184–186,
  200–201, 212
  undecidable 191, 194
  logical truths of 148
  as a synthetic theory 152

quantifiers 140
    connected 185
    relying on descriptive cross-identifica-
        tion 220
    relying on acquaintance 220
    quantification into 217, 219–221

reason, theoretical 80, 89, 95
    practical 80, 82, 89, 96
recollection (Plato) 59
reducibility to acquaintance (Russell) 210,
    226–231
remembering who 219
    with direct object 219
    past 219
res cogitans 114–121
rules of inference, natural 150

saying something, as saying something
    true 22–23
searching 199
self-knowledge 209
semantic information 156
sense-data 222, 226
    as values of perceptual quantifiers 222
    and the psychology of perception 223
sensible things always changing 62
sensorium, God's 128
sentences, eternal 51, 71
    occasion 51, 76
    standing 51
    indefinite 52
    temporally indefinite 51–54, 56–58, 60–
        61, 63, 65, 72–73, 75, 78
    temporally indefinite, expressing one
        and the same thought in Aristotle
        55, 69–70
setting-out 168–169
skeptics 82, 110
skill, and knowledge 13, 31–32
Socratic paradox 30, 41
sophia 31
sophist 39–40
sophrosyne 38
space, perceptual 128, 206
    as an intuition 164
    physical 206
    Kant on 128–129, 160, 162–163, 198,
        200, 203–205, 207
    spatiotemporal continuity 203, 205, 218

speaking what is (Plato) 23
speech-acts 110
    vs. thought-acts 106, 111
spoken words 74
    vs. written words 72
    vs. thought expressed 73
    primacy of 72
    as symbols for unspoken thoughts 69
statement, object of 22, 52–53
    and fact 53
    realizes itself in its object 22–23
    vs. sentence 105
    de dicto 227, 232
    de re 227, 232
substitutivity salva veritate 88, 215
surface information 184, 187, 191, 193
    not invariant with respect to logical
        equivalence 189
    what about? 190
    about reality 190
    as conceptual information 192–193
    both real and conceptual 192
surface probability 187
surface tautology 184, 187–188
syllogistic 157, 175
    Kant on 175
    syllogistic premisses 55, 76–77
synonymy 136
synthetic, syntheticity VII, IX, 127, 135,
        149, 152, 156, 170, 192
    synthetic proof 150
    synthetic a priori 184, 195
    synthetic, the history of the notion 153
    syntheticity and constructions 154, 171
    syntheticity and intuition 171
    mental synthesis 200

tautology 138, 145–146
    admits all alternatives 139
technology 44, 82, 86
    as imitating nature 44–45
tekhne 31, 35
teleology, conceptual 42
    implicit 5, 12, 42, 44–45
telos 5, 7, 42
tense-logic 78
that-construction 212
things in themselves 194
    as genuine class of entities 197
    as epistemological conventions 197, 200

vs. phenomena 197
as causes of sensations 198–199
and space and time 198
vs. empirical objects 200, 207–208
as ontological objects 200
inseparable from empirical objects 201
unknowability of 207, 210
thinking 119
as combination 25
thought, the objects of 17, 115
in Plato 61
as unspoken words 73
individuated by the Greeks in terms of
sentences 74
self-applied 115
thought-acts 112, 117
time 27, 56, 58, 67, 76
the notion of 50, 55
being in time 68
as an indication of value orientation 76
Kant on 128–129, 131, 162–163, 198,
200, 203, 207
timeless present 65–66, 68

transcendental method 198, 203
truth 136
and time 53, 55–57, 70, 75
and change 62, 65
degrees of 62
relativity of 64

undecidability of quantification theory
191
uniqueness presuppositions 217
unity of experience 207
universe, as mechanism 81

values, operate as ends in Aristotle 91
verb 58, 66, 76
tense of: past, present, future 56
present tense 65, 69
of intellection 116–117, 122, 125
virtue, as knowledge 30, 33, 40–41, 48
visual space 204, 219

Whorfian fallacy 43
world lines 203, 207, 219–220

SYNTHESE LIBRARY

Monographs on Epistemology, Logic, Methodology,
Philosophy of Science, Sociology of Science and of Knowledge, and on the
Mathematical Methods of Social and Behavioral Sciences

Editors:

DONALD DAVIDSON (The Rockefeller University and Princeton University)
JAAKKO HINTIKKA (Academy of Finland and Stanford University)
GABRIËL NUCHELMANS (University of Leyden)
WESLEY C. SALMON (University of Arizona)

1. J. M. BOCHEŃSKI, *A Precis of Mathematical Logic.* 1959, X + 100 pp.
2. P. L. GUIRAUD, *Problèmes et méthodes de la statistique linguistique.* 1960, VI + 146 pp.
3. HANS FREUDENTHAL (ed.), *The Concept and the Role of the Model in Mathematics and Natural and Social Sciences. Proceedings of a Colloquium held at Utrecht, The Netherlands, January 1960.* 1961, VI + 194 pp.
4. EVERT W. BETH, *Formal Methods. An Introduction to Symbolic Logic and the Study of Effective Operations in Arithmetic and Logic.* 1962, XIV + 170 pp.
5. B. H. KAZEMIER and D. VUYSJE (eds.), *Logic and Language. Studies dedicated to Professor Rudolf Carnap on the Occasion of his Seventieth Birthday.* 1962, VI + 256 pp.
6. MARX W. WARTOFSKY (ed.), *Proceedings of the Boston Colloquium for the Philosophy of Science, 1961–1962,* Boston Studies in the Philosophy of Science (ed. by Robert S. Cohen and Marx W. Wartofsky), Volume I. 1963, VIII + 212 pp.
7. A. A. ZINOV'EV, *Philosophical Problems of Many-Valued Logic.* 1963, XIV + 155 pp.
8. GEORGES GURVITCH, *The Spectrum of Social Time.* 1964, XXVI + 152 pp.
9. PAUL LORENZEN, *Formal Logic.* 1965, VIII + 123 pp.
10. ROBERT S. COHEN and MARX W. WARTOFSKY (eds.), *In Honor of Philipp Frank,* Boston Studies in the Philosophy of Science (ed. by Robert S. Cohen and Marx W. Wartofsky), Volume II. 1965, XXXIV + 475 pp.
11. EVERT W. BETH, *Mathematical Thought. An Introduction to the Philosophy of Mathematics.* 1965, XII + 208 pp.
12. EVERT W. BETH and JEAN PIAGET, *Mathematical Epistemology and Psychology.* 1966, XXII + 326 pp.
13. GUIDO KÜNG, *Ontology and the Logistic Analysis of Language. An Enquiry into the Contemporary Views on Universals.* 1967, XI + 210 pp.
14. ROBERT S. COHEN and MARX W. WARTOFSKY (eds.), *Proceedings of the Boston Colloquium for the Philosophy of Science 1964–1966, in Memory of Norwood Russell Hanson,* Boston Studies in the Philosophy of Science (ed. by Robert S. Cohen and Marx W. Wartofsky), Volume III. 1967, XLIX + 489 pp.
15. C. D. BROAD, *Induction, Probability, and Causation. Selected Papers.* 1968, XI + 296 pp.
16. GÜNTHER PATZIG, *Aristotle's Theory of the Syllogism. A Logical-Philosophical Study of Book A of the Prior Analytics.* 1968, XVII + 215 pp.
17. NICHOLAS RESCHER, *Topics in Philosophical Logic.* 1968, XIV + 347 pp.

18. ROBERT S. COHEN and MARX W. WARTOFSKY (eds.), *Proceedings of the Boston Colloquium for the Philosophy of Science 1966–1968*, Boston Studies in the Philosophy of Science (ed. by Robert S. Cohen and Marx W. Wartofsky), Volume IV. 1969, VIII + 537 pp.

19. ROBERT S. COHEN and MARX W. WARTOFSKY (eds.), *Proceedings of the Boston Colloquium for the Philosophy of Science 1966–1968*, Boston Studies in the Philosophy of Science (ed. by Robert S. Cohen and Marx W. Wartofsky), Volume V. 1969, VIII + 482 pp.

20. J. W. DAVIS, D. J. HOCKNEY, and W. K. WILSON (eds.), *Philosophical Logic*. 1969, VIII + 277 pp.

21. D. DAVIDSON and J. HINTIKKA (eds.), *Words and Objections: Essays on the Work of W. V. Quine*, 1969, VIII + 366 pp.

22. PATRICK SUPPES, *Studies in the Methodology and Foundations of Science. Selected Papers from 1911 to 1969*. 1969, XII + 473 pp.

23. JAAKKO HINTIKKA, *Models for Modalities. Selected Essays*. 1969, IX + 220 pp.

24. NICHOLAS RESCHER *et al.* (eds.), *Essay in Honor of Carl G. Hempel. A Tribute on the Occasion of his Sixty-Fifth Birthday*. 1969, VII + 272 pp.

25. P. V. TAVANEC (ed.), *Problems of the Logic of Scientific Knowledge*. 1969, XII + 429 pp.

26. MARSHALL SWAIN (ed.), *Induction, Acceptance, and Rational Belief*. 1970, VII + 232 pp.

27. ROBERT S. COHEN and RAYMOND J. SEEGER (eds.), *Ernst Mach: Physicist and Philosopher*, Boston Studies in the Philosophy of Science (ed. by Robert S. Cohen and Marx W. Wartofsky), Volume VI. 1970, VIII + 295 pp.

28. JAAKKO HINTIKKA and PATRICK SUPPES, *Information and Inference*. 1970, X + 336 pp.

29. KAREL LAMBERT, *Philosophical Problems in Logic. Some Recent Developments*. 1970, VII + 176 pp.

30. ROLF A. EBERLE, *Nominalistic Systems*. 1970, IX + 217 pp.

31. PAUL WEINGARTNER and GERHARD ZECHA (eds.), *Induction, Physics, and Ethics, Proceedings and Discussions of the 1968 Salzburg Colloquium in the Philosophy of Science*. 1970, X + 382 pp.

32. EVERT W. BETH, *Aspects of Modern Logic*. 1970, XI + 176 pp.

33. RISTO HILPINEN (ed.), *Deontic Logic: Introductory and Systematic Readings*. 1971, VII + 182 pp.

34. JEAN-LOUIS KRIVINE, *Introduction to Axiomatic Set Theory*. 1971, VII + 98 pp.

35. JOSEPH D. SNEED, *The Logical Structure of Mathematical Physics*. 1971, XV + 311 pp.

36. CARL R. KORDIG, *The Justification of Scientific Change*. 1971, XIV + 119 pp.

37. MILIČ ČAPEK, *Bergson and Modern Physics*, Boston Studies in the Philosophy of Science (ed. by Robert S. Cohen and Marx W. Wartofsky), Volume VII. 1971, XV + 414 pp.

38. NORWOOD RUSSELL HANSON, *What I do not Believe, and other Essays* (ed. by Stephen Toulmin and Harry Woolf). 1971, XII + 390 pp.

39. ROGER C. BUCK and ROBERT S. COHEN (eds.), *PSA 1970. In Memory of Rudolf Carnap*, Boston Studies in the Philosophy of Science (ed. by Robert S. Cohen and Marx W. Wartofsky), Volume VIII. 1971, LXVI + 615 pp. Also available as a paperback.

40. DONALD DAVIDSON and GILBERT HARMAN (eds.), *Semantics of Natural Language*. 1972, X + 769 pp. Also available as a paperback.

41. YEHOSUA BAR-HILLEL (ed.), *Pragmatics of Natural Languages*. 1971, VII + 231 pp.

42. SÖREN STENLUND, *Combinators, λ-Terms and Proof Theory*. 1972, 184 pp.

43. MARTIN STRAUSS, *Modern Physics and Its Philosophy. Selected Papers in the Logic, History, and Philosophy of Science*. 1972, X + 297 pp.

44. MARIO BUNGE, *Method, Model and Matter*. 1973, VII + 196 pp.

45. MARIO BUNGE, *Philosophy of Physics*. 1973, IX + 248 pp.

46. A. A. ZINOV'EV, *Foundations of the Logical Theory of Scientific Knowledge (Complex Logic)*, Boston Studies in the Philosophy of Science (ed. by Robert S. Cohen and Marx W. Wartofsky), Volume IX. Revised and enlarged English edition with an appendix, by G. A. Smirnov, E. A. Sidorenka, A. M. Fedina, and L. A. Bobrova. 1973, XXII + 301 pp. Also available as a paperback.

47. LADISLAV TONDL, *Scientific Procedures*, Boston Studies in the Philosophy of Science (ed. by Robert S. Cohen and Marx W. Wartofsky), Volume X. 1973, XII + 268 pp. Also available as a paperback.

48. NORWOOD RUSSELL HANSON, *Constellations and Conjectures* (ed. by Willard C. Humphreys, Jr.). 1973, X + 282 pp.

49. K. J. J. HINTIKKA, J. M. E. MORAVCSIK, and P. SUPPES (eds.), *Approaches to Natural Language. Proceedings of the 1970 Stanford Workshop on Grammar and Semantics*. 1973, VIII + 526 pp. Also available as a paperback.

50. MARIO BUNGE (ed.), *Exact Philosophy – Problems, Tools, and Goals*. 1973, X + 214 pp.

51. RADU J. BOGDAN and ILKKA NIINILUOTO (eds.), *Logic, Language, and Probability*. A selection of papers contributed to Sections IV, VI, and XI of the Fourth International Congress for Logic, Methodology, and Philosophy of Science, Bucharest, September 1971. 1973, X + 323 pp.

52. GLENN PEARCE and PATRICK MAYNARD (eds.), *Conceptual Change*. 1973, XII + 282 pp.

53. ILKKA NIINILUOTO and RAIMO TUOMELA, *Theoretical Concepts and Hypothetico-Inductive Inference*. 1973, VII + 264 pp.

54. ROLAND FRAÏSSÉ, *Course of Mathematical Logic – Volume I: Relation and Logical Formula*. 1973, XVI + 186 pp. Also available as a paperback.

55. ADOLF GRÜNBAUM, *Philosophical Problems of Space and Time*. Second, enlarged edition, Boston Studies in the Philosophy of Science (ed. by Robert S. Cohen and Marx W. Wartofsky), Volume XII. 1973, XXIII + 884 pp. Also available as a paperback.

56. PATRICK SUPPES (ed.), *Space, Time, and Geometry*. 1973, XI + 424 pp.

57. HANS KELSEN, *Essays in Legal and Moral Philosophy*, selected and introduced by Ota Weinberger, 1973, XXVIII + 300 pp.

58. R. J. SEEGER and ROBERT S. COHEN (eds.), *Philosophical Foundations of Science, Proceedings of an AAAS Program, 1969*. Boston Studies in the Philosophy of Science (ed. by Robert S. Cohen and Marx W. Wartofsky), Volume XI. 1974, IX + 545 pp. Also available as paperback.

59. ROBERT S. COHEN and MARX W. WARTOFSKY (eds.), *Logical and Epistemological Studies in Contemporary Physics*, Boston Studies in the Philosophy of Science (ed. by Robert S. Cohen and Marx W. Wartofsky), Volume XIII. 1973, VIII + 462 pp. Also available as a paperback.

60. ROBERT S. COHEN and MARX W. WARTOFSKY (eds.), *Methodological and Historical Essays in the Natural and Social Sciences. Proceedings of the Boston Colloquium for the Philosophy of Science, 1969–1972*, Boston Studies in the Philosophy of Science (ed. by Robert S. Cohen and Marx W. Wartofsky), Volume XIV. 1974, VIII + 405 pp. Also available as a paperback.

63. SÖREN STENLUND (ed.), *Logical Theory and Semantic Analysis. Essays Dedicated to Stig Kanger on His Fiftieth Birthday*. 1974, V + 217 pp.

64. KENNETH SCHAFFNER and ROBERT S. COHEN (eds.), *Proceedings of the 1972 Biennial Meeting, Philosophy of Science Association*, Boston Studies in the Philosophy of Science (ed. by Robert S. Cohen and Marx W. Wartofsky), Volume XX. 1974, VIII + 445 pp. Also available as a paperback.

65. HENRY E. KYBURG, JR., *The Logical Foundations of Statistical Inference*. 1974, IX + 421 pp.
66. MARJORIE GRENE, *The Understanding of Nature: Essays in the Philosophy of Biology*, Boston Studies in the Philosophy of Science (ed. by Robert S. Cohen and Marx W. Wartofsky), Volume XXIII. 1974, XII + 360 pp. Also available as a paperback.

In Preparation

61. ROBERT S. COHEN and MARX W. WARTOFSKY (eds.), *For Dirk Struik. Scientific, Historical, and Political Essays in Honor of Dirk J. Struik*, Boston Studies in the Philosophy of Science (ed. by Robert S. Cohen and Marx W. Wartofsky), Volume XV. Also available as a paperback.
62. KAZIMIERZ AJDUKIEWICZ, *Pragmatic Logic*, transl. from the Polish by Olgierd Wojtasiewicz.
67. JAN M. BROEKMAN, *Structuralism: Moscow, Prague, Paris*.
68. NORMAN GESCHWIND, *Selected Papers on Language and the Brain*, Boston Studies in the Philosophy of Science (ed. by Robert S. Cohen and Marx W. Wartofsky) Volume XVI. Also available as a paperback.
69. ROLAND FRAÏSSÉ, *Course of Mathematical Logic* – Volume II: *Model Theory*.

SYNTHESE HISTORICAL LIBRARY

Texts and Studies
in the History of Logic and Philosophy

Editors:

N. KRETZMANN (Cornell University)
G. NUCHELMANS (University of Leyden)
L. M. DE RIJK (University of Leyden)

1. M. T. BEONIO-BROCCHIERI FUMAGALLI, *The Logic of Abelard*. Translated from the Italian. 1969, IX + 101 pp.
2. GOTTFRIED WILHELM LEIBNITZ, *Philosophical Papers and Letters*. A selection translated and edited, with an introduction by Leroy E. Loemker. 1969, XII + 736 pp.
3. ERNST MALLY, *Logische Schriften* (ed. by Karl Wolf and Paul Weingartner). 1971, X + 340 pp.
4. LEWIS WHITE BECK (ed.), *Proceedings of the Third International Kant Congress*. 1972, XI + 718 pp.
5. BERNARD BOLZANO, *Theory of Science* (ed. by Jan Berg). 1973, XV + 398 pp.
6. J. M. E. MORAVCSIK (ed.), *Patterns in Plato's Thought. Papers arising out of the 1971 West Coast Greek Philosophy Conference*, 1973, VIII + 212 pp.
7. NABIL SHEHABY, *The Propositional Logic of Avicenna: A Translation from al-Shifā': al-Qiyās*, with Introduction, Commentary and Glossary. 1973, XIII + 296 pp.
8. DESMOND PAUL HENRY, *Commentary on De Grammatico: The Historical-Logical Dimensions of a Dialogue of St. Anselm's*. 1974, IX + 345 pp.
9. JOHN CORCORAN, *Ancient Logic and Its Modern Interpretations*. 1974, X + 208 pp.
11. JAAKKO HINTIKKA, *Knowledge and the Known*.

In Preparation

10. E. M. BARTH, *The Logic of the Articles in Traditional Philosophy*.
12. E. J. ASHWORTH, *Language and Logic in the Post-Medieval Period*.